NATIONAL GEOGRAPHIC
TRAVELER

Provence
& the Côte d'Azur

NATIONAL GEOGRAPHIC

TRAVELER
Provence
& the Côte d'Azur

by Barbara A. Noe
Photography by Gérard Sioen

National Geographic
Washington, D.C.

Contents

Page 1: Provençal sunflower
Pages 2–3: La Roque Alric
Left: Lavender festival in Sault

How to use this guide

See back flap for keys to text and map symbols.

The *National Geographic Traveler* brings you the best of Provence & the Côte d'Azur in text, pictures, and maps. Divided into three main sections, the guide begins with an overview of history and culture.

Following are six regional chapters with featured sites selected by the author for their particular interest. Each chapter opens with its own contents list for easy reference. A map introduces the parameters covered in the chapter, highlighting the featured sites and locating other places of interest. Walks and drives, plotted on their own maps, suggest

routes for discovering the most about an area. Features and sidebars offer intriguing detail on history, culture, or contemporary life.

The final section, Travelwise, lists essential information for the traveler—pretrip planning, special events, getting around, practical advice, and emergency contacts—plus provides a selection of hotels and restaurants arranged by area, shops, activities, and entertainment possibilities.

To the best of our knowledge, all information is accurate as of press time. However, it's always advisable to call ahead when possible.

Color coding

142

Each region of the country is color coded for easy reference. Find the region you want on the map on the front flap, and look for the color flash at the top of the pages of the relevant chapter. Information in **Travelwise** is also color coded to each region.

Visitor information

Musée du Tire-Bouchon

- 46 C2
- Domaine de la Citadelle, Le Chataignier, chemin de Cavaillon, Ménerbes
- 04 90 72 41 58
- Closed Sat.–Sun. Oct.–March
- $

Practical information for most sites is given in the side column (see key to symbols on back flap). The map reference gives the page number of the map and grid reference, if relevant. Other details are address, telephone number and website, days closed, entrance charge in a range from $ (under $5) to $$$$$ (over $25) and, for sites in Marseille, the nearest metro station and most important bus routes. Other sites have information in italics and parentheses in the text.

TRAVELWISE

AIX, MARSEILLE, & THE VAR — Color-coded region name

AIX-EN-PROVENCE — Town name

GRAND HÔTEL NÈGRE COSTE — Hotel name & price range
$$ ✪✪✪
33 COURS MIRABEAU — Address, telephone & fax numbers, e-mail address, website
TEL 04 42 27 74 22
FAX 04 42 26 80 93
One of Aix's better values, this 18th-century town house has friendly service and quiet rooms. — Brief description of hotel
⬛ 37 ⬛ P ⬛ All major cards — Hotel facilities & credit card details

LE CLOS DE LA VIOLETTE — Restaurant name & price range
$$$$
10 AVE. DE LA VIOLETTE — Address, telephone & fax numbers, e-mail address
TEL 04 42 23 30 71
Chef Jean-Marc Banzo runs Aix's top restaurant, blending artful presentation with his signature Provençal style; try the grilled sea bass stuffed with cured ham for starters. — Brief description of restaurant
⬛ Closed Sun.–Mon., & Wed. L ⬛ All major cards — Restaurant facilities & credit card details

Hotel & restaurant prices

An explanation of the price ranges used in entries is given in the Hotels & Restaurants section (beginning on p. 211).

REGIONAL MAPS

Drive start point

Important featured site

Department name

Grid letter

Important featured town

Point of interest

Road number

Adjacent chapter

- A locator map accompanies each regional map and shows the location of that area in Provence.
- Adjacent regions are shown, each with a page reference.

WALKING TOURS

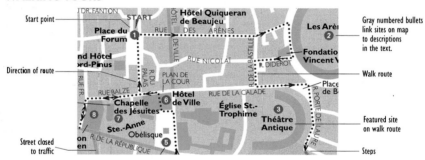

Start point

Direction of route

Street closed to traffic

Gray numbered bullets link sites on map to descriptions in the text.

Walk route

Featured site on walk route

Steps

- An information box gives the starting and ending points, time and length of walk, and places not to be missed along the route.

DRIVING TOURS

Drive start point

Drive route

Important featured site

Gray numbered bullets link sites on map to descriptions in the text.

Trail

Road number

- An information box provides details that include starting and finishing points, places not to be missed along the route, and the time and length of drive.

NATIONAL GEOGRAPHIC

TRAVELER

Provence
& the Côte d'Azur

About the author & photographer

Author Barbara A. Noe earned a B.A. in French and International Relations from the University of California at Davis, with a year of study at the Université de Bordeaux, France. After receiving an M.A. in Journalism from the University of Missouri School of Journalism, she moved to Washington D.C. for an internship with *National Geographic Traveler* magazine. Years later, she is now the senior editor of National Geographic Travel Books and, having visited France many times since her first visit, her favorite region is still Provence.

Gérard Sioen has traveled around the globe since 1974. His pictures appear in numerous photography books, including *Vive le Pays Cathare, Californie, Egypt, Camargue,* and *Provence.* For the past decade his work has focused on southern France, where he opened galleries in St.-Rémy-de-Provence, Gordes, and Carcassonne.

Christopher Pitts wrote the Hotels & Restaurants, Shopping, and Entertainment & Activities sections.

History & culture

The Marseillais fought fiercely against the Royals during the French Revolution.

Provence & the Côte d'Azur today

TO DEAL CARDS THE PROVENÇAL WAY IS TO THROW THEM DOWN ON THE table so they become as mixed as possible. This practice aptly describes Provence itself: a jumble of orchard-dotted valleys and snowcapped peaks, turgid rivers and bubbling springs. Mixed in are Roman ruins, pebbly beaches, bird-filled marshes, and deep, dark forests. There are lively cities like Nice and Marseille, and sleepy medieval hill towns. Old and new, traditional and modern, natural and man-made all combine to make up this most enchanted land, a varied and contradictory realm indeed.

There's one thing, however, that's universally agreed upon. Cross into Provence and you succumb to its charms. The translucent light, the dazzling blue skies, the exquisite scenery all work together to seduce you. Sitting at the Café de France's terrace in Lacoste, sipping an

apéritif and overlooking the patchwork fields far below, Bonnieux's golden medieval buildings rising on a hill beyond. Coming upon a field of blooming lavender on the plain near Buoux, the tiny buds creating an effervescent blue-violet aura. Watching a *santonnier* meticulously paint a tiny terra-cotta figure in the Côtes du Rhône village of Ségurat, as artisans have for centuries. Sampling a bowl of savory bouillabaisse by Marseille's raucous fish market. Scanning the Camargue sky for flocks of flamingos ...

Provence is a glorious place, celebrated for its fruity wines, abundant fruits and vegetables, indigenous Romanesque architecture, year-long calendar of festivals, friendly people,

lilting accent, famous beaches ... all good reasons to explain why everyone from ancient Romans to movie stars have been lured here.

There's a certain *je ne sais quoi* about the Provençal style, a flair that is both rustic and sophisticated, traditional and elegant—and nothing is accidental: The stone for the walls is faded by centuries of sun, the bright and distinctive fabrics for table and bed come from designers working in a centuries-old tradition, the pottery and glassware are the product of local craftsmen.

Even those who haven't visited know Provence's joyful vibrance, thanks largely to the parade of artists who have passed through: Matisse, Renoir, Picasso, Bonnard, Chagall, and Aix-native Cézanne, to name a few. But the artist most affected by the landscape was certainly Vincent van Gogh, who moved to Arles in 1888 and frenetically painted more than 150 canvases over the next two years. It's these tableaus that have given us the most quintessential image of Provence: the bold, colorful irises, sunflowers, starry nights, outdoor cafés. He wrote his sister Willemien in 1888: "Nature in the south cannot be painted with the palette of a mauve for instance which belongs to the north ... how the palette is distinctly colorful, sky blue, orange, pink, vermillion, a very bright yellow, bright green, wine and violet."

But, as with most things, there's more than meets the eye.

MOTHER NATURE

Porous limestone is the basic ingredient of the Provençal landscape, nurturing an arid vegetation that features silvery olive trees and prickly succulents, the thick *maquis* and *garrigue* (shrublands). Water is greatly cherished, noted by the myriad fountains in towns and villages. In a few days, or a few hours, it can rain here as much as it does in Paris in a year. Then the mountains blur into torrents, as the water races toward the Verdon, the Durance, the

Marseille faces a sparkling future, with millions of euros being poured into its economy as part of the Euroméditerrannée project's goal of making it the most important Mediterranean port by 2010.

Rhône, the Mediterranean Sea. After, the land can remain parched for months. Adding to this hardship, the mistral wind rages down from the north more than a hundred days a year, ravaging farm crops, influencing the positioning of houses, and affecting people's moods. It overturns cars, rips off roof tiles, uproots trees. Provençal writer Marcel Pagnol eloquently portrayed nature's fury in *Jean de Florette* and *Manon des Sources,* the story of a kind farmer's demise due to conniving neighbors who hide the source of a nearby spring from him, and his daughter's revenge upon his death.

AGRICULTURAL PARADISE

"How can this rocky, seemingly forsaken land give us such richness?" asks food writer Patricia Wells in the introduction to her book, *At Home in Provence.* Indeed, the hardy Provençaux coax an Eden of produce from this brutal climate: exquisite truffles, luscious red cherries, quinces, pears, olives, rich wines,

pungent goat cheeses. The farmers' markets are always full of such delicacies, along with bundles of sunflowers, *coquelicots* (red poppies), or whatever other seasonal flowers are blooming in nearby fields.

Such bounty defines the root of the Provençal character—resilient, hardworking, making much from little. Historically farmers and fishermen, the Provençaux have always been tied close to the earth. Rather than dominating, they have adapted, planting trees for

Purple waves of lavender roll across the Plateau de Puimichel. Cutting machines do most of the work these days, though some of the smaller, older fields lack sufficient space for tractors and must be harvested by hand.

shade from the hot Midi sun, facing houses away from the relentless north wind, adding heavy shutters to their homes to keep out harsh temperatures.

The rural way of life was jeopardized after

World War II, when Provence, with the rest of France, embraced industrialization. The economic focus moved to Concorde supersonic aircraft, nuclear power, and other pursuits. Farmers were encouraged to modernize their equipment. Many went bankrupt, since their small farms were not suitable for new tools designed for larger plots. In the early 1980s, only 10 percent of the Provençaux worked as farmers, compared with 35 percent before World War II.

But then a global trend toward organic, biologically sound produce came to the rescue. People could not get enough fresh, organic pressed olive oil, herbs, wines—Provence's forte. Provence reinstated the family farms, a back-to-tradition trend that persists to this day. Indeed, Provence holds the top spot in France for the production and exporting of produce.

All this is not to say that modernity is bypassing the region. Not at all. Nuclear research continues at Cadarache, while La

to Europe, this fully fledged urban development operation, covering nearly 740 acres (300 ha) in the city's heart, aims to bring major professional and technology companies together in one place. In addition, new cultural venues and modern housing are being built, museums are being renovated, and fine restaurants are opening. In this way, it is hoped that by 2010 Marseille will become the center of the Mediterranean free-trade zone.

THE HEART OF TRADITION

Wrapped in heirloom lace, the Queen of Arles speaks fluent Provençal, the traditional regional dialect—a distinction much more important than beauty. Elected every three years by a panel of seven judges, l'Arlesienne, as she is called, epitomizes the region's enduring devotion to tradition, embedded throughout the Provençal culture in myriad ways.

Each village has its own coat of arms, for instance, its own fruits, cheeses, wines, and specialty sweets. The yearly calendar is filled with local festivals, many including traditional dance, music, and costumes. Most are religious—the festival in Les-Stes.-Maries-de-la-Mer, for example, which venerates the gypsies' patron saint—or tied closely to the earth around the harvests of lavender, wine, olive oil. Some are obscure. Take Gorbio's snail-lantern festival, in which townspeople wander through the streets carrying empty snail shells aglow with flames. Or Nice's gourd festival, symbolizing the end of winter and a time to make public amends to one's spouse after having been cooped up together all winter.

Of all the festivals that embody Provence's singular traditions, however, the most cherished is Christmas. It all starts with the *gros souper,* the large supper served on Christmas Eve before midnight Mass. The family gathers around a table decorated with sprigs of myrtle and St.-Barbe's wheat and lentil sprouts, which are symbols of prosperity. Additional places are laid for the poor or for parents who have

Gaude is world famous for its contributions to electronics. Marseille devotes much energy to biological research, while atomic and metereological exploration takes place on Mont Ventoux, as well as at Michel-de-Provence and Nice. The Fos-Lavera-Berre industrial and port complex, specializing in petrochemicals, polymers, and fine chemicals, is one of the major chemical platforms in Europe.

And the visitor will hear much about Marseille's Euroméditerranée project. Unique

died, and for three days the table is not cleared, so as to allow angels to take part in the feasting. The Nativity scene is integral to the atmosphere. Everywhere you see *santons* (literally, little saints), the colorful, meticulously carved wooden or clay figures of the Christmas story that have been a traditional local craft since the 18th century.

But perhaps what best defines Provence are its daily traditions, suggesting that the people who live here know how to take life slowly, to take the time to enjoy friends and family, and never get too harried. Shops and businesses (and most museums) close between noon and two or three, even four, as their owners enjoy a long lunch and siesta. Dinners are often long conversational affairs as well, starting with an apéritif—perhaps pastis, the region's popular licorice-flavored liqueur, or a glass of Muscat—and negotiating through several courses of dishes prepared from the freshest of local ingredients.

Provence, it seems, has stayed Provençal by existing separately from the world, creating a special essence all its own. And yet southern France has drawn the world to its borders since the Greeks arrived in 600 B.C. Centuries ago, West Indies traders brought the bold ornamental cottons called *indiennes,* for instance, today so instantly recognizable as Provençal. The salt cod, so prevalent in local dishes, originally came from New England. Marseille, long a

Portside cafés, such as this one in Toulon, promise fresh bouillabaisse and other seafood delectables.

mondial crossroads, is a city of immigrants, with a quarter of its population of North African origin.

And that's the beauty of this beguiling land. There's more than meets the eye. You could spend a lifetime getting to know it. And you should. ■

Goat cheese from Banon has been prepared the same way since Gallo-Roman times: Each piece is wrapped in chestnut leaves and tied with raffia or straw to be kept fresh over winter.

Cuisine du soleil

IN NEARLY EVERY PROVENÇAL TOWN, MARKET STALLS BURGEON WITH sun-kissed goods—cherries, melons, dried sausages, bright red tomatoes, olive oils, goat cheeses—that hint at the region's simple, aromatic, healthy cuisine. Based on the seasons and on age-old tradition, it's a Mediterranean gastronomy, an ode to olives and garlic and tomatoes, that stands apart from the rest of France. Elements hark back to the Greeks—indeed, the Greeks introduced the first olives to the region—with an even greater influence coming from its proximity to Italy. But the Provençaux have ensured that their *cuisine du soleil*—cuisine of the sun—is distinctly their own.

There are three essentials to Provençal cuisine. Garlic anchors most dishes, providing a tangy (and healthy) kick. Olive oil, used as flavoring as well as to cook, is regarded nearly as highly as wine, some even possessing their own AOC *(appellation d'origine contrôlée),* a stamp of quality in which *oléiculteurs* (olive growers) comply with a rigid set of rules. Finally, Provence's wild herbs—basil, thyme, and rosemary especially—season all kinds of dishes, from chicken to ice cream. Sage, chervil leaves, tarragon, aniseed, and lavender are other ubiquitous seasonings.

The region's singular sauces and condiments are working variations of these basic ingredients. The most famous is aïoli, a garlicky mayonnaise that's served with codfish, raw vegetables, or soup. *Anchoïade* is an anchovy paste made with garlic and olive oil, while tapenade is a black-olive-based purée seasoned with garlic, capers, anchovies, and olive oil and served on toast or celery.

Prevalent vegetables include spring asparagus, *aubergines* (eggplants), *courgettes* (zucchini), young artichokes, tomatoes, and mushrooms. Ratatouille is one of the most common vegetable dishes, a savory mixture of onions, tomatoes, aubergines, and courgettes stewed with green peppers, garlic, and *herbes de Provence.* Stuffed vegetables are also popular, including *aubergines farcies à la provençale,* eggplant stuffed with meat, onions, and herbs

Olives for sale at the St.-Rémy-de-Provence farmers' market. More than 15 different varieties are grown in Provence, destined for olive oil or the table.

in a tomato sauce; and *fleurs de courgettes farcies*, stuffed zucchini flowers. From Nice comes *salade Niçoise* (containing most of the following: tomatoes, cucumbers, hard-boiled eggs, onions, green peppers, green beans, olives, sometimes tuna, but never potatoes) and *pissaladière* (onion tart with olives and anchovies). Grilled tomatoes with garlic and breadcrumbs is a common side dish throughout Provence. *Soupe au pistou* is the signature soup, a hearty vegetable, bean, basil concoction served with pistou (a basil, garlic, and olive oil sauce that's stirred in). And no list is complete without *truffes*—truffles—Provence's black gold (see sidebar p. 58).

Lamb is the most common meat dish. The greatest delicacy is *agneau de Sisteron*, roasted with herbs and listed on menus as *gigot d'agneau aux herbes*. Game includes rabbits, hare, wild boar, and birds including snipe and thrush (served in stews and *saucissons*). Beef appears on most menus, served in rich, slow-cooked *daubes*. In the Camargue, you'll come across *taureau* everywhere—bull's meat, served grilled; stewed in red wine, often with olives and tomatoes; or in *boeuf à la gardiane*, usually served with the delicious local nutty rice.

Along the coast, fresh fish is the treat: anchovies, cod, sea bass, sea bream, and whiting, to name a few *délices*, while inland you'll be treated to freshwater trout. In fishing ports west of Marseille you'll find *oursins* (sea urchins), *violets* (sea squirts), and bowlfuls of *bulots* (whelks). But the queen of all seafood dishes is bouillabaisse, Marseille's classic seafood stew that's available up and down the coast (see sidebar p. 124). *Bourride* is a less expensive variation, made with white fish served with aïoli; while *baudroie* is another fish soup with vegetables and garlic.

Provence is celebrated for its fruits, among them Luberon cherries, Cavaillon cantaloupes (grown here since the Avignon papacy), apricots, table grapes, and sumptuous late summer figs from Marseille. The best place to find the seasonal specialties is at a local farmers' market—most towns hold one at least once a week.

As far as cheeses go, goat cheese *(chèvre)* is Provence's forte. Banon is the most famous (it's also made from sheep milk). *Picodon* is a small, tangy goat cheese, while *pelardon* is similar, but ripened and firm. *Brousse* is typically a soft and mild sheep's milk cheese, used in ravioli or served as a dessert with olive oil and honey.

For desserts, see sidebar p. 186. ■

Provence's wines

Provence's fecund soils and sunny climate—with a dash of brutal mistral wind—are ideal for grape growing. The Greeks brought the first vines here, introducing the syrah, a grape variety originally from Shiraz, Persia. Since maceration was not yet known, it was a rosé that through the ages has become Provence's quintessential cool summer swill. Though the region is France's second largest wine-producing area, its quality hasn't always been highly acclaimed. Indeed, "tourist pink" and "hard-to-swallow red" are more common descriptions than "fine" or "rare." Bit by bit that's all changing, as a new generation of winemakers has begun to emphasize quality.

The River Rhône is one of the world's greatest wine rivers, nurturing some of the world's finest wines along its banks. In Provence, these appellations include Tavel, Muscat de Beaumes-de-Venise, and the fabled Châteauneuf-du-Pape. Farther east, the Côtes de Provence is where most of Provence's rosés derive, while pocket vineyards along the Côte d'Azur coastline produce an assortment of wines, including Cassis's illustrious whites. Here is a primer on some of Provence's better known appellations.

Côtes du Rhône This appellation, focusing mostly on reds, extends through six *départements* and three regions, covering more than 148,300 acres (60,000 ha). The southern half, known as *vins méridionaux,* is Provence's segment, located north of Avignon along the Rhône's eastern bank.

The most celebrated vintage is Châteauneuf-du-Pape, harking back to papal days (see pp. 76–77). High in alcohol and easy to enjoy, the strong, full-bodied reds are a complex blend of at least 8 and up to 13 different *cépages* (grape varieties). The dominant grape is Grenache. More rare is the Châteauneuf-du-Pape white, which accounts for 7 percent of production. Outstanding producers include Beaucastel and Rayas.

Other highly regarded reds from the area include hearty and robust Gigondas. From the vicinity, too, come the delicate fruity reds of the 17 Côtes du Rhône villages, noted for their good soil and microclimates. The wines are best when made by the traditional barrel fermented techniques and not the newer carbonic maceration technique.

Provence's most famous (and expensive) rosé is Tavel, originating 8 miles (13 km) west of Châteauneuf-du-Pape. Dry, full-bodied, it's best enjoyed as young as possible. Domaine de la Forcadière and Domaine de la Genestière produce some of the most excellent Tavels.

Finally, Beaumes-de-Venise makes a sweet, fortified muscat that's been entitled its own AOC; it's served as a popular apéritif.

Côtes de Provence Provence's principal AOC (annual production a hundred million bottles), and France's sixth largest, it comprises 44,480 acres (18,000 ha) between Nice and Aix-en-Provence, including the Varois hinterland and bordering the Mediterranean from Hyères to Fréjus. Its diversity of *terroirs* and climates—ranging from coastal maritime to inland hills—means that the appellation covers a wide range of wine types. The majority—75 percent—is fresh and fruity rosé, with 20 percent being multiflavored reds and 5 percent the much rarer whites. Côtes de Provence is always drunk young and served at a crisp 46°F to 50°F (8°C to 10°C). Excellent producers: Domaine Gavoty and Domaine Richeaume.

Vignoble de Bandol Bandol is famed for its round, deep-flavored reds, produced from the dark-berried Mourvèdre grape that requires a minimum of 18 months to age in oaken *foudres.* It's good for immediate consumption but is best known for its *grands vins* that need aging. There's also a rosé produced for local demand, aged a minimum of eight months in wood (unusual for a rosé), giving the wine an orange tinge.

Vignoble de Cassis The tiny seaport of Cassis is renowned for its crisp, nutty whites (75 percent of production), perfectly matching such local specialties as sea snails with garlic mayonnaise. The white wine is good, while reds and rosés are also made. Clos Ste.-Magdelaine produces one of Cassis's most distinctive whites, its grapes grown on a sunny sliver of limestone soil on the edge of the Mediterranean.

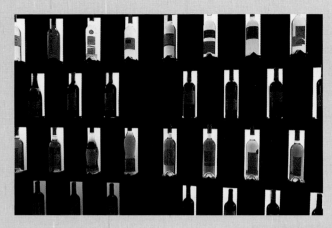

Left: The end product for sale at the Maison des Vins, Les Arcs. Below: The aging process at Domaine Ste.-Roseline. Bottom: Grape gathering near Cotignac, Côtes de Provence.

Tasting, visiting, & buying You can buy directly from the *domaine* (wine-growing estate) of the *producteur* (wine producer) at a lower price than most shops. Most places offer *dégustations* (wine-tastings).

To visit, phone ahead to confirm opening days and times. The best wine-touring is in the Châteauneuf-du-Pape area, Les Dentelles (see drive pp. 68–69), and the Varois hinterland near Les Arcs (see drive pp. 132–133). See p. 230 for information on reading wine labels. ∎

The land

PROVENCE'S DISTINCTIVE LOOK—A JUMBLE OF DAZZLING WHITE LIME-
stone and deep-red ocher cliffs, fields of lavender and a glittering blue sea—derives from
a long geological past.

The story began more than 200 million years ago, when a giant sea covered southeastern France. Then, during the Mesozoic (245 to 66.4 million years ago), emerged the landmass of Tyrrhenia, created by an arc of volcanoes extending from the present-day French Riviera in the north, down to Italy's Tyrrhenian Sea. Slowly leveled by erosion, Tyrrhenia's particles were carried south by rivers and deposited at the bottom of the Tethys Sea, where they transformed into horizontal layers of limestone, clay, shale, and sandstone. In the middle Tertiary, subterranean forces folded these rock layers—the ancient seabed—into the east-west-running limestone ridges so characteristic of Provence today. The remnants of ancient Tyrrhenia include the Massif de l'Estérel west of Cannes, the Massif des Maures, and Sicily and Corsica.

Provence is divided into six *départements* (Vaucluse, Bouches-du-Rhône, Var, Alpes-de-Haute-Provence, and Alpes-Maritimes, plus part of Hautes-Alpes). In the 1960s, these départements became one administrative region called Provence-Alpes-Côte d'Azur, with the capital at Marseille. Tucked into southeastern France, this 160-by-140-mile (257 by 225 km) region is bounded by the River Rhône to the west, the Mediterranean Sea to the south, Italy to the east, and the Alps to the north.

THE DÉPARTEMENTS

With the River Rhône delineating its western edge and the Durance to the south, much of the **Vaucluse** comprises fertile lands for vineyards and fruit growing. But the Vaucluse's character is also defined by the plateau de Vaucluse, speckled with caves and underground rivers that emerge here and there as springs, like that at legendary Fontaine-de-Vaucluse. To the north rises the Ventoux Massif, with Mont Ventoux, at 6,263 feet (1,909 m), the region's highest peak.

The varied **Bouches-du-Rhône**—bounded by the Rhône, the Durance, the Mediterranean, and the Massif de Ste.-Baume—creates a microcosm of Provence. In the west alluvial deposits comprise open plains. South of Les Alpilles, a chain of limestone hills, is La Crau, an enormous field of river pebbles marking the Durance's ancient delta. South of that, the River Rhône melds into the bird-rich marshlands of the Camargue as it nears the sea. In the east, the Arc Valley separates the Ste.-Victoire mountain range from the Étoile chain.

Eastward, wedged between the Mediterranean, the southern Alps, and the Bouches-du-Rhône, the **Var** is Provence's most forested region. Along the coast, great massifs push up against the sea, while the Îles d'Hyères lie offshore.

A borderland between the Var's rocky plateaus and the full-fledged Alps, the **Alpes-Maritimes** features rocky coastline—the fabled Côte d'Azur—backed by the southern Alps foothills.

In the **Alpes-de-Haute-Provence,** Alpine peaks grow sky high. Its Gorges du Verdon is Europe's largest canyon, while, on the Durance's southeast bank, sprawls the plateau de Valensole, Provence's lavender kingdom.

PREVAILING FLORA

Oak-pine forest covers 38 percent of Provence, featuring evergreen, pubescent, and cork oaks and maritime, Aleppo, and umbrella pines. Greeks brought the first olive trees in 600 B.C. The palm tree arrived in the 19th century with the English, who also imported the mimosa, eucalyptus, and succulents from Australia. Lemon and orange trees have been grown along the coast since the Middle Ages, while limes, chestnuts, and almond trees also flourish.

In the scrubby underbrush, called the *maquis,* grow many herbs, including rosemary, basil, tarragon, thyme, fennel, and oregano. Adapted to hotter, drier conditions, the plants of the *garrigue*—including juniper, kermes oak, and ferns—can survive on chalk soil and are well-adapted to the caprices of water. ∎

Pretty as a picture, Montagne Ste.-Victoire

Drystone dwellings, called *bories*, have been built in the Luberon since prehistoric times.

History of Provence

PEACEFUL, PICTURE-PERFECT PROVENCE IS A PRODUCT OF CONFLICT— cities against cities, province against crown, authority against individual, Catholics against Protestants, borders shifting all the while. Along the way, a fierce nationalism took root, renewed by Frédéric Mistral at the turn of the 20th century, and, later, Marcel Pagnol and Jean Giono, and surviving today in a regional loyalty toward all things Provençal—including its proverbial cuisine, traditions, and language.

PREHISTORIC TIMES

Provence's strategic position along the Mediterranean made it attractive to visitors early on. The first arrived in the Monaco area about a million years ago, where they etched drawings on the Grotte de l'Observatoire (today a museum). By 400,000 B.C., early humans were living around the beaches of

Terra Amata in Nice (now the Boulevard Carnot). A series of shallow dwellings contain the remains of hearths scattered with coprolites (fossilized human feces); analyses found seeds grown in the late spring to early fall, suggesting this was a seasonal camp.

Neandertal man showed up about 60,000 years ago, during the Middle Paleolithic period. Modern man—*Homo sapiens*—arrived some 25,000 years later, leaving behind weapons in the Grimaldi grottoes. Shell and fishbone necklaces and bracelets uncovered with skeletons in the coastal Rochers Rouge, outside Menton, indicate a hunting, fishing, and gathering culture.

About 20,000 B.C.—the peak of the last ice age—hunter societies left ornate wall paintings of bison, seals, and ibex in caves such as the Grotte Cosquer in the massif near Cassis—discovered only in the 1960s. The Neolithic period—also known as the New Stone Age—arrived as early as 6000 B.C., during which time the first fixed populations appeared. They raised sheep and cultivated crops, and built drystone houses, called *bories*—that still dot the Luberon, including an entire village at Gordes. They laid their dead to rest in collective stone burial mounds, called dolmens, some of which can be seen in the Massif des Maures.

Sometime between 2800 and 1300 B.C., shepherds journeyed to the remote Vallée des Merveilles near Tende, where they scratched tens of thousands of rock carvings into caves at the foot of Mont Bégo; among them are witchlike figures called *orants,* suggesting this corner might have been a place of worship. Tende's Musée des Merveilles provides a fascinating account of these ancient peoples.

It's difficult to pinpoint the origin of the Ligurians—the next group of people to inhabit Provence—but the term generally refers to anyone living in the Mediterranean area as the Neolithic Age spilled over into the Iron Age. Beginning about 800 B.C., this disparate group built fortified villages on hilltops, today referred to by the Latin name *oppidum.*

About the same time, waves of Celts, a Germanic tribe, invaded Provence from the north. They intermingled with the Ligurians, eventually forming a fierce tribe called the Celto-Ligurians, which established a stronghold at Entremont, just north of present-day Aix-en-Provence.

THE GREEKS
(600 B.C.–118 B.C.)

Western civilization came to Provence in 600 B.C. in the form of Greeks, who settled at Massalia (Marseille). Over a couple of cen-turies, they established trading colonies at Antipolis (Antibes), Nikaia (Nice), Olbia (Hyères), Monoïkos (Monaco), and Glanum (near St.-Rémy). Their introduction of grape vines and olive trees established an economic base that would serve Provence for millennia to come.

As the Romans began their centuries-long domination of the West, the Massalians allied with them, if only because their common enemies included the Etruscans, who occupied lands between the two; the Phoenicians; and the Celts and Ligurians. When Hannibal, the famous general of Carthage (North Africa), crossed the Alps with elephants to attack Rome, the Massalians were quick to join forces with the Romans. In 212 B.C., Massalia switched over to a Roman form of municipal government.

The alliance reached its apex in 125 B.C., when Celto-Ligurians, who had been waiting for just the right moment, banded together to attack Massalia from Entremont. The overwhelmed Massalians called on Rome for help. The Romans destroyed Entremont, establishing the Roman stronghold of Aquae Sextiae Salluviolum (Aix-en-Provence) at its base, the first Roman city of transalpine Gaul. Addressing the need to develop a buffer between Rome and the Celto-Ligurians, as well as to protect their trade route to Spain, the Romans established garrisons in towns between the Alps and the Pyrenees, and the huge Provincia Romana—the first Roman province outside Italy—was born.

PROVINCIA ROMANA
(118 B.C.–A.D. 472)

After Julius Caesar's total conquest of Gaul in 58–51 B.C., the Romans created a prosperous province, where they would remain for 600 peaceful years. Nîmes, Aix, and Arles became important Roman cities, while colonies at Glanum and Vaison-la-Romaine thrived. Throughout Roman Provincia, enormous monuments and landmarks were built, including amphitheaters, arenas, bathhouses, temples, and stadiums, many of which remain standing in well-preserved glory. Roman engineering was applied to transportation (including a road system that spread from Italy to Spain) and the water supply (the Pont du Gard near Nîmes being one of the most striking reminders). One remainder of these culture-rich times was the development of a regional language, Provençal, derived from Latin.

Meantime, Massalia, in recognition of its support for Rome, was allowed to stay an independent state within the Roman territory. However, the city made the lethal mistake of siding with Pompey rather than Caesar during Rome's civil war in 49 B.C. After Caesar rose to power, he punished the town for its lack of allegiance by taking away its independence and transferring its possessions to Arles, Narbonne, and Fréjus. The city nevertheless went on to flourish as an intellectual center whose universities rivaled those of Athens—the last outpost of Greek culture in the west.

The conversion of Constantine the Great to Christianity in A.D. 312 marked the beginning of the end for the Roman Empire. He ruled from Constantinople rather than Rome, and his attention was directed mainly within the Middle East. At the same time, the new religion reached Provence, and soon monasteries and churches were replacing Roman temples.

AGE OF INVASIONS (5TH–10TH CENTURIES A.D.)

The Western Roman Empire expired in A.D. 476, heralded by invasions from several Germanic tribes: the Burgundians (of Scandinavia), Ostragoths (East Goths, from the Black Sea area), and, most notably, the Visigoths (West Goths, from the Danube Delta region in Transylvania). In the sixth century, another Germanic tribe, the Franks, gained the upper hand. Marseille, Arles, and Avignon rebelled and were brutally squashed, and Provence was absorbed into a mix of duchies and kingdoms of western and central Europe that would form the historic kernel of modern-day France and Germany.

Provence remained under Frankish rule beneath the great Carolingian rulers

(including Charlemagne) until 843, when the Treaty of Verdun broke up their kingdom. The ninth and tenth centuries saw further invasions, by the Normans, even the Hungarians, who sacked Nîmes in 924.

But it was the Saracens—a generic term for Muslim invaders, including Turks, Moors, and Arabs—who raised most havoc. Although Provence at first formed an alliance with this marauding force in order to fight the Franks and establish their own independence, skirmishes soon erupted between the forces that lasted for centuries. The villagers withdrew to hilltops where they built fortified towns—many of Provence's *villages perchés* (perched villages) come from this chaotic time. The Saracens were defeated in several battles, but only in A.D. 972, when William the Liberator (Guillaume le Libérateur), count of Arles, attacked their stronghold at La Garde-Freinet in the Massif des Maures was their threat eliminated once and for all.

MEDIEVAL PROVENCE (1000–1300)

In 1032 Provence was absorbed into the Holy Roman Empire. With the power base so far away in southern Germany, however, towns became fiercely independent, and battling barons and shifting alliances occurred with little interference from overlords.

One bright light in these dark times was the huge expansion of church institutions throughout the region, led by Marseille's Abbaye de St.-Victor. This was the era of pilgrimages, especially to St-Trophime in Arles and St.-Guilhem near Aniane, while the Crusades were launched in 1095. At the same time, Provence (as elsewhere in Europe) experienced a spectacular flowering of architecture, poetry, and music. Traveling from castle to castle, troubadours sang Europe's first lyric poetry.

Sometime in the 11th century, a small dynasty awarded itself the title of Counts of Provence, ruling the land between the Rhône and the Alps. When the line died out in 1113, the title passed to the Counts of Barcelona. The clever Raymond Bérenger V (1209–1245), the first Catalan count to reside permanently in

Left: Charlemagne, emperor of the Franks between 800 and 814. Above: Many Crusaders left from Provence's shores to fight the Holy War in the Middle East.

the new Provençal capital of Aix, had high hopes of creating a great Mediterranean empire. He married his daughter Béatrice, heiress of Provence, to Charles d'Anjou, brother of Louis IX (St.-Louis), king of France. After Bérenger's death in 1245, the Comte de Provence (county of Provence) passed to the House of Anjou.

THE POPES COME TO AVIGNON (1309–1417)

Fed up with constant bickering in Rome, French-born Clément V (R.1305–1314)

moved the papal court to Avignon in 1309. Eight more popes followed, ruling the Roman Catholic Church between 1309 and 1376 from this vassal city of the Holy See. The third pope, Benoît XII (R.1334–1342), widely criticized for being arrogant and greedy, began work on the Palais des Papes (Palace of the Popes). More than an acre in size, the palace's over-powering stature exemplified the church's absolute power.

Benoît's successor, Clément VI (R.1342–1352), was an aristocrat used to a life of luxury. He found Benoît's palace austere and simple,

For nearly the entire 14th century, the popes ruled Christendom from Avignon.

and so he built a second, more elegant one. This "New Palace" was admired at the time for being one of the world's most handsome residences and greatest strongholds.

During this time, Avignon and the surrounding area, called the Comtat-Venaissin, experienced a cultural renaissance, with the expansion of new industries such as glassmaking and paper manufacturing and the rise of an artistic school, now known as the Provençal Primitives or the school of Avignon. At the same time, the venality of the papal court caused the city to become infamously corrupt—a fact condemned by

the poet Petrarch, who lived in the city at the time.

Grégoire XI (R.1370–1378) is the pope who finally succeeded in reestablishing the Holy See in Rome, in 1377. However, the French cardinals were so displeased with the next elected pope, Urban VI, an Italian, that they decided to call for a new vote. They selected their own pope, Clément VII, which led to the Great Schism of the Occident, during which time there were two popes, one in Rome and one in Avignon. The schism lasted for nearly 40 years, until 1417, when Martin V established himself in Rome.

MORE MEDIEVAL HAPPENINGS (1348–1536)
The Black Death entered through the port of

The French language is the product of the Roman conquest. The Romans brought both classical Latin (taught in schools and used for literature) and the colloquial Latin of soldiers and merchants. The latter drove out Celtic and gradually evolved into the Romance vernacular known as French. However, a single language did not take root. Various dialects in the south evolved (Provençal, Aquitain, Languedocien, Auvergnat, and Dauphinois), collectively called the *langue d'oc*, while in the north arose a separate set of dialects, called the *langue d'oïl*. The subjection of the southern provinces in the 13th century assured that the northerner's langue d'oïl would dominate— this is today's French language. Provençal survived as a regional spoken language, but its literature died out until its revival in the 19th century. ■

Marseille in 1348, decimating the city's population. At the same time, feudal despots such as the seigneurs of Les Baux added to a general sense of fear and confusion.

By 1409, however, things seemed to be improving. Louis II of Anjou, a most capable ruler, founded the University of Aix. His son, Bon Roi René of Anjou (Good King Rene; 1409–1480), one of the most literate and enlightened men of his time, brought an artistic revival to his court, and during his reign, Aix became Provence's star city. René was the last count of Provence to rule, and, after his death, Provence became part of France. Holy Roman Emperor Charles V took the opportunity to invade Provence between 1524 and 1536 as part of the French-Italian Wars.

WARS OF RELIGION & BEYOND (1545–1720)

Brought on by the Reformation that was sweeping Europe, the Wars of Religion between the Catholics and "heretic" Protestants occupied much of the latter part of the 16th century. Protestant enclaves had taken hold in Orange, Haute-Provence, the Luberon, and especially in Nîmes, where three-quarters of the population became Huguenot (French Protestant). The Catholics became determined to rout them all out.

The wars' opening salvo in Provence occurred in 1545, when the population of 11 Vaudois (a Protestant sect) villages in the Luberon was massacred in six days. Most of Orange's Protestant population was killed in 1563 by neighboring Catholics, while 200 Catholics died in an attack in Nîmes in 1567. The wholesale destruction of churches (including St.-Gilles) and their art took place throughout the region.

Hostilities officially ended with the 1598 Edict of Nantes, in which Henri IV guaranteed Protestants civil and religious liberties. The uneasy peace lasted until 1685, when

Thanks to the efforts of Frédéric Mistral and other Provençal poets and writers, the Provençal language and culture has not been lost to history.

Louis XIV revoked the edict and outright persecution of Protestants ensued again. Many Huguenot leaders were killed or imprisoned in Tour de Constance in Aigues-Mortes and Chateau d'If in Marseille.

In the 17th and 18th centuries, regional alliances decreased as a national awareness grew. Towns expanded with elegant town houses *(hôtels particuliers),* and châteaus proliferated. Despite economic development in the textile industry and the growth of the ports at Toulon (famous for boatbuilding) and Marseille, this was a tough period for many, culminating in the devastating plague of 1720. Introduced in Marseille by a ship from Syria, the plague killed more than half of the city's population. All contact with Marseille was banned and a huge wall was built to halt the epidemic; nevertheless, it spread as far as Toulon, Aix, and Arles before abating the following year.

REVOLUTION (1789–1795)

Sharing the general population's discontent with the royalty, the Provençaux enthusiastically joined forces with the revolutionaries in 1789. In Marseille a guillotine was set up along La Canebière, which some say saw as many royalist heads rolling as the one in Paris. One of Provence's biggest contributions came from Marseille's National Guard, who, as they marched north to Paris, sang a cheery little tune composed several months earlier during the war against Prussia, called "Chant de Guerre de l'Armée du Rhin" ("Battle Hymn of the Rhine Army"). Later it was rechristened "La Marseillaise" and adopted as the French national anthem.

During this time, anarchy reigned throughout France. Many châteaus were destroyed, while churches were desecrated and cathedrals turned into temples of reason. Fearful of religious persecution, people created little clay figurines depicting biblical scenes, called *santons,* which they used to pray in private.

TERRITORIAL RESHUFFLINGS (1790–1860)

In 1790 Provence was divided into three départements: the Var, Bouches-du-Rhône, and Basse-Alps (Lower Alps). France's annexation of papal Avignon and the surrounding Comtat-Venaissin two years later paved the way for the creation of another département—the Vaucluse.

Revolutionary forces seized Nice from Italy in 1793, as well as Monaco, which heretofore had been recognized as an independent state ruled by the Grimaldi family. The British, taking advantage of the confusion, occupied Toulon in 1793, only to be chased away by 24-year-old Napoléon Bonaparte. The young Corsican would go on to take power in 1799 (see feature pp. 158–159).

In 1814 France lost the territories it had seized in 1793. Nice and its surrounding lands went to Victor Emmanuel I, king of Sardinia.

The next year, Napoléon escaped from his exile on Elba, stepping ashore at Golfe-Juan with his boatfuls of supporters. They marched north via Cannes, Grasse, Castellane, Dignes-les-Bains, and Sisteron (today called the Route Napoléon) to Paris, where he returned to power.

Revolting against high taxes, Menton and Roquebrune declared themselves independent from Monaco in 1848. In 1860 Charles III, king of Monaco, ceded rights to these towns to France in exchange for Monaco's recognition as an independent state.

The last major territorial shift saw Nice and its hinterlands returned from the House of Savoy in 1860, when Napoléon III made a pact with the king of Italy, Victor Emmanuel II, to help chase Austrians from northern Italy. In exchange, France repossessed Savoy and Nice.

BELLE ÉPOQUE (1840–1910)

With the Second Empire (1852–1870) came the effort to revive the Provençal culture and language, spearheaded by Frédéric Mistral, author of the epic poem *Mirèio (Mireille).* He was one of seven young poets who in 1854 began the Félibrige Movement, devoted to the cause (see sidebar p. 38).

At the same time, industrialization was transforming the region. The Suez Canal's opening in 1869 and the expansion of France's colonies brought increased port traffic—and wealth—to Marseille. The coastal railway, an engineering marvel with its tunnels and high bridges, reached Toulon in 1856, Nice in 1865, and Monaco in 1868. In 1864 work began on the road between Nice and Monaco.

Above all, this era saw the development of coastal Provence as the playground of the rich and famous. The first regular visitors to the region were English gentlemen, who came to coastal Provence as part of their culture-polishing Grand Tour. Little by little, wealthy French, English, Americans, and Russians learned about the coast's beguiling climate and beautiful scenery and began passing their winters in Nice and Hyères, where they built grandiose villas. Nice's chic Promenade des Anglais was built in 1822.

Cannes's emergence as a tourist resort came in 1834, when Lord Brougham, former lord chancellor of England, was held over at

The belle époque saw the rise of tourism to the French Riviera, advertised as a peaceful Eden.

the then small fishing village and declared that he liked it so much he would build a villa there, which he did. His friends and countrymen followed. Beaulieu and Antibes were also discovered about this time.

Royalty, too, wintered along the Riviera, including Queen Victoria, Aga Khan, and

Empress Eugénie, the wife of Napoléon III. After Stéphane Liégeard published the first guidebook to the French coast in 1887, titled *La Côte d'Azur,* the region had a name. Between 1890 and 1910 the number of foreign visitors to Nice grew nearly sixfold, to more than 150,000—making Nice Europe's fastest growing city.

WORLD WAR I & THE INTERWAR

Provence lost one out of every five men in World War I. The bright side was that the south's reliance on tourism rather than industry meant that it recovered more quickly from the postwar financial crisis that struck elsewhere.

The 1920s and '30s saw the explosion of the glitz and glamour typically associated with the Côte d'Azur. Grandiose hotels were built along the waterfronts of Nice and Cannes. Socialites Sara and Gerald Murphy built Villa America on Cap d'Antibes and invited their friends—including Ernest Hemingway and F. Scott Fitzgerald (who based *Tender is the Night* on his exploits here)—to frolic in the summer sun, thereby inventing the Summer Season. The first casino opened in the Palais de la Méditerranée in Nice in 1929, the creation of American railroad magnate Frank Jay Gould.

A paid summer vacation under the Socialist Front Populaire in 1936 meant even more tourists flocked to the region.

WORLD WAR II

After Paris fell in June 1940, the south became part of the *zone libre,* or free zone (though Menton and its northern Vallée de la Roya were occupied by the Italians). The Côte d'Azur, especially Nice, became known as a safe haven from occupied France, and by 1942 some 43,000 Jews had come to seek refuge. Monaco remained neutral throughout the war.

With Nazi Germany's invasion of Vichy France in 1942, Provence was at war. German troops occupied the south, and the southern Résistance (or maquis, named after the scrubland they hid in) became active.

When the Nazis moved to confiscate French warships at Toulon in 1942, the French scuttled the major portion of their fleet to prevent Germans from seizing them. The Germans responded by invading Toulon, while Italians took over Nice. In January 1943 Hitler gave the 40,000 residents of Marseille's Le Panier quarter—a popular refuge for Jews and Résistance leaders—24 hours to pack up and leave, or face incarceration. The whole neighborhood was duly razed.

Provence was finally freed 10 weeks after D-Day, on August 15, 1944, when Allied forces landed in a two-pronged attack centered on the Var. The southern assault was planned to echo the Normandy invasion on a smaller scale, in which thousands of soldiers parachuted inland overnight ahead of amphibious landings that brought troops to beaches between Cannes and Toulon. Within 14 days, all of Provence had been liberated. The Italian-occupied Vallée de la Roya was not returned to France until 1947.

MODERN PROVENCE

Cannes's International Film Festival in 1947 brought back a sense of normalcy to postwar Côte d'Azur, as well as rocketing Cannes into the role of Europe's film capital. Over the next couple decades, the Côte d'Azur went on to become known worldwide as the glittery enclave of stars, money, and high living. Prince Rainier III's fairy-tale wedding in 1956 to Hollywood film princess Grace Kelly, as well as Brigitte Bardot's role that same year in *Et Dieu Créa la Femme (And God Created Woman),* filmed in St.-Tropez, added to the mystique.

Algeria in 1962 achieved independence, sending some 750,000 impoverished, newly homeless *pieds noirs* ("black feet," as Algerian-born French people were known) to France. Many settled in Provence, especially in Marseille, Toulon, and Nice, setting off a wave of strong anti-immigrant sentiment.

Provence saw rapid industrialization in the 1960s, including five hydroelectric plants on the River Durance and, in 1965, the construction of a 24,710-acre (10,000 ha) petrochemical zone and an industrial port at Fos-sur-Mer.

More and more outsiders (mostly British) began coming to Provence in the late 1970s to restore charming old *mas* (farmhouses), exemplified by Peter Mayle's *A Year in Provence*—whose publication

Members of the maquis Résistance, who helped fight the Nazi garrison in Marseille before the entry of Allied troops, celebrate the city's liberation in September 1944.

in 1990 brought even more hordes, especially to the Luberon.

Corruption reigned in the 1980s and '90s, topped off with the antics of Jacques Médécin, Nice's right-wing mayor who, during his 38-year stint, was found guilty twice of income tax evasion. Socialist President François Mitterand, elected in 1981, created regional governments across France—a major turning point in the centuries-old pursuit of Parisian centralism.

In the mid-1990s, the extreme-right Front National (FN), spearheaded by Jean-Marie Le Pen, won victories in municipal elections in Toulon, Orange, and Marignane in 1995, and in Vitrolles in 1997. The FN failed to make any headway in national politics until the 2002 presidential elections, when Le Pen stunned the nation by earning 4.8 million votes (16.7 percent) in the primary election. His greatest support came from the PACA

(Provence-Alpes-Côte d'Azur) region, where he defeated then-president Jacques Chirac in the first round. Since then, the FN has weakened somewhat with many voters opting instead for Nicolas Sarkozy, who won the 2007 presidential election by wooing away far-right supporters with talk of increased security and anti-immigration policies.

With the new millennium came the opening of the TGV Méditerrannée, cutting travel time between Paris and Marseille to three hours. The whole region awaits the effects of the Euroméditerranée free trade zone, of which Marseille has been chosen to be the central hub. As part of this international economic initiative, due to be in place by 2010, the city will receive three billion euros to transform itself into a booming business center and tourist attraction—a far cry from the rural image that has been associated with Provence since its beginnings. ■

The arts

THE PROVENÇAL LANDSCAPE HAS INSPIRED COUNTLESS ARTISTS, MOST notably van Gogh, Cézanne, Dufy, and others who set off the postimpressionist movement at the turn of the 20th century. After World War II, Pablo Picasso's style took on a lighthearted, colorful mood, directly linked to Provence's ever shining sun and blue skies. Writers, too, have been seduced by Provence—including Frédéric Mistral, determined to preserve its traditional language and culture, and F. Scott Fitzgerald, who recorded the birth of the Summer Season in *Tender is the Night*. Movies were invented on the Côte d'Azur, and the industry is celebrated every May at the Cannes International Film Festival.

ARCHITECTURE

While taking on French and Italian influences through the ages, Provence's architecture has evolved a distinct look all its own. The region's earliest structures were stone megaliths from the Neolithic period (4000–2400 B.C.), of which numerous can be seen in the Vallée des Merveilles. Other early edifices were the Luberon's bories (igloo-shaped drystone huts), dating back as early as 3500 B.C.

Provence's greatest architectural influence came from the Romans. During their 600-year occupation of Provincia Romana, they built classical-style aqueducts, fortifications, marketplaces, temples, amphitheaters, triumphal arches, and bathhouses using large blocks of limestone. While they copied Greek architectural forms, they added their own flourish—massive rounded arches, vaults, and domes, for instance. And while the Greeks used the column as an important focal point, the Romans relegated it to decoration. The Maison Carrée in Nîmes, a perfectly preserved temple, is a prime example.

The Romans may have departed in 476, but their buildings stayed around for centuries—some still exist, including the great amphitheaters at Nîmes and Arles, where modern bullfights are staged to this day; and the theater at Orange, where summer concerts and performances unfold. Elements of other buildings were redeployed by early Christians into new structures. St.-Sauveur's cloister in Aix-en-Provence, dating from the 12th century, for example, typifies this recycling, in which different kinds of columns, pilasters, even tombstones were harmoniously integrated into the new creation.

Invaders chased villagers to hilltops beginning in the Middle Ages, where they built towns protected by fortified walls and gates.

Communication between houses was often by underground passages, streets were roughly paved, and sewage was carried away by a central gutter. These villages perchés have survived as today's picturesque hill towns—Bonnieux, Gordes, and Grimaud among them.

A religious renewal in the 11th century allowed Provence to develop its own distinct architectural approach, the first real Western European style, called Provençal Romanesque. Combining the classic order and perfection of Roman design with new styles from northern and southern Europe, it featured round Roman arches, barrel vaulting, heavy walls with few windows, and little ornamentation. The works were predominantly ecclesiastical in nature, the best examples including the three Cistercian abbeys: Sénanque (1148), Le Thoronet (1160), and Silvacane (1175).

The Gothic style, which flourished throughout northern France in the mid-12th through 16th centuries, did not make much headway into southern France. Ribbed vaults, large stained-glass windows (to teach the largely illiterate congregation the story of their faith in pictures), and, above all, soaring pointed arches (to draw the spirit of man to the heavens) are features of the style. Avignon's Palais des Papes is the south's supreme showcase, while other important examples are the Val de Benediction Charterhouse in Villeneuve-lez-Avignon, the basilica at St.-Maximin-de-la-Ste.-Baume, and Carpentras's Cathédrale St.-Siffrein.

The Renaissance and its illuminating rebirth of culture barely touched Provence, which was otherwise preoccupied with the

Great military architect Vauban oversaw the construction of Entrevaux's 17th-century hilltop citadel.

Wars of Religion. During the 1600s, citadel architecture, spearheaded by Sébastien le Prestre de Vauban (1633–1707), was the period's most notable contribution (see sidebar p. 156). His works in Provence include the Fort Carré in Antibes and the fortification of the hilltop villages of Entrevaux and Sisteron.

Moving into the 18th century, the Italian baroque spilled over Provence's eastern borders, especially into the churches of Menton and Nice. With classic architecture as a base, the style dripped with a profusion of paintings, sculptures, and gilded adornments, creating an overall dramatic effect. Nice's St.-Jacques and Cathédrale Ste.-Réparate and Menton's St.-Michel show off full-blown baroque style. In its later stage, the baroque became known as rococo, which was reduced in scale, moving toward lighter, more frivolous features.

Beginning about 1740, neoclassicism encompassed a renewed interest in classical forms normally associated with antiquity—columns, simple geometric shapes, traditional ornamentation—that showed stability and permanence during increasingly turbulent times. In domestic buildings it's seen in elegant facades graced with elaborate doorway carvings and windows (as in the buildings of Aix's Mazarin Quarter). The style came into its own in the mid-1800s under Napoléon III, who used it to convey a sense of grandeur and imperialism in his monumental architecture.

Belle époque architects—who reigned between 1870 and 1914 and based their eclectic works on teachings of the École des Beaux-Arts—made play with all historical styles according to their fantasies: Arabesque palaces rose beside medieval and neo-Gothic châteaus, "wedding cakes" beside "chocolate boxes." The extravagant trimmings often included decorative stucco friezes and trompe l'oeil paintings. The finest collection of belle époque villas is

Peille's vaulted passageways and cobbled lanes epitomize the architecture of medieval *villages perchés*, villages built on hilltops to protect citizens from marauders.

Ironwork bell towers

Skeletal bell towers grace Provence's church steeples, a centuries-old design that yields to damaging mistral winds. Gusts blow right through the light, open, wrought-iron framework, carrying the bells' melodic tolling far and wide. Some bell towers are highly ornamental, others plain and simple, but all are exclusively Provençal. ∎

found in Nice (see sidebar p. 171).

France's most celebrated 20th-century architect is Charles Edouard Jeanneret, better known as Le Corbusier (1887–1965), one of the major instigators of the International Style. Le Corbusier interpreted objects akin to cubist painters, pioneering a philosophy of functionality summarized in his famous dictum: "Buildings are machines to live in." His greatest work in Provence is Marseille's Unité d'Habitation (1946–1952), a massive housing project of 340 superimposed villas raised above ground on freestanding supports *(pilotis)*.

More recently, ultramodern styles have been used for many art galleries, including the Musée d'Art Moderne et d'Art Contemporain in Nice (1990), with its square towers linked with glass passageways; and Sir Norman Foster's award-winning Carré d'Art in Nîmes (1993), its glass walls between concrete columns harmonizing with the adjacent Roman temple.

A discussion of Provence's architecture is not complete with touching upon the vernacular—seen most prominently in the traditional stone-built mas (farmhouses) speckling the countryside, as well as the *cabanes* of the Camargue *gardians* (bull herdsmen or cowboys). Both types of buildings are squat, sturdy structures with thick, stone walls, small windows, heavy shutters, and reinforced doors that ward off the brutal mistral wind and relentless summer sun. On their northern sides, rows of cypresses break the wind, while windows are usually nonexistent. To the south, plane and locust trees provide shade.

PROVENÇAL LITERATURE

Beautiful writings have graced Provence's culture since the Middle Ages, when troubadours sang lyrical poems throughout the region's courts. Written in the ancient *langue d'oc* (see sidebar p. 29), with strict conventions regarding rhyme and meter, these works consisted of *cansos* (elaborate love songs), *sirventes* (satires), and *partimen* (debate poetry). Provence's most celebrated troubadours included Bernart de Ventadorn and Raimbaut de Vacqueyras.

Provençal literature declined after Provence was annexed to France in 1481 and French evolved into the official language. Some writers, however, continued to write in the ancient tongue. Among the more notable was Grasse native Louis Bellaud, better known as Bellaud de la Bellaudière (1532–1588), whose *Obros et Rimos Provensalos (Provençal Works and Rhymes)* comprises 160 sonnets. Nicolas Saboly of Avignon (1614–1675) was the classic age's greatest Provençal writer. His *Noëls Provençaux,* a series of poems about a nativity scene, later influenced the work of Frédéric Mistral and Joseph Roumanille.

The name most closely related to the Provençal movement is that of poet Frédéric Mistral (1830–1914), who wrote solely in the ancient language and was also largely responsible for the late 19th-century revival in Provençal literature (see sidebar p. 38).

Provence's French-language literature

Physician and astrologer Nostradamus, born in St.-Rémy in 1503, became famous with *Les*

Frédéric Mistral

Early on a lover of the Provençal traditions and language—the ancient *langue d'oc*, the tongue of the troubadours—poet Frédéric Mistral (1830–1914) devoted his life to preserving the age-old ways of Provence. While presenting the purity of the Provençal language in his writings, he extolled the beauty of Provence's countryside and people. Among his most famous works are *Mirèio* (1859), the epic story of two star-crossed lovers; *Calendau* (1867), about Provençal fishermen; and *Nerto* (1884), about the popes' last days in Avignon. Over 20 years he also compiled a dictionary of the Provençal language, dialects, beliefs, and traditions, the *Lou Tresor doù Felibrige (Treasury of Félibres)*. With six other writer friends, including Théodore Aubanel, Jean Brunet, and Alphonse Tavan, Mistral in 1854 founded the Félibres, a group of militant Provençal writers determined to save southern France's original language. He went on to win the Nobel Prize for Literature in 1904 and used his prize money to establish the Museon Arlaten in Arles that same year. For the most part, however, Mistral and his group were celebrating a time of the past, and the movement could not be sustained. While there are vestiges of a lively Provençal literature, it's increasingly the language of the elderly and those living in Provence's remote corners. ∎

Centuries (1555), a book of more than a thousand prophesies in verse quatrains. He died in Salon-de-Provence in 1566, of gout, as he had predicted.

The controversial Marquis de Sade (1740–1814), who owned as castle at Lacoste in the Luberon, led a life of criminal debauchery for which he was condemned to death in 1772. He passed his sentence both at the Bastille and the Vincennes dungeon, writing his best known works: *Justine, ou les Malheurs de la Vertu; Juliette, ou les Prospérités du Vice;* and *La Philosophie dans le Boudoir.* The Revolution freed him, after which he busied himself with the publication of his books. While many consider his writings licentious and obscene, some critics stress his importance as a precursor of Nietzsche's Superman. His style is said to also have influenced such 19th-century writers as Charles Baudelaire and Alphonse de Lamartine.

Nîmes-born Alphonse Daudet (1840–1897) spent a considerable amount of time with Mistral in Maillane, though he wrote in French, not Provençal. His romantic drama *L'Arlésienne* was later set to music by Bizet, but the novelist is chiefly remembered for *Lettres de Mon Moulin (Letters from My Windmill)*, published in 1866. Based on Daudet's visits to Fontvieille, the collection of sentimental yet humorous sketches portrays Provençal life and culture.

In the 20th century, Jean Giono (1895–1970), a native of Manosque, celebrated the Provençal Alps and their people in rich poetic language. Among his most famous works is *The Horseman on the Roof (Le Hussard sur le Toit)*, made into a movie in 1995. His contemporary, Marcel Pagnol (1895–1974), is primarily a playwright and only incidentally a novelist. In 1952 he filmed *Manon des Sources* near La Treille, and the movie was so successful that he wrote a novel, *L'Eau des Collines* (1962), comprising *Jean de Florette* and *Manon des Sources.*

One of the most highly regarded, yet controversial, 20th-century French poets was René Char (1907–1988), born in L'Isle-sur-la-Sorgue. He began as a surrealist, then settled into his own style of elliptical, abrupt verse and prose-poems. A strong cultural force in the French Résistance, and a militant

Sporting a bullfighter's hat, Pablo Picasso (center) enjoys a mock bullfight in Vallauris in 1955 with artist pal Jean Cocteau (to his right). Picasso revitalized the town's ceramics industry.

demonstrator against nuclear proliferation, he confronted major 20th-century moral, political, and artistic issues in his writings.

The early writings of St.-Tropez resident Françoise Sagan (1935–2004) addressed the rebelliousness and cynicism of her peers in French bourgeoisie. Her 1954 novel, *Bonjour Tristesse (Hello Sadness),* about a jealous, 17-year-old girl whose meddling in her father's impending remarriage leads to tragic consequences, was set on the Côte d'Azur.

Answering Provence's muse

Many foreign writers have succumbed to Provence's allure. The earliest was Italian poet Petrarch (1304–1374), who moved to Avignon with his father at age nine. There in 1327 he cast eyes on the lovely but married Laura de Noves, to whom he wrote 366 love sonnets and ballads. Tortured by his unrequited love (and fed up with papal corruption), he moved to Fontaine-de-Vaucluse, where he wrote his *Canzoniere* songbook for her. With that, he became one of the greatest Renaissance poets and, along with Dante, among the first to write in vernacular Italian.

Many centuries later, during the "great days" of the 1920s and '30s, British novelist Somerset Maugham lived on Cap-Ferrat. He set little of his fiction in Provence, however, apart from two short stories: "The Three Fat Women of Antibes" and "The Facts of Life." American F. Scott Fitzgerald (1896–1940) is probably the most famous expat author. He and his wife, Zelda, spent summers on Cap-Ferrat, playing and partying with Ernest Hemingway and other Americans.

Other foreign writers came to the French Riviera for health reasons. Sick with tuberculosis, D. H. Lawrence stayed at Bandol in 1929, then moved to Vence, where he died. Katherine Mansfield resided in Bandol, then moved to Menton in 1920–1921, where she did some of her finest writing. But even Menton's idyllic weather could not cure her consumption, and she died in 1923.

PAINTING

Provence's first painters were Upper Paleolithic-era inhabitants who adorned the recently discovered Grotte Cosquer, near Marseille, with dozens of painted and etched horses, stags, bison, auks, and human hands. Any significant contribution to the painting movement, however, didn't come about until the 14th century, when the popes moved to Avignon (1309–1417) and hired some of Italy's finest artists to decorate their Palais des Papes. Foremost among the talented group was Simone Martini of Siena (1280–1344), one of the most original and influential artists of the Sienese school, and his assistant, Matteo Giovannetti of Viterbo. Their magnificent frescoes fuse Italian naturalism with French Gothic in a refined, elegant style that became known in Western European courts as International Gothic.

The school of Avignon developed in the early 15th century, assimilating International Gothic with the precise techniques of Flemish masters and producing some of the greatest paintings in the history of French art. Two northern masters headed the movement, Enguerrand Charenton (or Quarton; circa 1416–1466) and Nicolas Froment (1435–1486). Charenton's tragic "Avignon Pietà," his best-known work, now hangs in the Louvre, but one major painting survives in Provence: his panel of "The Coronation of the Virgin" (1453), now in Villeneuve-lez-Avignon's Musée Municipal. Froment is best known for his "Le Buisson Ardent" ("Burning Bush"; 1475–1476), a minutely observed triptych hanging in Aix's cathedral (see p. 111). It was commissioned by Bon Roi René, count of Provence, who did much to foster the arts in the 15th century and made Aix into an important cultural center.

The Bréa family, above all Louis Bréa (1450–1523), dominated the school of Nice, which flourished in the 15th and 16th centuries and marked the transition between medieval and Renaissance art (Nice was then a part of Italy). They illuminated the altarpieces of many churches in Nice and the nearby countryside. Louis's first known work is a triptych of the Pietà (1475), in the parish church at Cimiez, thoroughly Provençal in derivation with its similarities to Charenton's Pietà. Apart from the Bréas, Provence missed out on the great

flowering of the Renaissance—preoccupied as it was with the Wars of Religion, as well as with its annexation to France, after which time artists moved to Rome and Paris for better opportunities.

Great baroque sculptor (and architect) Pierre Puget (1620–1694) made a name for himself as the Michelangelo of Provence. He began his career painting figureheads, then moved to Rome to study under the master Bernini, leaving behind in his native Marseille the Vieille-Charité renovation and sculptures in its Musée des Beaux-Arts.

An interest in sentiment and emotion in the 18th century rooted itself in the painting world as romanticism, headed by Eugène Delacroix and Jean-Auguste-Dominique Ingres. Provence's virtuoso romantic painter was Grasse-born Jean-Honoré Fragonard (1732–1806). Celebrated for his highly sensual, graceful depictions of lovers, cupids, and youthful Venuses, Fragonard's fame heightened in 1771, when he painted for Louis XV's pleasure-loving court. Some of his works are on display at the Villa-Musée Fragonard in Grasse. Another influential Provençal artist of this period was Avignon native Claude-Joseph Vernet (1714–1789), one of the finest landscape painters of the day. His unusually subtle observations of the play of light on water is reflected in his dramatic seascapes, shipwrecks, and conflagrations. His best works include the series of 15 "Ports of France," hanging in the Louvre.

Postimpressionism & modern art

In the 19th and 20th centuries, artists discovered Provence's luminescent light and unparalleled scenery, and the region will ever be associated with this crucial period of art. One of the most influential artists of this time is Paul Cézanne (1839–1906), of Aix-en-Provence. Having spent some time in Paris and Auvers-sur-Oise, he returned south in 1870 to escape the Franco-Prussian War. Here the Impressionist contemporary entered a later phase built around a few basic subjects: still lifes of studio objects focused on recurring elements such as apples, statuary, and tablecloths; studies of bathers; and, above all, successive views of nearby Montagne

Vincent van Gogh captured a clear St.-Rémy night in "Nuit Etoilée" ("Starry Night"; 1889), just one of his flurry of canvases completed during his stay in Provence in 1888–1889.

Ste.-Victoire. He captured this stark limestone mountain on canvas more than a hundred times, trying to see the "cylinder, the sphere, and the cone in its form," a thought process that heralds abstract painting. Though no major Cézanne works are in Provence, a handful of minor ones are found at Aix's Musée Granet.

In 1907 in Paris, artist Georges Braque rediscovered Paul Cézanne at memorial exhibitions at the Salon d'Automne and Galerie Bernheim-Jeune. He—along with his new friend Pablo Picasso—saw in Cézanne's late works a new geometrization of form and new spatial relationships that became the basis of cubism.

Vincent van Gogh's (1853–1890) greatest paintings were done during his two years in Provence, including "Le Café de Nuit Sur l'Endroit Lamartine, Arles" ("The Night Café on the Place Lamartine, Arles"), "La Chambre à Coucher" ("Bedroom"), and "La Maison Jaune" ("The Yellow House"), all painted in 1888. He came to Arles from Paris that year, in the hopes of establishing an Académie du Midi. He persuaded his friend and mentor Paul Gauguin (1848–1903) to join him, but Gauguin found Arles ugly and wanted to move back north. Seesawing between elation and depression, fighting his own demons, van Gogh finally threatened Gauguin on the street with a razor, then cut off his own ear. He was taken to the Hôtel-Dieu (now Éspace Van Gogh), then in May 1889 voluntarily confined himself to an asylum in St.-Rémy. Here he painted flowers (including his famous "Irises") and views of the asylum garden. He left for Auvers-sur-Oise in May 1890, where the disturbed artist, at the height of his genius, produced 76 more paintings before committing suicide on July 27.

Though van Gogh failed to establish an

artistic school, he greatly influenced the fauvists.

Henri Matisse and André Derain, who happened upon some of his paintings at the Galerie Bernheim-Jeune in Paris in 1901, along with Georges Rouault, Maurice de Vlaminck, Raoul Dufy, and Kees van Dongen, were inspired by his simplified forms and vibrant colors. They showed their own van Gogh-inspired works—mostly painted along the Côte d'Azur, especially La Ciotat, Cassis, and L'Éstaque—at the Salon d'Automne in 1905. An art critic described the room as a *cage aux fauves* (cage of wild beasts)—the term "fauve" was hence born.

Other artists discovered the Côte d'Azur's allure around the turn of the 20th century. In 1892 pointillist painter Paul Signac (1863–1935) visited St.-Tropez and was so bedazzled by its beauty that he bought a house there. Fauvist Pierre-Albert Marquet (1875–1947) lived in Marseille beginning in 1916. One of the founders of the Nabis, Pierre Bonnard (1867–1947) lived in Le Cannet for more than 20 years until his death. During this time he depicted the personal environment of the artist—picnics, garden views, lunchtime with friends—and developed a style that united color and light, offering a transition from Impressionism to abstract art.

The biggest name of this period, however, was an aging Pierre-Auguste Renoir (1841–1919), one of the founders of the Impressionists, who visited the coast in the late 1890s for health reasons. He lived in Le Cannet, Villefranche, and Antibes, finally buying a house and studio at Cagnes-sur-Mer. He painted "Les Grandes Baigneuses" here in 1887, though he despised painting outdoors and focused more on sculpture.

Interwar & beyond

Henri Matisse (1869–1954) began developing an interest in color after seeing a group of Impressionist works in a collection of an Australian painter in Brittany. His real discovery, however, had come when he visited Paul Signac in St.-Tropez in 1904, which inspired his "Luxe, Calme, et Volupté." The next year, Matisse went to Collioure in Roussillon with his friend Derain, where he created the first major work of his career, "Le Bonheur de Vivre" ("The Happiness of Life").

From there, he took his own road, full of color and Middle Eastern mystique. He first visited Nice in 1917 and, enchanted by the brilliant and sensual environment, began spending his winters there two years later. His last major work, the one he believed was his crowning achievement, was the Chapelle du Rosaire in Vence, a chapel that he designed in its entirety, from the stained-glass windows and Stations of the Cross drawings to the candlesticks and priest vestments.

Inspired by Cézanne and early cubism, Fernand Léger (1881–1955) developed a distinct style in which he used simple lines and blocks of color to depict urban and machine imagery, as well as scenes of proletariat life. Upon his death, his wife opened a museum devoted to him in Biot.

Probably the south's most influential artist in this world of influential artists was Pablo Picasso (1881–1973). After spending the bleak war years in Paris, the flamboyant Catalan came to Antibes in 1945 where, beneath the brilliant Midi sun, he produced exuberant masterpiece after masterpiece. His works contain a certain playfulness, full of fauns and goats and sea urchins. Picasso once stated: "It's strange that in Paris I never drew fauns, centaurs, or mythical heroes like this. You would think they only existed here." The standout is his "Joie de Vivre" ("Joy of Life"; 1946), a lighthearted, whimsical depiction of his latest lover, Françoise Gilot, as a dancing woman-flower bathed in light and surrounded by flute-playing centaurs and fauns. Most of his works, including "Joie de Vivre," hang at the Château Grimaldi in Antibes, where he had his studio. While in Provence, Picasso also stumbled across the ancient art of pottery-making at Vallauris's Madoura workshop, beginning a long adventure in ceramics.

French-Russian painter Marc Chagall (1887–1985) is best known for his joyful illustrations of folk tales and Bible stories, though he also worked as a designer of book illustrations, stage sets, and stained-glass windows. He moved to Vence in 1950, where he first attempted painting and modeling ceramics and, a few years later, created his first mosaics. Nice's Musée National Message Biblique Marc Chagall showcases his interpretations of the Bible on vast, colorful canvases. He is buried in St.-Paul-de-Vence.

Hungarian-born Victor Vasarely (1908–1997) began as a graphic designer and turned completely to abstract painting in 1947. He is a major pioneer of op art, a style that uses hard-edged black and white or colored patterns that appear to vibrate and change their shape as the viewer looks at them. The Fondation Vasarely in Aix-en-Provence showcases 42 of his works.

CINEMA

When cinematography pioneers Auguste and Louis Lumière showed their two-minute reel of a train pulling into La Ciotat's train station (*L'Entrée d'un Train en Gare de La Ciotat* or *The Arrival of a Train at La Ciotat Station*), moviegoers were startled out of their seats. The year was 1895, the place their father's Château Lumière in La Ciotat (three months before the Paris premiere), and Provence has been involved in the film world ever since.

Grace Kelly and Cary Grant lounge on a beach in the 1955 classic *To Catch a Thief.*

Eventually, as the focus of art shifted across the Atlantic, Provence lost its artistic limelight. There are still pockets of innovation, however. In the 1960s, Nice became the center of nouveau réalisme, the French version of pop art. Leading members were Yves Klein, Martial Raysse, and Arman, all of whose works can be seen in Nice's ultramodern Musée d'Art Moderne et Contemporain. The geometrically abstract Support, Surface Group emerged in Nice in 1969, founded by Claude Villat (1936–). Modern artists from Provence include Gilles Barbier, Stéphane Magnin, and Francesco Finizio.

Seeking greater independence, Hollywood producer Rex Ingram (1893–1950) bought Victorine film studios in Nice in 1925, thereby turning the city into the Little Hollywood of the Côte d'Azur. The first silent movie he created there, *Mare Nostrum* (1926), was a spy story involving German submarines.

Writer and director Marcel Pagnol (1895–1974) built studios near Marseille in 1934, and during the '30s devoted himself almost entirely to making films—including *La Femme du Boulanger (The Baker's Wife,* 1938), based on Jean Giono's novel about a baker's wife who runs off with a shepherd, thereby shattering the village's tranquility when the

Brad Pitt and Angelina Jolie arrive at the premiere of "A Mighty Heart" during the 60th Cannes Film Festival in 2007.

baker stops baking. All of Pagnol's films were set in Provence, with dialogue written for the southern accent. Toulon native Raimu, one of Pagnol's greatest stars, is best remembered for his amusing portrayals of Provençal characters.

Cannes donned its cloak of glamour in 1947 when movie stars hit La Croisette during the first Cannes International Film Festival. Every May, the city still fills with stars, as films from all over the globe are judged, including documentaries, short films, and feature-length films. Considered one of the world's most prestigious film festivals, it is also a serious marketplace, where much wheeling and dealing of films and talent take place.

After a wartime slump, Provence's movie industry perked up in 1956 with *Et Dieu Créa la Femme (And God Created Woman)*, a low-budget flick directed by young Roger Vadim and starring his wife, an unknown Brigitte Bardot. In no time, of course, BB became an international sex symbol, one of the few to be created outside Hollywood. The movie is also significant because it proved to French film financiers that young directors could make commercial successes, helping to pave the way for the *nouvelle vague.*

"New wave" is a term journalists used to describe the swell of new directors making their first feature films in France in the late fifties and beyond. Aggressive, unorthodox, influential, these directors have become some of the film industry's biggest names: Jean-Luc Godard, François Truffaut, Louis Malle. Claude Chabrol's *Le Beau Serge* (1959) was the earliest film to draw attention, though it wasn't particularly successful. The real breakthrough came in 1959 with Truffaut's *Les Quatre Cents Coups,* which won a prize at Cannes for direction, and Alain Resnais's *Hiroshima Mon Amour,* which won the French Syndicate of Cinema Critics award.

Though the new wave has lost its edge, and the Victorine today makes only TV commercials, Provence continues to be a favorite backdrop among filmmakers and a playground for the stars. ■

Beyond majestic Avignon, the popes' medieval center of power, awaits a storied land of vineyards, lavender fields, piled-high market stalls, and hill towns, with Roman ruins abounding throughout.

Avignon & the Vaucluse

Capturing the Abbaye de Sénanque on canvas

Avignon & the Vaucluse

NAMED AFTER THE CLOSED VALLEY THAT HARBORS THE FONTAINE-DE-Vaucluse, this dreamy region of perched villages, ocher cliffs, rocky limestone mountains, and endless vineyards fans out north and east from its capital of Avignon. The Romans left behind columns, bridges, and triumphal arches, but it was the arrival of the popes in the 14th century that changed the area forever. Known for their ostentatious lifestyle, bringing grapes, melons, and an entire new outlook on art, architecture, and theater, the popes heralded a new era of culture and good living that's still celebrated today.

Snuggled inside ancient city walls along the River Rhône, Avignon is the area's largest town, its high point being the impressive Palais des Papes. But there's much more here, including several art and cultural museums installed in centuries-old *hôtels particuliers*.

Eastward lies the fabled Luberon, the idyllic countryside that everyone pictures at the mention of Provence, with its vibrant fields, blooming flowers, and toylike hill towns. The Marquis de Sade left his imprint in Lacoste's château (recently bought by Pierre Cardin for summer theater), while the villages of Menèrbes, Bonnieux, and Oppède-le-Vieux have their own charms. Lesser known Luberon includes tiny hamlets far off the tourist track,

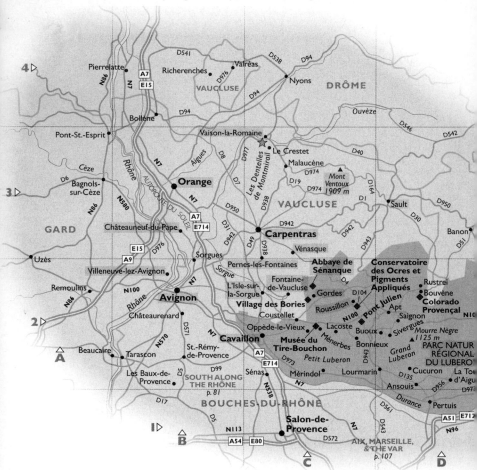

... of farmland are a Roman legacy (see sidebar p. 79).

...ose château is known ... ovence" for the ...tists it has fostered

...ter tinges the soil ...ssillon, where a short ...wanders through the whimsical formations of a disused ocher quarry.

Gordes has perched on its clifftop aerie since the 16th century, its Renaissance château towering above. Older is the nearby Village des Bories, a small settlement of drystone dwellings dating from the 17th century (though the technology is much older) and, even older, the Abbaye de Sénanque, founded in 1148.

The towns of L'Isle-sur-la-Sorgue and Fontaine-de-Vaucluse grew up on the River Sorgue. The former is best known for its antique markets, while the latter's mystique swirls around the seemingly endless spring that feeds the river. How deep is it? No one knows. Both are picturesque but touristy towns, with Vaucluse offering a plethora of museums, including one devoted to former resident Petrarch and another to the Résistance movement during World War II.

Roman ruins abound in Vaison-la-Romaine, a picturesque town with an upper and lower village, spanned by an ancient Roman bridge. Vaison is the starting point for a drive around Les Dentelles de Montmirail, showcasing the hilly, vine-striped beauty of the Côtes du Rhône countryside. More Roman relics await in Orange, including the world's best preserved amphitheater, where performances still are held. ■

Map labels

ALPES-DE-HAUTE-PROVENCE

D951
N96
D13
D4

N100
• Forcalquier
D13

ALPES PROVENÇALES
p. 187

0 ____ 12 kilometers
0 ____ 12 miles

N96 **A51**
E712
•osque

Valensole

D952
D23

VAR

AVIGNON & THE VAUCLUSE
ITALY

Area of map detail

△
E

Avignon
🅰 46 B2
**Visitor
information**
✉ 41 cours Jean-Jaurès
☎ 04 32 74 32 74
www.ot-avignon.fr

Note: Avignon's PASSion
provides reductions
on entrance fees to
all monuments and
museums; available
at the tourism
office, or at the
various sights.

Avignon

THE POPES BUILT THE PALAIS DES PAPES—AVIGNON'S
Gothic fortress-palace—in the 14th century to rule the Roman
Catholic Church from here. Today, a lively university city bustles in
its empty shadow. A longtime papal tradition, the city's devotion to
the arts springs alive every July with the joyful Festival d'Avignon.

Avignon's role as Vatican of the
north began in 1309, when Pope
Clément V fled Rome to escape
political infighting. His successor,
John XXII, chose to stay in town,
and the third pope, Benoît XII,
built the magnificent palace. Over
the next several decades, the
ecclesiastical lordships held
extravagant court with much
feasting, arts, and culture as
befitting their high office, while
the city became an international

meeting place of pilgrims, diplo-
mats, ecclesiasts, and courtiers.
The acclaimed poet Petrarch spent
much of his early life here, but
Simone Martini, the great Sienese
painter, served the pope most
effectively. He and his assistant,
Matteo Giovanetti, decorated the
palace and cathedral with refined,
elegant frescoes in a style that
became known as International
Gothic. In 1376, when Pope
Gregory XI was persuaded to return

to Rome, Avignon elected its own rival pope—setting off a schism that split the Christian world. The struggle ended in 1417 with the disbanding of the papal cult.

Medieval walls surround Avignon, and you will most likely enter through the **Porte de la République,** where cours Jean Jaurès (which becomes rue de la République) bisects the town, leading straight to the **place de l'Horloge.** This lively, vibrant square, with its cafés, restaurants, and belle époque merry-go-round, is the city's tourist heart. One of its most beautiful buildings is the **Opéra-Théâtre,** finished in 1847. Boasting a year-round bill of theater and opera performances, it showcases some of the most important plays during the annual Festival

d'Avignon (see sidebar p. 55).

To visit the papal heart of the town, head uphill from the place de l'Horloge.

PALAIS DES PAPES

Part fortress, part showplace, this vast stone residence—once crammed with paintings, sculptures, tapestries, and silverware—has little furniture or artworks to visually illustrate the pope's once luxurious way of life; the audioguide allows visitors a colorful and detailed historical account.

The Palais des Papes comprises two palaces—the Palais Vieux (Old Palace), built by Benoît XII on the east and north sides, and the Palais Nouveau (New Palace) expansion, a graceful Gothic residence that Benedict's successor, Clément VI, built on the south and west sides. Linking the two is the **Cour d'Honneur** (Courtyard of Honor)—where the tour begins. This courtyard has been the main venue for the annual Avignon theater festival since 1947.

From the courtyard, enter into the enormous **Grande Trésorerie** (Great Treasury Hall), where the Apostolic Chamber took care of the popes' financial matters—including accounting for taxes taken from Christendom's religious establishments, the minting of pontifical coins, among other aspects of the treasury's responsibilities.

Walk up the stairs to the **Salle de Jésus** (Jesus Hall), where faint monograms of Christ (I.H.S., Latin abbreviation for "Jesus, Hominum, Salvator") still adorn the walls. This room was the vestibule hall to the wing housing the pope's private apartments, where cardinals waited for the pope as he dressed. You can peruse facsimiles of papal documents, and read up on different popes described on panels.

Next you visit the **Chambre du Camérier** (Chamberlain's

Palais des Papes

✉ Place du Palais

☎ 04 90 27 50 00

www.palais-des-papes.com

$ $$. Combined ticket available with the Pont St.-Bénezet: $$$. Audioguides available.

Grand Tinel

PALAIS DES PAPES

Main Entrance

Chamber), once divided into several rooms but now one large room featuring eight masonry vaults in the floor, where valuable documents were hidden. The chamberlain was the church's highest ranking dignitary after the pope and oversaw the Apostolic Chamber.

Now peek into the ornate **Revestaire Pontifical** (Papal Vestry), with its pale green and gold decorations featuring cherubs and coats of arms. In this small room the pope put on his consistorial robes: the amice, the alb, and the stole, along with red sandals, a cape adorned with a breast plate, gloves, red velvet cape, and white miter.

Next you enter the **Salle du Consistoire** (Reception Room), a long dark hall with four tall, narrow windows along the east side.

The pope sat on a dais against the southern wall, with his assembly perched on wood-paneled stone

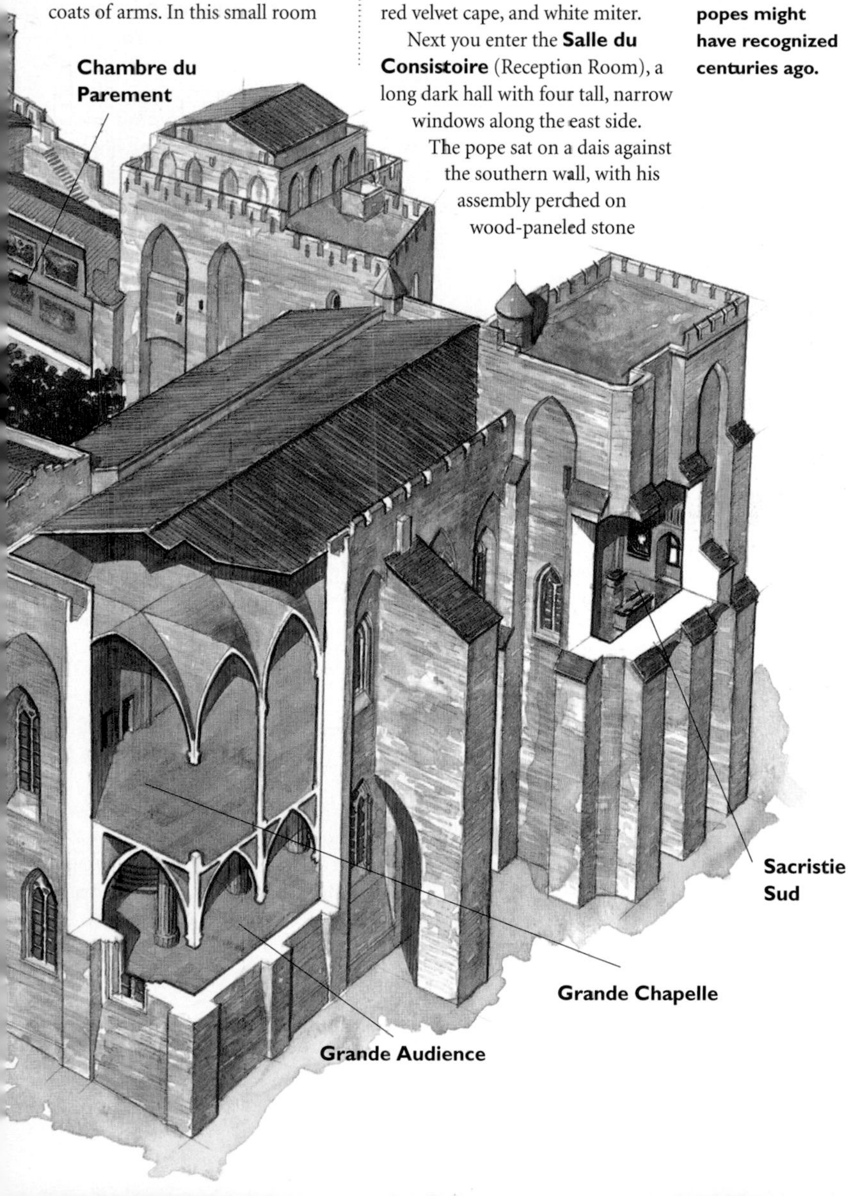

The River Rhône glides peacefully past Avignon, in a scene the popes might have recognized centuries ago.

Chambre du Parement

Grande Chapelle

Sacristie Sud

Grande Audience

Cathédrale
Notre-Dame
des Doms
✉ Place du Palais
☎ 04 90 82 12 24
🕐 Treasury: Open
by appt.

benches along the walls. The hall was used as a tribunal, as well as an audience, where the pope would receive visitors, sovereigns, and ambassadors, plus hear legal, theological, and political matters.

Don't miss the small **Chapelle de St.-Jean**—St. John's Chapel—with its richly hued frescoes by Giovanetti, painted between 1346 and 1348 and narrating the lives of

Detailed carvings grace the 1619 Hôtel des Monnaies, one of Avignon's best examples of baroque style.

St. John the Baptist (on the north and east walls) and St. John the Evangelist (on the south and west walls).

The **Cloître de Benoît XII** (Benoît XII's Cloister) provides some fresh air before going up the stairs to the vast **Grand Tinel.** Banquets were held here (*tinel* has its roots in *tina,* the Latin word for "barrel" or "cask") on feast days. Beside the fireplace you enter the **Grande Cuisine** (Upper Kitchen), devoid of the grills and spits that once cooked the piles of meat that formed the centerpiece of medieval banqueting.

Backtrack through the Grand Tinel, pausing to peek into **Chapelle St.-Martial** (*undergoing restoration*). Featuring more elaborate murals painted by Giovanetti between 1344 and 1346, these portray scenes from St. Martial's life.

Next you enter the **Chambre de Parement,** the antechamber to the pope's chambers. Parement

was used to describe the tapestries that covered the walls and seating (the ones hanging now are Gobelins). Here is where the pope and cardinals held secret consistories.

The adjacent **Studium** (Study Tower) boasts the palace's only original 14th-century floor: Green and brown tiles alternate with decorative scenes of critters and geometric designs.

The **Chambre du Pape** (Pope's Bedroom) gives an idea of the popes' devotion to lavishness, with its frescoes of intertwining vines and oak leaves against a rich blue background.

At this point, you leave Benoît XII's Old Palace and enter Clément VI's New Palace. The first room, the **Chambre du Cerf** (Stag Room), was Clément's study and bedroom. Its walls are covered with frescoes of a stag hunt.

Down some wooden stairs awaits the **Sacristie Nord** (North Sacristy), where the pontiff changed vestments during ceremonies in the adjoining Great Chapel. The vaulted bays with intersecting ribs and carved decoration on the walls mark the difference between this and the old palace, in which wood-paneled vaults and ceilings were more common. The plaster busts, portraying political and religious figures, were gifts from European cities.

Hold your breath as you enter the heavenly **Grande Chapelle** (Great Chapel), with its soaring ceiling and light-filled space. Clément VI was behind this magnificent room—measuring 170 by 49 by 65 feet (52 x 15 x 20 m). Despite the threat of Black Death, the chapel was completed in less than a year, in 1348. Of its 16th- and 17th-century frescoes, only a handful faintly remain. Next door, in the **Sacristie Sud** (Cardinals' Vestry), the cardinals put on their habits.

The tour now leads to a room where the French film "The Other Rome" is shown. Up the stairs is the **Terrasse des Grands Dignitaires** (Terrace of Great Dignatories), with marvelous panoramas over Avignon and beyond.

You are then led to the **Loggia,** overlooking the Court of Honor, where the pope gave his triple blessing to the crowd below and downstairs to the dark **Grande Audience** (Great Audience Hall), a two-nave hall that housed the court of apolistic causes; thousands of appeals were heard here, against whose judgments no appeal was possible. Giovanetti graced these walls in 1352 with frescoes of the prophets, of which only one remnant is apparent in one corner, with traces elsewhere.

You exit through the **Petite Audience** (Small Audience Hall), where you originally bought tickets. From here, you can follow signs to a tasting room of the popes' wines and onward to the gift shop.

AROUND THE PALAIS

Next door, the **Cathédrale Notre-Dame des Doms** was built in the 12th century atop a paleo-Christian basilica and has been remodeled many times since. It contains the Flamboyant Gothic tomb of some of the apostate popes. The gold statue topping its steeple is the Virgin, from the 19th century.

Farther up the hill, on the north end of Palace Square, is the **Musée du Petit Palais.** Built for Cardinal Bérenger Frédol circa 1318–1320, it holds two collections: the Avignon school paintings from the Musée Calvet, and a large group of Italian paintings from the 13th to 16th centuries. You'll want to stop and study many of these fine works, but be sure to seek out the "Virgin and Child between Two Saints and Two Donors" (Room XVII; 1450–1455) by Enguerrand

Quarton, one of the founders of the Avignon school. Its simplicity and use of light in the construction of form are typical of the Avignon school in its attempt to bridge Flemish realism and Italian abstract stylism. Other masterpieces include "Virgin in Majesty" by the Master of 1310, an altarpiece showcasing the masterwork of early 14th-century Italian painters (Room III); the "Virgin of Mercy" by Pietro di Domenico da Montepulciano (Room VIII); and the graceful "Virgin and Child" by Botticelli (Room XI). Spiral stone stairs lead to the second floor, where in Room XVIII awaits more Italian art.

Outside the Petit Palais, a ramped walkway leads up to the

Shops fill Avignon's historic buildings, purveying everything from postcards to regional pottery to trendy clothes.

Musée du Petit Palais

✉ Place du Palais

☎ 04 90 86 44 58

🕐 Closed Tues.

💲 $$

Avignon's famous bridge lost more than half its span in 17th-century floods.

Pont St.-Bénezet

 Rue Ferruce

 04 90 27 51 16

$. Combined ticket with Palais des Papes: $$$.

Papalines

For a heavenly treat, try these chocolate truffles filled with liqueur distilled from 60 herbs picked from nearby Mont Ventoux. ∎

Jardin du Rocher des Doms
(Garden of the Rock of the Lords), a 19th-century public park with splashing fountains, classical statuary, a rock grotto, and a pond with floating swans. Overlooking the River Rhône where it splits in two, this spot was strategic as far back as the Neolithic age. During papal times, it was the private aerie of cardinals and bishops. In one corner, the popes' private vineyard still exists.

Take the staircase down to the River Rhône and the **Pont St.-Bénezet,** Avignon's famous bridge (*"Sur le pont d'Avignon, on y danse, on y danse …"*). No one knows who built the original bridge, but the story goes that a young shepherd was instructed by voices to build a bridge over the Rhône at Avignon. He finally convinced the bishop—

by performing the miracle of moving a boulder all by himself—and he became a hero. It's a miracle any of the bridge survives: Built between 1177 and 1185, it was destroyed in 1226 during the siege of the city, rebuilt, then endured more flood damage and repairs until 1660, when the Rhône swept away half of it—only four of its original 22 arches survive. Also surviving is the bridge's little **Chapelle St.-Nicholas,** which preserved the remains of St.-Bénezet until they were lost in French Revolution.

AVIGNON'S MUSEUMS
Wandering the labyrinth of Avignon's little streets, you'll come across a handful of delightful small museums. Facing rue de la République, the **Musée Lapidaire,** the Musée Calvet's archaeological annex, is housed in the 16th-century chapel of the Collège des Jésuites. Four different civilizations are featured here: Egyptian; Greek and southern Italian; Etruscan; and Roman, Gallo-Roman, and paleo-Christian. Of particular interest are the many Roman works found locally,

including carved busts dating from the first century A.D. and floor mosaics from the first and second centuries A.D.

Nearby, near Église St.-Denis, is the **Musée Angladon,** a former hôtel particulier featuring the magnificent art collection of Jacques Doucet—the celebrated Parisian haute-couture designer who cultivated several young artists, including Pablo Picasso, Georges Braque, and Max Jacob. The ground floor's modern, stark white walls are the backdrop for 19th- and 20th-century masterpieces, including several Picassos ("Arlequin," 1915; "Nature Morte Cubiste," 1920; and "Nature Morte à la Guitare," 1919); Amedeo Modigliani's lovely "La Blouse Rose"; and Provence's only van Gogh—the dark "Wagons de Chemin de Fer," painted in Arles in 1888. You'll also spot works by Degas, Manet, Cézanne, and Sisley. Upstairs, rooms furnished in period style show rare antiques and objets d'art, including Chinese porcelains from the 16th through 18th centuries.

Another fine art museum, housed in another beautiful hôtel particulier, is the **Musée Calvet,** located across rue de la République on tiny rue Joseph-Vernet. Its wide range of works include paintings and sculptures from the 15th to 20th centuries, decorative arts, and arts from Asia, Oceania, and Africa. One of the museum's most treasured works is Jean-Pierre David's 19th-century statue "Barra," which portrays the drummer boy who was killed during the Revolution for refusing to shout "Vive le Roi" instead of "Vive la République." Well-known 19th-century works include "Mazeppa and the Wolves" by romantic artist Horace Vernet; Edouard Manet's "Nature Morte au Châpeau Espagñol" ("Still Life with a Spanish Hat"), and an Italian landscape by Jean-Baptiste-Camille

Corot. The progression to modern styles is well represented by Raoul Dufy and Maurice Utrillo, plus three outstanding works by expressionist Chaïm Soutine: "The Village Idiot," "The Old Man," and "The Downfall." Several period rooms are devoted to Asian art, including a 14th-century Chinese bodhisattva and a circa 1200 Cambodian Khmer clay head.

Down a few crooked streets is yet another museum in a hôtel particulier, the **Musée Louis Vouland,** featuring a quirky collection of 17th- and 18th-century decorative arts collected by businessman and art collector Louis Vouland (1883–1973). You'll find faïences from Moustiers and Marseille, Asian porcelain, furniture (including four Regency armchairs from 1736 depicting fables by Jean de la Fontaine), an 18th-century Gobelins tapestry, and a cheerful "L'Enfant aux Cerises" by Joos van Clève (1485–1540), all the while serenaded by birds in the garden outside. ■

Festival d'Avignon

Avignon's celebrated three-week July festival began in 1947, when actor-director Jean Vilar was invited to the city to perform T. S. Eliot's "Murder in the Cathedral"—and he refused. Instead, he proposed to perform three plays: Shakespeare's *Richard II*, Paul Claudel's *Tobie et Sara,* and *La Terrasse de Midi* in an entirely new way: using young talents, aimed at younger audiences. And thus was launched a renewal in French theater. Avignon's festival today maintains the tradition with 40 new French and foreign drama and dance productions shown to an audience that numbers more than 120,000. ■

Musée Lapidaire
✉ 27 rue de la République
☎ 04 90 85 75 38
www.musee-lapidaire.org
🕐 Closed Tues.
💲 $

Musée Angladon
✉ 5 rue Laboureur
☎ 04 90 82 29 03
www.angladon.com
🕐 Closed Mon. & a.m. mid-June–Nov.; closed Mon.–Tues. & a.m. rest of year
💲 $$

Musée Calvet
✉ 65 rue Joseph-Vernet
☎ 04 90 86 33 84
www.musee-calvet.org
🕐 Closed Tues.
💲 $$

Musée Louis Vouland
✉ 17 rue Victor Hugo
☎ 04 90 86 30 79
www.vouland.com
🕐 Closed Mon., & a.m. Nov.–April
💲 $$

The Luberon
46 C2, 46 D 1&2,
& 47 E2

Musée du Tire-Bouchon
46 C2
✉ Domaine de la
Citadelle, Le
Chataignier, chemin
de Cavaillon,
Ménerbes
☎ 04 90 72 41 58
🕐 Closed Sat.–Sun.
Oct.–March
💲 $

Bonnieux
46 C2
Visitor information
✉ 7 place Carnot
☎ 04 90 75 91 90

Musée de la Boulangerie
✉ 12 rue de la
République,
Bonnieux
☎ 04 90 75 88 34
🕐 Closed Tues.
💲 $

Maison du Parc Naturel Régional du Luberon & Musée de la Paléontologie
✉ 60 place Jean-
Jaurès, Apt
☎ 04 90 04 42 00
🕐 Closed Sun.
💲 Museum: $

The Luberon's splendid lavender fields burst into bloom in July.

The Luberon

MEDIEVAL *VILLAGES PERCHÉS*, HONEY-COLORED FARM-houses, vineyards, bounties of cherries, melons, and goat cheese, and fragrant fields of red poppies, sunflowers, and lavender: The Luberon is classic Provence. The fact that Luberon has officially dropped its accent—so it is pronounced Lubouran rather than Lubéron—reflects the English invasion to the region.

The fecund expanse ranges from Cavaillon in the west and Manosque in the east, and from Apt south to the Durance River. Dominating the landscape is the Montagne de Luberon, the rocky, oak-covered massif for which the area is named. This powerful barrier is broken only in one place, at the Combe de Lourmarin, creating the Grand Luberon—rising to 3,691-foot (1,125 m) Mourre Nègre—to the east, and the Petit Luberon to the west. Much of the area is preserved as the Parc Naturel Régional du Luberon, established in 1977.

The hill towns hark back to a time when Ligurians, Romans, then Saracens settled here. The most dramatic period, however, came in the 1500s, during the Wars of Religion, when the Vaudois (a Protestant sect), who had taken refuge in the Luberon, were perse-cuted by the Catholics. Villages were razed, whole populations decimated.

PETIT LUBERON
In the shadow of the Luberon massif, tiny lanes wander through a potpourri of vineyards, cherry orchards, and lavender fields to some of Provence's most delightful villages perchés. Enjoy this charm-ing niche at a leisurely pace, taking time to visit farmers' markets and to stop in some of the more esoteric museums, including one devoted to corkscrews (*tire-bouchon*) and another to bread.

Oppède-le-Vieux is a virtual ghost town now, its empty build-ings and silent streets begrudgingly giving away secrets of its past. The town's name belies its former importance as a Roman stronghold. Indeed, among artifacts that have been found here are coins, tiles, and an altar for worshiping Mercury

(now at the museum in Cavaillon; see p. 78). Its entire Vaudois population was massacred by Catholics in 1545, in the throes of the Wars of Religion; afterward, its remaining residents left the old village for the plains below.

You will have to leave your car in the parking lot at the base of the village and follow the picturesque path up the hill. Upon entering the village, climb time-worn cobblestoned lanes past empty noble facades to the top of the hill. Perched at the village's highest point, the **Collégiale Notre-Dame d'Alidon** was built in the 16th century on the site of an ancient church. Romanesque in style, it received Gothic touches in 1592. In the simple interior, nearly all ornamentation comes from frescoes, some of which have been restored. Above the altar is a 17th-century painting by Reynaud le Vieux, portraying Mary handing a rosary to St. Dominic and St. Catherine of Siena. Above the church are the broken-down walls of a château-fort constructed in the 13th century under Raymond VI of Toulouse and enlarged in subsequent centuries.

Follow little lanes 3 miles (5 km)

more than a year. The Catholics took it back using similar methods. Despite the unwanted fame bestowed upon the town thanks to Peter Mayle, who lived here from 1986 to 1993 and wrote about it in *A Year in Provence,* Ménerbes remains an unassuming, friendly place.

In the valley nearby, you can visit the **Musée du Tire-Bouchon,** established by Yves Rousset-Rouard, village mayor, movie producer, and former MP. It presents more than a thousand different corkscrews dating from the 17th century to the present. You'll see an early French corkscrew, hand-forged from iron in the 1600s, and more modern corkscrews, some several feet tall. The museum is part of the Domaine de la Citadelle, and wine-tasting is included at the end.

The infamous Marquis de Sade retreated to his castle crowning **Lacoste,** 4 miles (6 km) east of Ménerbes, in the late 1700s between various prison terms, where he hosted wild parties. The French nobleman's perverse sexual preferences and erotic writings gave rise to the term "sadism"; his best-known work is the notorious novel *Justine* (1791). Designer Pierre Cardin recently bought the ruined castle and converted it into an open-air theater; the Festival de Lacoste *(tel 04 90 75 93 12)* now takes place within its walls every summer. The town itself is beautifully restored, with

Bonnieux's Église Neuve (New Church)

TRUFFLE MARKETS (in season)

Apt
Sat. a.m., place de la Bouquerie

Carpentras
Fri. a.m., in front of Hôtel Dieu

Richerenches
Sat. a.m., main street

Valréas
Wed. a.m., place Cardinal Maury

east of Oppède, past cherry and fig trees to pretty **Ménerbes.** Another ridgetop fortress town, its old château sits atop the highest point *(closed to visitors).* The castle was considered impregnable, yet during the 16th-century Wars of Religion, 120 Protestants entered by ruse in 1577 and sheltered here for

Truffles

The gourmet's black diamond, it's called, the exquisite, earthy black winter truffle. And the ever-green oak that grows on the dry, poor land covering the Luberon massif's south face offers it one of the world's best environments to grow. Provence's Romans knew this delicacy, and Avignon's popes incorporated them into many a fine banquet dish. Truffles cost hundreds of dollars per pound, and local restaurants create entire truffle menus during the season— November through March. Called *rabasse* by the Provençaux, they are hunted with a dog or a sow, often secretly at night. ■

steep cobbled lanes winding up to the castle. Be sure to enjoy an apéritif at the **Café de France,** with its sublime views across farmlands to Bonnieux, perched on its hilltop 3 miles (5 km) away.

The biggest of the Petit Luberon villages is magnificent **Bonnieux,** its sand-colored buildings clinging to a pyramidal mound that rises up to the 12th-century **Haute Église.** You'll have to climb 86 steps, past tiny plazas and fine old houses, to reach the often closed church—the views, however, are amazing, taking in an Impressionist patchwork of vines, lavender, and fruit trees set against the Monts de Vaucluse. Tucked away on a quiet street hides the **Musée de la Boulangerie,** complete with period bread oven. At the base of the hill is the newer **Église Neuve,** built in 1870.

Nearby, on the D149, the three-arched **Pont Julien** is the only remaining bridge on the old Roman road between northern Italy and Provence.

GRAND LUBERON

The wilder brother to the Petit Luberon's gentleness, the Grand Luberon is a deeply forested, canyoned land dotted with small bourgs lost in time. **Apt,** its major hub, however, possesses an industrial air. The city's beauty lies in its old town, with its ancient vaulted passageways and fountains. On Tuesdays and Saturdays, the open-air market unfurls on place Lauze de Perret. Keep an eye out for crystallized fruits *(fruits confits),* a local specialty. Hidden away in a courtyard off rue des Marchands is the **Maison du Parc Naturel Régional du Luberon,** with a museum focusing on the area's natural history, as well as helpful tourist information. The bones of Ste.-Anne, the Virgin Mary's mother, were supposedly discovered in

the town's eighth-century crypt, inspiring the construction of **Cathédrale Ste.-Anne** in the 11th century. Look for the saint's shroud among the treasury's reliquaries, and admire the set of 14th-century stained-glass windows at the end of the apse that describe

her life. The town's major museum, the **Musée Archéologique** *(27 rue de l'Amphithéâtre, tel 04 90 74 78 45, undergoing renovation at press time)* houses Roman artifacts excavated in the surrounding area.

Wee roads south of Apt wander through some of the Luberon massif's wildest lands, with forests stretching to the horizon and every imaginable Provençal herb scenting the air. Follow the GR92 to lovingly restored **Saignon.** Here, *boules* players while away hot afternoons in the shade of plane trees, and *le rocher de Bellevue*—what's left of the old château—offers sublime 360-degree views over fields, mountains, and villages (follow signs for "Le Rocher").

Nearby are the peaceful bourgs of **Sivergues,** offering a popular trailhead for hikes up the Grand Luberon, and **Buoux,** in the middle of lavender fields. Buoux's fortress, which provided refuge to the Vaudois during the religious

Apt

🏛 46 D2

Visitor information

✉ Office de Tourisme, 20 ave. Philippe de Girard

☎ 04 90 74 03 18

St.-Symphorien priory, Buoux

Ancienne Cathédrale Ste.-Anne

✉ Rue de la Cathédrale, Apt

☎ 04 90 74 36 60

🕐 Treasury: open July–Sept. Guided tours only, at 11 a.m. & 5 p.m. Mon.–Sat., & 11 a.m. Sun.

Lourmarin

🏛 46 D2

Visitor information

✉ 17 ave. Philippe de Girard

☎ 04 90 68 10 77

www.lourmarin.com

**Château de
Lourmarin**
☎ 04 90 68 15 23
🕐 Closed Jan. Mon.–Fri.
💲 $$

Ansouis
🗺 46 D2
Visitor information
✉ Place du Château
☎ 04 90 09 86 98

**A Saignon
fountain**

wars of the 16th century, was destroyed in 1660 by Louis XIV— only pieces of the rampart and chapel walls survive today.

The twisty D943 brings you farther south to **Lourmarin.** Its Renaissance **château** has lorded over town since the 16th century. Since restoration in the early 1900s, it has received writers and artists in residence, earning it the title the "Médicis Villa of Provence." The village has been turned over to chic restaurants and cafés, boutiques and antique shops, frequented by well-coiffed clientele—possibly a French movie star or two. Nobel Prize–winning writer Albert Camus (1913–1960) was a longtime resident; he and his wife rest in peace at the village

cemetery, his tombstone planted with rosemary, hers with lavender.

Another **castle** rises from the vineyards in **Ansouis,** southeast of Lourmarin via the D135, inhabited by the Sabran family since 1160 *(rue Cartel, tel 04 90 09 82 70, closed Tues. March–Nov.; open Sun. only rest of year, $$).* The tour takes in the kitchens with their shiny copperware, the salons with their Flemish tapestries, plus the Room of Saints, devoted to the family's St.-Elzéar and Ste.-Delphine. The saintly couple married in 1299 and vowed to live together in chastity—no doubt made easier by the fact that he rarely spent any time at home. The terrace gardens are magnificent. Also in town, the **Musée Extraordinaire** *(rue du Vieux Moulin, tel 04 90 09 82 64, open p.m. & by appt. a.m., $)* is an eclectic assemblage of life-size sculptures, paintings, shells, and fossils; and the **Musée de la Vigne et du Vin** *(Château Turcan, rte. de Pertuis, tel 04 90 09 83 33, $)* has viticulture tools.

Scenes for Claude Berri's *Horseman on the Roof* were filmed in quiet **Cucuron,** east of Lourmarin. Walk through the 18th-century ramparts to see the **Église Notre-Dame-de-Beaulieu,** with a baroque altarpiece and Gothic side chapels; and the medieval *donjon* of **St.-Michel** *(closed to public).* The **Musée Marc-Deydier** houses 3,000 photographs of Luberon and of the Vaucluse, taken between 1885 and 1917.

On the Grand Luberon's eastern fringe, the town of **La Tour-d'Aigues** has the remains of another Renaissance château. In its cellars is the **Musée des Faïences** *(Château de la Tour-d'Aigues, tel 04 90 07 50 33, closed Sun. & Mon. a.m. & Tues. p.m., $),* showcasing local pottery, and another gallery with temporary exhibits. ∎

Roussillon

IT'S THE TOWN'S VIBRANT RED-OCHER COLOR AGAINST THE dark green hills that's so striking, perched on the edge of a dramatically red canyon. This is the heart of one of the world's biggest ocher deposits, where 17 different shades of soil—violet, blood red, orange, yellow, and everything in between—once were worked. The incredible beauty, alas, draws hordes of tourists in summer.

Market day
Wed.

Roussillon
⛰ 46 C2
Visitor information
✉ Place de la Poste
☎ 04 90 05 60 25

The spectacle is rooted in a 230-million-year-long history, when Provence was covered by the sea. Sands containing iron were deposited, later to be oxidized in brilliant tints of color—ocher. The Romans used the tinted earth for pottery glazes. In the 18th century, local Roussillonnais figured out how to waterproof the pigment—and a whole new industry of pot and housepainting was born. Production dropped in the 1950s, and today only one company still operates.

You can visit the old ocher quarries via the 0.6-mile (1 km) **Sentier des Ocres** (*$*), through a mini-canyon of fantastically shaped formations set against a pine backdrop (don't wear white to avoid staining). The village is worth a stroll as well:

Tiny, steep streets wind past flowery facades painted in the local ochers, many filled with tourist shops.

Less than a mile (1 km) east of town on the D104, guided tours at the **Conservatoire des Ocres et Pigments Appliqués** show the stages of pigment production at an old ocher factory.

Another old quarry, the **Colorado Provençal,** a few miles away near Rustrel, comprises an even larger site of rock formations. Seven walking trails wind past giant columns of red ocher. The **Sentier des Cheminées des Fées** and **Sentier du Satard,** both 0.6 mile (1 km) long, are the most dramatic; they start from the municipal parking lot in Bouvène, off the D22 south of Rustrel village. ■

Colorado Provençal, at its most beautiful at sunset

Conservatoire des Ocres et Pigments Appliqués
✉ Usine Mathieu, D104
☎ 04 90 05 66 69
🕐 Closed Mon. Nov.–March
💲 $$

Colorado Provençal
✉ S of D22 toward Rustrel from Apt
💲 $

A Renaissance-
era château
dominates the
hilltop village
of Gordes.

Market day
Tues.

Gordes
🅰 46 C2
**Visitor
information**
✉ Le Château
☎ 04 90 72 02 75
www.gordes-
village.com

**Château de
Gordes/Musée
Pol Mara**
💲 $

Gordes & Abbaye de Sénanque

MAJESTICALLY SPIRALING UP A WHITE ROCK OVERLOOKING the Luberon's patches of farmland, the tiered village of Gordes is strikingly handsome—perhaps too much for its own good. It's the Luberon's No. 1 tourist site, overwhelmed with cars and visitors in summer. A springtime visit, when the cherry trees are in bloom, or fall, as the leaves turn golden, is a better bet. Peace and quiet can be found at the nearby Cistercian abbey of Sénanque, one of Provence's three great Cistercian monasteries, and the Village des Bories, rock dwellings inhabited since Ligurian times.

GORDES

The obviously strategic site has been occupied since prehistoric times. In the Roman period an *oppidum* was built here, and, in the Middle Ages, inhabitants living on the plain sought refuge in the fortified town. It was never taken, even during the brutal Wars of Religion. What almost did Gordes in was attrition at the turn of the 20th

century, as residents migrated to cities for factory jobs. Modern art came to the rescue. Cubist painter André Lhote discovered the village in 1938, drawing Marc Chagall, Victor Vasarely, and other modern artists to visit and summer here as well. Their painting bliss was cut short, however, when German troops in 1944 destroyed much of the village in retaliation for a

Résistance attack. A monk from the nearby abbey of Sénanque intervened to avoid even further damage.

Though the town has been largely rebuilt, Gordes has managed to retain its old-world charm. A labyrinth of cobbled lanes edged with drystone walls harbors beautifully restored houses, many now occupied by shops selling the usual Provençal goods and cafés where well-heeled people sip regional muscat. Dominating the entire site is the **château,** dating from the Renaissance and constructed on the site of a medieval fortress. The 12th-century crenellated tower is all that remains from its earlier days, while three stories of Renaissance windows pierce the tall curtain walls. The main room has an outstanding Renaissance fireplace. To see it, though, you must buy a ticket for the **Musée Pol Mara** installed inside. The exhibition showcases the works by the contemporary Flemish artist. Nearby, the **Église St.-Firmin** was constructed in the 18th century. Its murals are dedicated to the Virgin and a parade of saints, including St. Firmin. Continue down rue de l'Église, which brings you to **rue du Belvédère** and its glorious valley vista.

VILLAGE DES BORIES

A *borie* is a stone, igloo-shaped hut constructed with no mortar. Ligurians in the Bronze Age built the first examples in the area, which were continuously used, repaired, and renovated until the 18th century. You'll find single bories throughout Provence's fields. Their original purposes are not known, but for centuries they have been used for shelter and storage. The village has 20 restored structures, inhabited between the 16th and 19th centuries, including dwellings, an oven, sheep pen, and

wine cistern. Some contain exhibits on life in a borie, the reconstruction process, and historic Gordes.

ABBAYE DE SÉNANQUE

It took a hundred years to build this austere ensemble of buildings, beginning in 1148. The community thrived in the 13th and 14th centuries, adding a mill, seven granges, and large areas of land throughout Provence. It was partially destroyed

Mortar-free structures dot the *bories* village.

during the religious wars in the 16th century and sold off during the Revolution. A new community returned in 1854, only to be expelled due to new laws on religious consecrations in 1903. A new group of monks returned in 1988; they cultivate lavender and produce honey to help maintain the community.

Several guided visits—the only way to see the monastery—are offered throughout the day. They are in French, but a translated pamphlet helps explain some of what you see. The tour takes in the abbey's five 12th-century buildings: the abbatial church, the cloister, the dormitory, the chapter room, and the calefactory (heating room).

If you time your visit for late June and early July, you will see crowds, but also the abbey's lavender fields in bloom. ∎

Village des Bories
- 🅰 46 C2
- ✉ Les Savournins
- ☎ 04 90 72 03 48
- 💲 $$

Abbaye Notre-Dame-de-Sénanque
- 🅰 46 C2
- ✉ 1.9 miles (3 km) N of Gordes on D177
- ☎ 04 90 72 05 72
- 🕐 Closed Sun. a.m.
- 💲 $$

Market days
Thurs. & Sun.;
daily in summer

L'Isle-sur-la-Sorgue
⚠ 46 C2
Visitor information
✉ Office de Tourisme,
place de la Liberté
☎ 04 90 38 04 78
www.ot-
islesurlasorgue.fr

**Collégiale Notre-
Dame-des-Anges**
✉ Place de la Liberté
🕒 Closed Sun.

**Hôtel Donadeï de
Campredon**
✉ 20 rue du Docteur
Taillet
☎ 04 90 38 17 41
🕒 Closed Mon. &
Nov.–March
$ $$

L'Isle-sur-la-Sorgue

Water appears at every turn in this compact medieval mill town, built on islands dotting five branches of the River Sorgue. Today, France's second largest antique market (after Paris) spreads out on weekends along the riverbanks, while six antique malls exist around town, open daily.

The region was swampland in the 12th century, when a handful of fishermen and their families built houses on stilts where the town now stands. Before long, the river was reined with waterwheels and canals, providing energy for burgeoning silk, wool, and papermaking industries, and L'Isle-sur-la-Sorgue became the most important town of the Comtat-Venaissin (now known as the Vaucluse). Several waterwheels still churn around town; the structures on rue du Dr. Jean-Roux and rue Jean-Théophile are especially picturesque.

The Sorgue meanders in and about the old town, its slow-moving green waters mirroring timeworn houses—many now containing tourist shops—and plane trees. In the heart of town, the **Tour Boutin,** also called Tour d'Argent, is the oldest structure, dating from the Middle Ages, when the counts of Toulouse ruled. Its purpose remains a mystery.

Nearby, the **Notre-Dame-des-Anges,** with an Italianate belfry, dates from 1222 but received its Italian flair in the 17th century, making it one of Provence's most beautiful baroque examples. Note that the windows on the north side have been walled up (since 1666) in defense against the mistral winds. Inside, over the Carrara marble altar looms the 1630 painting by Reynaud Levieux, "Ascension of the Blessed Virgin," looked on by 22 statues by Jean-Baptiste Peru and 220 cherubs. ■

Fontaine-de-Vaucluse

**Fontaine-de-
Vaucluse**
⚠ 46 C2
**Visitor
information**
✉ Office de Tourisme,
chemin de la
Fontaine
☎ 04 90 20 32 22

Quiet jade waters reflect leafy plane trees in this peaceful medieval hamlet, tucked in a closed valley at the edge of the plateau de Vaucluse. Its intense beauty has been the inspiration of writers and poets through the ages, most famously the Italian Renaissance poet Petrarch. This unassuming little town also possesses one of France's most extraordinary phenomena, for which it is named—the Fontaine de Vaucluse.

You'll have to leave your car in a pay lot and walk into town. Be forewarned that this is an extremely popular summer tourist destination.

The River Sorgue is the town's centerpiece, colored emerald green by water parsnips. Restaurants, shops, and a handful of museums, mostly on the river's right bank, make for a pleasant stay. Overlooking all is a ruined château built to protect pilgrims visiting the tomb of the eighth-century hero St.-Véran, who, the story goes, saved villagers from a dragon.

Follow the souvenir-shop-lined pathway up the River Sorgue to the base of a rocky cliff face, where a deep, emerald pool forms the **Fontaine de Vaucluse.** The *fontaine* is the collapsed part of a cave system filled with water. Many divers and speleologists have tried in vain to determine the spring's depth, including the late Jacques Cousteau and, in 1985, a small submarine robot—and still no bottom has been found. The deepest explorations have reached 1,043 feet (318 m). What *is* known is that at its springtime peak, the spring produces 660,430,128 gallons (2.5 million cubic m), about

to the dark world of war, with more than 10,000 objects and documents combined with a detailed narrative in French (*audioguide available in English*). In the first section, describing daily life of the French under occupation, period rooms provide a visual account of those days, including a living room with blacked-out windows. The

Le Monde Souterrain de Norbert Casteret

⊠ Chemin de la Fontaine
☎ 04 90 20 34 13
$ $$

Peaceful Fontaine-de-Vaucluse

the same amount that flows over Niagara Falls in 17 minutes. It is always at a constant temperature of 53°F to 55°F (12–13°C). Learn more at **Le Monde Souterrain de Norbert Casteret** (Underground World of Norbert Casteret), which includes an underground stroll along the river.

Probably the town's biggest surprise is **L'Appel de la Liberté–Musée d'Histoire 1939–1945,** located on the busy path to the spring and completely out of place with its excellent, thoughtful account of the French Résistance movement during World War II. You are transported

second section focuses on the men and women who risked their lives in their underground fight against the Nazis, and the third section, the "freedom of the spirit," ponders the rationality of war. It's a heavy dose of reality, and you should allow plenty of time to take it all in.

The **Musée Pétrarque,** on the river's left bank, stands on the site where 14th-century Italian poet Francesco Petrarca (1304–1374) wrote *Canzoniere.* The small house museum features lithographs and watercolors of Petrarch and Laura, his unrequited love, as well as early editions of his books—including a 1645 edition of *De Remediis.* ■

L'Appel de la Liberté–Musée d'Histoire 1939–1945

⊠ Chemin de la Fontaine
⊕ Closed Tues., & Jan.–Feb.
$ $

Musée Pétrarque

⊠ Quai du Château Vieux
☎ 04 90 20 37 20
⊕ Closed Tues. & Nov.–March
$ $

House columns (above) and statues (below) hint at Vaison's once grand Roman town.

Vaison-la-Romaine

BOASTING RUINS OF A ONCE WEALTHY ROMAN TOWN AND narrow medieval streets winding up to an ancient château, Vaison-la-Romaine has plenty of history to explore. But the picturesque little city offers much more, including Provence's largest market *(on Tues.)* and a summer filled with theater and music and dance festivals.

Known for centuries simply as Vaison, the town didn't gain the second part of its name until the early 20th century, when Roman ruins were discovered beneath the streets of its Basse Ville (Lower Town). From beneath the ground emerged the vestiges of a splendid Roman city that once covered 148 to 173 acres (60–70 ha)—only 15 of which have been excavated (the rest of it remains under the modern city). What makes this site unique is the fact that it is made up of streets with shops and town houses, rather than individual landmarks (as at Arles and Orange), so you get a sense of the overall urban layout. While little

remains of the grand town that formerly flourished here, the literature provided helps re-create the Roman way of life.

Comprising the largest archaeological site in France, two quarters can be visited (both in the Basse Ville): Puymin, adjacent to the Office de Tourisme; and La Villasse, across the street and closer to the river.

Begin with the cypress- and pine-shaded **Quartier du Puymin,** where you can purchase one ticket for both sites. Immediately to your right as you enter is the enormous **House of the Laureled Apollo,** named for the head of Apollo in white marble found here. Up the hill, the **Musée Théo Desplans** displays sculptures, mosaics, and other objects found on the site. The site's coup de grâce, however, is the **Théâtre Antique,** built in the first century A.D. It measured 315 feet (96 m) across, large enough to seat 6,000 spectators. The stage's front wall, complete with 12 hollows used to work the curtain, are all that remain of the stage area. At the wall's base, you can make out the location of three doors that actors would have taken. The theater has been used since the 1930s for summer concerts. There are also remains of a sanctuary, a craftsmen's district, and another villa to see.

The **Quartier de La Villasse** features the splendid rue des Boutiques, made from large limestone slabs on which horse-drawn chariots could easily drive. Under the pavement is a huge sewer system, while an overhang on the street's west side protected pedestrians from inclement weather; look for the supporting column. The nearby **House of the Silver Bust,** covering 1.2 acres (0.5 ha), is the largest urban dwelling thus far unearthed in Vaison. The adjacent *thermae* and *palestra,* built in 20 to 10 B.C., is where Romans bathed and exercised.

MEDIEVAL VAISON

Cross the 2,000-year-old Roman bridge—which has survived many floods through the ages, including a devastating torrent in 1992—to Vaison's lovingly restored **Haute Ville** (Upper Town). During the tumultuous Middle Ages, Vaison's residents took to this towering hill for protection from raiding countrymen under a rival lord, hiding behind ramparts and a defensive fortress. You enter through the fortified *porte* (gate), dating from the 14th century and featuring a belfry. Narrow cobbled lanes wander up the hill, past tiny fountain-graced squares and grand stone houses, many

now occupied by shops and restaurants. Flowery gardens spill over the walks and gates, providing a very picturesque setting. If you take rue de l'Év.eque to the left, you will eventually come to the ruins of the 1192 **château,** built by Raymond V, count of Toulouse. The only way to visit the castle is by guided tour through the tourist office (in French only). Magnificent views take in the distant wine-carpeted Ouvèze valley and Mont Ventoux.

Back in the **Basse Ville,** there are two more medieval sights to visit. Once the heart of a medieval village that has long since disappeared, the **Cathédrale Notre-Dame-de-Nazareth** is a fine example of Romanesque architecture with its lovely arches (*from Quartier de la Villasse, head to the river; cathedral will be on right*). It was built in the 11th century, using stones from preceding Roman buildings. Note the 11th-century white marble altar, decorated with carved grapes and leaves.

The little **cloister** behind is charming with its single olive tree and four galleries supported by columns with leaf-carved capitals dating from the 11th and 12th centuries. ■

Stepping up the hillside, medieval Vaison overlooks the Basse Ville.

Market day
Tues.

Vaison-la-Romaine
🅰 46 C3
Visitor information
✉ Place du Chanoine-Sautel
☎ 04 90 36 02 11
www.vaison-la-romaine.com
🕐 Closed Sun. Oct.–April

Quartiers du Puymin et de La Villasse
💲 $$ (includes entry to cathedral cloister)

Cathédrale Notre-Dame-de-Nazareth
✉ Place de la Cathédrale

A drive around Les Dentelles

Circling Les Dentelles de Montmirail—the mountain ridges named for their resemblance to lace—this pastoral drive takes in quintessential Provence: hill towns, bucolic views, ancient vineyards, and plenty of opportunities to stop and sample the local wine.

Leave the lower town of **Vaison-la-Romaine** ① (see pp. 66–67) by crossing the Roman bridge and turning left on the D938. Just beyond the hamlet of Crestet, turn right on the D76 for 1.9 miles (3 km), winding up to the hill town of **Le Crestet** ②. Park at the base of town and continue on foot. There's the 11th-century church of **St.-Sauveur** to peek in, as well as the ruins of a 12th-century castle atop the hill, the old residence of Vaison's bishops.

Continue on the D938 to Malaucène, where you take the D90 toward Suzette, 5.5 miles (9 km) away. Midway awaits the **Col de la Chaîne,** with its wide-sweeping vistas. Onward, the road cozies up to Les Dentelles, providing close-up looks at the finely chiseled limestone crests. The many signs for *sentiers* (trails) hint at the abundant hiking and mountain-biking opportunities.

You know you're approaching **Suzette** ③ by the signs for *caveau* and *dégustation*. The view is the star in this hamlet, looking out over the mountains and Crête St.-Amand.

Still following the D90, pass through tiny Lafare and onward to **Beaumes-de-Venise** ④. Beaumes is best known for its muscat wine, drunk cool as an apéritif, which you can taste in wine cellars along avenue Raspail. Or stop by the tasting room of the **Vignerons de Beaumes de Venise** (*Quartier Ravel, tel 04 90 12 41 00*), just outside town in the direction of Vacqueyras. Another site worth a mention is the blue-shuttered **Cathédrale Notre-Dame-d'Aubune,** down the street from the Vignerons. Built in the eighth century in gratitude for the French victories against the Saracens near Tours and Poitiers, its unusual tower was added in the 13th century.

The drive continues via the D81 and D7 through the flatlands, with wine-tasting opportunities at every turn. **Vacqueyras,** fortified in the 15th century, was the birthplace of troubadour Raimbaut de Vacqueyras. You soon come to the turnoff for sleepy **Gigondas** ⑤, celebrated worldwide for its powerful, robust wine. The shaded central

Côtes du Rhône vineyards carpet the countryside surrounding Les Dentelles.

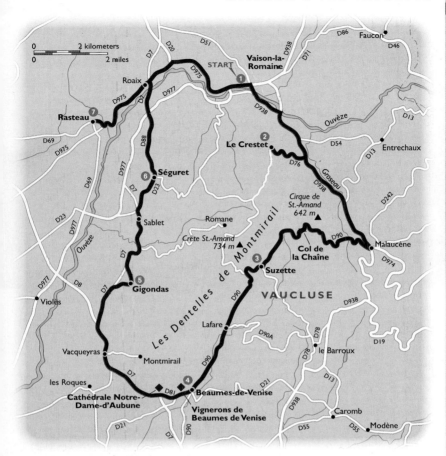

place **Gabriel Andéol** has a few cafés and the ubiquitous wine-tasting cellars. Leave your car here to wander lanes that will bring you to Ste.-Catherine's parish church, with its lovely 14th-century facade.

The king of hill towns awaits down the road: **Séguret** ⑥, classified as one of France's most beautiful villages, a distinction it absolutely deserves. Cobbled lanes wind past noble houses, now containing restaurants, galleries, and wine-tasting shops. There are two santon shops here, including one where you can watch a master artist painstakingly paint these tiny ceramic figures. An interesting aside: This fortified hill town is where the word "security" was coined. Yellow areas lead to sites associated with this legacy.

Onward, a detour via the D88, D7, and D975 leads to **Rasteau** ⑦, where the **Musée**

See area map p. 46
► Vaison-la-Romaine
⟷ 40 miles (65 km)
⏱ Half a day
► Vaison-la-Romaine

NOT TO BE MISSED
- View from Le Crestet
- Gigondas
- Séguret

du **Vigneron** *(rte. de Vaison-la-Romaine, tel 04 90 83 71 79, closed Tues. & Sun., & a.m. Sept.–June, $)* features more than 2,500 winemaking tools. The adjacent **Domaine de Beaurenard** offers one last chance for wine-tasting before returning to Vaison-la-Romaine. ∎

Market day
Thurs.

Orange
46 B3

Visitor information
✉ 5 cours Aristide-Briand
☎ 04 90 34 70 88
www.otorange.fr
🕐 Closed Sun. Oct.–March

Théâtre Antique
✉ Place des Frères-Mounet
☎ 04 90 51 17 60
💲 $$ (combined ticket with museum)

Orange

EUROPE'S BEST PRESERVED ROMAN THEATER LOOMS OVER Orange's old town, a monumental reminder of the important Roman colony founded here in 35 B.C. A splendid triumphal arch, plus plenty of statuary, mosaics, and pottery, are other souvenirs of these early residents. While Orange today is a fairly large, busy city, its historic core is charming to explore.

The idea was ingenious: The Romans headed by Augustus founded a colony in a land they had conquered (Provence) and used it as a veteran's retirement home, peopling it with soldiers from the Second Gallic Legion. The residents farmed the lands and henceforth enjoyed wealth in their later years. Called Colonia Firma Julia Secundanorum Arausio, the city had all the features of a civilized Roman town, including a forum, religious quarter, and theater. It was organized on a checkerboard layout based on the width of the theater's huge wall.

THÉÂTRE ANTIQUE

Dominating the town center, the old Roman theater rises in its well-preserved state, a honey-colored stone edifice with a 338-foot-long (103 m) front wall, wings, passages for spectators, and storage rooms still standing.

In the 2nd century A.D., Roman citizens entered this very theater to enjoy the entertainment du jour—perhaps a mime show, or juggling act, or popular farce. Such diversions were used to propagate Roman culture and also to distract locals from political action and nationalistic claims. As the Roman Empire declined in the 4th century, the theater was officially closed and remained abandoned until it took on the role of defensive post in the Middle Ages and then a refuge by townspeople during the 16th-century wars of religion. Prosper Merimée, the director of

Monuments Historiques in the 19th century, began extensive restoration work that brought the theater back to its former glory.

With an audioguide in hand, you enter via stage right, at the base of the great stage, the seats at your back forming a half circle that can hold 8,000 to 10,000 people. In Roman times, the massive stone wall in front was divided into several stories and, at its high point, was plaid with marble. Sound bounced off the facing hillside, providing perfect acoustics—a system that still works today. The wall is covered with columns, blocks, and statue niches. The only remaining authentic statue is the 13-foot-tall (4 m) statue of Augustus in the central niche, used to symbolize the emperor's universal presence. Other statues and columns are found in the Musée Municipale across the street (see below). Note the new roof built to protect the stage wall.

The tour next takes you through dark, earthy arched galleries, with the option of climbing more stairs for a panoramic view over Orange. You then descend on the theater's backside to a café overlooking further ruins, which you can visit (up to a point) as well. These include a temple and outhouses whose uses have been difficult to determine.

MUSÉE MUNICIPAL & MORE ANCIENT ORANGE

Housed in the 17th-century hôtel particulier of a Dutch nobleman, the Musée Municipal traces Orange's history. Downstairs is a remarkable collection of Roman treasures from 25 B.C. to A.D. 10, including famous friezes from the theater, mosaics, and objects of daily Roman life. Particularly interesting are the land registry plans, engraved on marble tablets, which have provided modern archaeologists with valuable clues about Roman land distribution (essentially, the Romans got the good

Les indiennes

The bold, sun-drenched cottons gracing Provence's tables, windows, and beds are not indigenous to the region. Dutch and Portuguese traders introduced the fabric in the 1600s from India (hence their name, *les indiennes*). The fabric was highly popular throughout France, even at Louis XIV's Versailles. By the early 1770s, local manufacturers began making their own indiennes, incorporating French motifs into the design—cicadas, sunflowers, poppies. They were produced entirely by hand, including natural dyes derived from plants and minerals. Today, of course, the process is entirely mechanized, but the result is just as charming. ■

Musée Municipal

✉ Rue Madeleine Roch

☎ 04 90 51 18 24

💲 $$ (includes theater)

Eighteenth-century Indian cottons inspired Provence's quintessential fabrics.

land, the conquered locals the less desirable plots).

Exhibits on the second floor focus on Orange's later history. Much of it spotlights William I, count of Nassau. In 1544, Orange became a principality inherited by William I, who proceeded to lead the Dutch revolt against Spanish rule. He became ancestor to both William III of England and the present-day royal Dutch family. One of the most interesting rooms has five paintings once housed in Orange's Maison Wetter, dating from 1764. They depict the story of how *indi-*

THÉÂTRE ANTIQUE

Orchestra

Seating
(up to 10,000)

Performances still unfold on the Théâtre Antique's stage, as they have for centuries.

ennes fabrics were brought to Provence (see sidebar p. 71).

Be sure to walk up **St.-Eutrope Hill,** behind the theater, for a splendid view over town. Here, too, are the ruins of the château built by the Orange-Nassau family. Then follow rue Victor Hugo (which approximates the ancient Roman imperial road) to the **Arc de Triomphe,** built about 20 B.C. to celebrate the victories of the Second Gallic Legion. Unfortunately, the roads surrounding it are quite busy.

THE CHURCH & AROUND

Beyond the Roman ruins, the restored **Église Notre-Dame-de-Nazareth,** consecrated in 519, was reconstructed in the 12th century in typical Romanesque style. From here, explore tiny pedestrianized squares and streets (rue de la République, rue St.-Martin), with their ancient, pastel-colored town houses now holding restaurants, terrace cafés, and small shops. ■

Église Notre-Dame-de-Nazareth

✉ Rue Notre-Dame

Statue of Augustus

Stage wall

Basilicae

Wooden stage

Roman life & culture

The Romans left vast ruins throughout Provence, hinting at a complex, intriguing way of life more than 2,000 years ago. What was their life like? Their cities? Their homes? Their clothes? Here are a few descriptions to help fill in some of the blanks.

VILLAS

Wealthy Romans' houses, which survived more often than less elaborate homes, consisted of a series of open and closed spaces with splashing fountains, statue-dotted pathways, and wall hangings to divide space. Porticoes and colonnades graced exteriors. Inside, rugs, hangings, furniture, and art objects richly decorated the rooms. The decor followed a simple rule of concentration: If something was hung on the wall, the floor was left bare; if there was nothing on the wall, inlaid marble or multihued mosaics covered the floor. The kitchen was often located on the north side, which was cooler and could better preserve foods. Sinks had water under pressure, connected to gutters that carried waste to outside sewers. Water inside a home was a luxury, so only the wealthiest Romans had it. The less fortunate had to fetch their water from fountains or wells.

CULINARY MATTERS

Not every Roman was rich enough to feast. Breakfast (*ientaculum*) and lunch (*prandium*) were typically light and consisted mostly of bread and accompaniments, while dinner (*cena*) was the main meal, taking place in the late afternoon. A simple meal was mostly cold, including bread; salad of lettuce, beans, and lentils; olives; and cheeses. Hot dishes might include hams and pigs' heads, sausage in semolina, and bacon. Fancier dishes might have incorporated teats from a sow's udder or a lamb's womb stuffed with sausage. A recipe survives for a platter of small songbirds in asparagus sauce, carefully arranged with quail's eggs. *Mulsum* (wine), flavored with honey or spices, was the usual drink of choice.

BATH TIME

A daily public bath not only refreshed Romans from the hot Midi climate, but also served as a highly sociable affair. First the women would bathe, then the men. The first step was to toss off garments and perhaps work out in the exercise yards at the *palaestra* (open courtyard). Then came the plunge into the *natatio,* a great swimming pool of cool water. The *tepidarium* (warm room) was next, where bathers warmed themselves amid rich decoration. The floors were made of hollow tiles through which warm air was continuously forced from a great system of charcoal furnaces located in the substructures of the *thermae* (baths). The *caldaria* (hot baths), were next, followed by the *laconicum,* a marble-floored room filled with intense dry heat where the bathers perspired and then were scraped down with thin bronze strigils. Then they would go to the *frigidarium* (cold bath) to close their pores. Afterward, they were rubbed down with towels and anointed with perfumed oils; the more elite partakers would finish with a massage.

FASHION À LA ROMAN

The purpose of Roman clothing was generally to indicate social standing. Slaves and workers wore plain tunics. Stripes on a tunic revealed an equestrian or senator. A uniform and cloak specified an army general, while an emperor wore a laurel wreath on his head. Only men who were Roman citizens could wear a toga, a semicircular piece of fabric draped around the body from the shoulders and worn everywhere in public. A normal toga was always wool, usually of dull white. In the Republican days, men seeking election would often bleach their togas, hence their name—*candidati,* "extra-white" men. The man wearing a purple toga with golden embroidery could only be the emperor.

Women wore a tunic topped by a *stola,* an ample draping of cloth closed with ornate clasps and pins. Outdoors, they would don a *palla* (shawl), of which wealthy women had many colors. ■

Roman ruins at Glanum, near St.-Rémy-de-Provence

Market day
Fri.

**Châteauneuf-
du-Pape**
🗺 46 B3
Visitor information
✉ Place du Portail
☎ 04 90 83 71 08
🕐 Closed Sun. & Wed.

**Musée des Outils
de Vignerons**
✉ Le clos
☎ 04 90 83 70 07
www.brotte.com

Châteauneuf-du-Pape

STRIPING 7,000 ACRES (2,800 HA) ON THE RHÔNE'S EAST
bank just north of Avignon, the Châteauneuf-du-Pape wine region is
known worldwide for its majestic, full-bodied reds. The magical hilltop
village at its heart is charming as can be, with its shuttered medieval
houses, narrow lanes, and *caveaus de dégustation* at every turn.

Bishop Geoffroy of Avignon decided
in 1157 to follow the ancient Roman
tradition of making wine. Clément V
planted vines in 1308. But the
region's true winemaking tradition
came with Pope John XXII, the
"wine pope," who built his summer
château here in 1318 to 1333 and
planted vines on surrounding lands.
    John XXII probably didn't real-
ize that his lands possessed a happy
geological coincidence for produc-

ing excellent wines. You'll not see
fertile brown earth, but cream and
rust-tinted river pebbles deposited
by Ice Age glaciers. The stones act
as heat storers to absorb the Midi
sun's warmth and reflect it back to
the vines long after sunset. The
result: full ripeness in the grapes
yielding robust and full-bodied
wines. The alluvial soil beneath,
widely spaced vines, and the mistral
winds also add to the wine's success.

Châteauneuf can officially be made using a mixture of 3, 7, or 13 kinds of grapes, though in practice only a few traditionalists use all 13. The predominant grape is Grenache, with Mourvèdre, Syrah, and/or Cinsault often added.

VISITING

The beautifully preserved medieval town has few shops or boutiques. Instead, the business at hand is apparent in the many *caveaux de dégustation* offering tastings. A good place to start is at place de la Fontaine, where a number of wine-tasting cellars are located. Or stop by **Vinadéa,** a retailer that represents 80 domaines and *châteaus d'appellation* (8 rue Maréchal Foch, tel 04 90 83 70 69, *www.vinadea.com*).

Wine rating

Châteauneuf-du-Pape is the first wine region to have received its own *appellation d'origine contrôllée,* France's strict quality-control rating. Baron Le Roy de Boiseaumarié, a distinguished local vintner, proposed specific geographical boundaries and minimum standards for wines to be given the Châteauneuf-du-Pape label. In 1923 area vintners won exclusive rights to market their Côtes du Rhône under that label. From this came the government-controlled rating system used today. ■

The *vendange* takes place every September beneath bright blue skies.

Narrow lanes lead up to the papal castle, **Château du Pape—** at least what's left of it, after being sacked in 1562 by Protestant troops during the Wars of Religion. It overlooks the sweeping vineyards first planted by the popes, with the River Rhône and Les Dentelles beyond (see drive pp. 68–69).

There's one small museum in town, the **Musée des Outils de Vignerons,** which has wine-making tools and machineries of yore. A shop and tasting room await at the end. ■

Touring wineries
To tour a particular vineyard, call ahead to make a reservation. The local tourist office offers a list of vineyard visits.

More places to visit in Avignon & the Vaucluse

CARPENTRAS

In bustling, crowded Carpentras, the quintessential medieval town center is lovely to wander. One interesting sight is the 14th-century **synagogue** *(place de l'Hôtel de Ville)*, France's oldest. It appears very plain on the outside, but is richly decorated inside; the prayer room, for instance, resembles a Louis XIV salon, with gold-painted paneling, jade green

Market day in Carpentras

wood, and a sky blue ceiling full of gold stars. The synagogue has baths used in the monthly ritual purification of women as well as ovens where unleavened bread was baked. The former Cathédrale St.-Siffrein (place St.-Siffrein) is a pastiche of styles, from the 15th-century Provençal Gothic to an early 20th-century bell tower. St. Siffrein's feast day (Nov. 27) is Carpentras's largest fair and signals the start of truffle season. The market, one of Provence's largest, is held every Friday morning on place Aristide Briande.

🅼 46 C2 **Office de Tourisme** ✉ Place Aristide Briand ☎ 04 90 63 00 78

CAVAILLON

This lively city is famous for its sweet cantaloupes, introduced during the Italian Wars by Charles VIII. Filling market stalls May to September, they are celebrated during the mid-July Fête du Melon. Roman artifacts found in the surrounding area are on display at the **archaeological museum** *(Hôtel Dieu Porte d'Avignon, tel 04 90 76 00 34, closed Nov.–April, $, combined ticket with Musée Juif)*. A Roman arch stands on place François Tourel *(in front of tourist office)*. Here, too, is the 12th-century **Cathédrale St.-Véran** and a beautiful synagogue (1772–1774) with its **Musée Juif-Comtadin** (Jewish Museum; *rue Hébraïque, tel 04 90 76 00 34, closed Tues., & Sun. Nov.–April, $, combined ticket with archaeology museum)*, exhibiting objects used for worship, books, and documents on the prayers.

🅼 46 C2 **Office de Tourisme de Cavaillon** ✉ Place François Tourel ☎ 04 90 71 32 01, www.cavaillon-luberon.com

MONT VENTOUX

Italian poet Francesco Petrarch (1304–1374) climbed Mont Ventoux in 1336 for no other reason than "a desire to see its conspicuous height"—thereby inventing the sport of mountain climbing. When he reached the top he "remained immobile, stupefied by the strange lightness of the air and the immensity of the spectacle." These days, there's a hairpin road that snakes to the top, crowded with cyclists in summertime (now and again the road is included in the Tour de France). The vegetation changes as you climb, from lavender fields and vineyards, through a forest of beeches and cedars, then pines. The lunar summit, at 6,263 feet (1,909 m), is a parched, bald semidesert, snow-capped at least half the year and nearly always blasted by winds up to 250 mph (402 kmph) (Ventoux means the "windy one"). A great portion of the mountain was declared a UNESCO biosphere reserve in 1990. Hiking and skiing are popular seasonal pursuits. You can access the main summit route (D974) at **Malaucène,** a busy bourg with a fortified 14th-century church and fountain-filled historic heart. Or, take the quieter, prettier D19, which you can pick up south of Malaucène before Le Barroux. While in the region, be sure to taste the local specialty, *épeautre,* or wild barley (also known as "poor man's wheat"), washed down with a local Côtes du Ventoux.

MUSÉE DE LA LAVANDE
Gleaming copper stills, flacons, and old-style labels take you through the story of lavender at this excellent museum in Coustellet. A bilingual video describes the cultivation process, then, audioguide in hand, you wander through a series of informative displays. The whole museum smells of lavender, and a shop at the end gives you the chance to bring home many forms of the herb.
N 46 C2 ⊠ Rte. de Gordes, Coustellet ☎ 04 90 76 91 23, www.museedelalavande.com **$** $$

PERNES-LES-FONTAINES
Thirty-six fountains from the mid-18th century grace this quiet medieval town, a former capital of the Comtat-Venaissin. Near the

chapel of Notre-Dame-des-Grâces, incorporated into the old city walls, is the town's most striking fountain, the baroque **Fontaine du Cormoran,** with its majestic statue of an open-winged cormorant. If you drink from the **Fontaine de la Lune,** say locals, you will go crazy. The visitor center has a map for a fountain-themed walking tour.
N 46 C3 **Office de Tourisme** ⊠ Place Gabriel Moutte ☎ 04 90 61 31 04

SAULT
In the heart of lavender country—at its full glory in June and July—Sault's tourism office offers a plethora of lavender-related activities, including maps for scenic (and aromatic) lavender drives and hikes. Learn all there is to know about lavender at **Le Jardin des Lavandes** (rte. du Mont Ventoux, tel 04 90 64 13 08, by guided tour only). Note that the town's Wednesday market is famed for its lavender-related goods.
N 46 D3 **Office de Tourisme** ⊠ Ave. de la Promenade ☎ 04 90 64 01 21, www.saultenprovence.com

VÉNASQUE
This quiet little hill town, built on a rock spur in the heart of the Forêt de Vénasque, once reigned as the region's capital. During

Field patterns

Provence's field patterns differ from those of northern France, part of the lingering influence of the ancient Romans. While fields in the north tend to be either large patchworks bounded by hedges or stone walls, or long and open spaces, Provençal fields are small, an artistic mingling of cultivated strips, vines, and fruit trees.

The Romans divided Provence into squares called "centuries," thereby creating a grid pattern for the rural landscape just as they created a town plan. Thanks to Roman inheritance laws, in which all sons were allocated equal shares of land, rather than just the eldest, field sizes were small.

Tools also influenced the region's field patterns. Since Roman times, southern fields have been tilled with the *araire,* a small, light tool

that opens the earth without turning it over. It's conducive to sandy, stony limestone soil and can be drawn by a single animal—perfect for Provence's small, hilly plots. To prepare the ground for sowing, the farmer must plow each field twice, once up and down and once crosswise—hence the unique pattern.

There are no walls, in addition, in southern fields—another Roman touch. Physical barriers were not necessary to mark property lines, since everyone knew that enforcement of the legal code was taken seriously.

Finally, groves of trees are prominent features. The Romans planted clusters of olive and fruit trees in the middle of fields, providing a cool place to rest and store the water gourd while working in hot weather—an inspiration for artists for centuries to come. ■

A sidewalk flower market in Sault purveys dried lavender and other regional sundries.

the barbarian invasions in the Middle Ages, the bishops of Carpentras retreated to this strategic spot, explaining the impressive collection of early Christian and medieval buildings. (In fact, the town gave its name to the Comtat-Venaissin.) As you stroll the pretty streets, seek out the **Église de Notre-Dame** *(at the spur's northern point),* whose well-preserved baptistery, built in the sixth century, is one of France's oldest religious buildings.

◭ 46 C3 **Office de Tourisme**
✉ Grand'Rue ☎ 04 90 66 11 66

VILLENEUVE-LEZ-AVIGNON

In 1307 King Philippe le Bel built a castle across the Rhône from Avignon's papal palace, around which sprung up a "new town." As the popes' importance grew, so did the king's watchtower, the **Tour Philippe Le Bel** *(rue Montée de la Tour, tel 04 32 70 08 57, closed Mon. & Dec.–Feb., $),* which stands exactly where the Pont St.-Bénezet once joined the west bank. The tower still affords a marvelous view. In the town center, the 14th-century **Église de Notre-Dame** *(place du Chapître)* rises in medieval splendor—don't miss the peaceful cloister. Nearby, the **Musée Municipal Pierre de Luxembourg** *(rue*

de la République, tel 04 90 27 49 66, closed Mon. & Feb., $) has among its four floors of artworks two masterpieces: the 14th-century "Madonna and Child," delicately carved of ivory; and the "Coronation of the Virgin" (1454) by Enguerrand Quarton, one of the Avignon school's leading lights. Down the street is the **Chartreuse du Val de Bénédiction** *(rue de la République, tel 04 90 15 24 24, $$),* once France's largest and most important Carthusian charterhouse. Established by Pope Innocent VI in 1352, much of it now lies in ruins. Nevertheless, the intimate cloisters and the monks' cells give a sense of yesteryear's spirit. The small chapel off Cloître du Cimetière has beautiful frescoes by Matteo Giovanetti. Overlooking the charterhouse is the **Fort St.-André** *(montée du Fort, fort: tel 04 90 25 45 35, abbey: by appt., fort tower: $, abbey: $$),* its 14th-century fortifications giving magnificent views over the Rhône to Avignon. Inside are the remains of the **Abbaye St.-André,** a tiny Romanesque chapel set amid a garden of roses, lavender, and wisteria.

◭ 46 B2 **Office de Tourisme** ✉ 1 place Charles David ☎ 04 90 25 61 33, www.villenevelesavignon.fr ∎

The heart of the Provençal spirit, this agricultural realm offers a sampling of varied charms: chalky peaks, vibrant farm fields, beaches, medieval towns, and—a surprise—a bird-rich marshland where flamingoes are king.

South along the Rhône

Van Gogh's chair

South along the Rhône

SOUTH OF AVIGNON, THE RIVER RHÔNE BECOMES SLUGGISH AND WIDE AS IT approaches the Mediterranean Sea. Part of the Bouches-du-Rhône administrative region, this diverse landscape also possesses some of Provence's oldest history: The first humans settled along the river's banks more than a million years ago. The Romans followed long after, establishing flourishing cities at Nîmes, Arles, and St.-Rémy—today buzzing cities mingling old and new. But the region is probably most associated with Vincent van Gogh, who in 1888 and 1889 madly captured its sunflower fields, starry nights, and groves of olive trees in many of his best known works.

Roman Nîmes possesses some of the best preserved monuments from its toga-clad forbears, including Les Arènes, the world's finest example of a Roman amphitheater, and the Maison

Carrée, a beautifully preserved temple that once stood among other important buildings on the city forum. Today it's a lively city with both Spanish and Provençal flair—

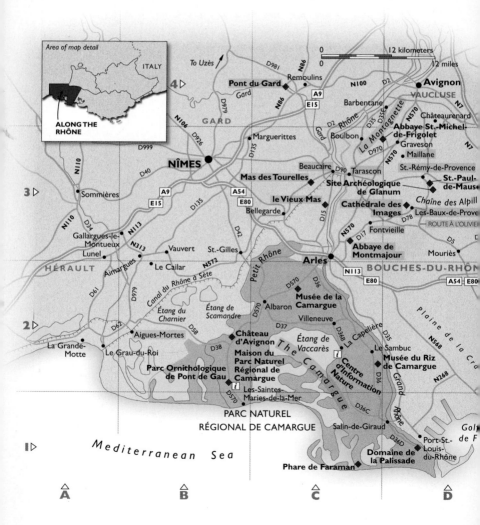

bullfights and flamenco music and lazy café afternoons. The nearby Pont du Gard, the Roman aqueduct, is one of Rome's most famous legacies, built to supply water to ancient Nîmes.

Southward, the landscape becomes flat and marshy, as the Rhône nears the Mediterranean. This lonely realm, called the Camargue, is the domain of the French *gardian* (cowboy), master of

The ancient Roman city of Nîmes features plenty of historical monuments, but also sunny cafés to while away hours at a time.

the indigenous white horse and wild black bull. Millions of birds gather here year-round, luring bird-watchers by the hordes.

Arles is one of Provence's most charming towns, with medieval lanes and café-ringed squares. The Romans once thrived here, leaving behind many monuments, including the Arènes, a twin to the amphitheater in Nîmes. North is Les Baux, former stronghold of the terrible medieval warlords, its lower town since invaded by souvenir shops. The peak-top remains of the citadel, with its far-off view over fields and mountains, proves that the strategic position was not lost on early inhabitants.

Lesser known, and much less touristy, La Montagnette—"little mountain"—to the north of Tarascon provides a scenic wander through forests sprinkled with medieval towns and a fascinating abbey.

On the nearby plains, van Gogh locked himself in the insane asylum at St.-Rémy, where he painted in a flurry of productivity. The Romans knew St.-Rémy long before, the remains of their town (called Glanum) providing a good primer on ancient Roman life. Today St.-Rémy is a pleasant market town with upscale shops installed in historic buildings. ■

Nîmes

Market day
Daily

Nîmes
⚓ 82 B3
Visitor information
✉ Office de Tourisme, 6 rue Auguste
☎ 04 66 58 38 00
www.ot-nimes.fr

Musée Archéologique
✉ 13 bis blvd. Amiral Courbet
☎ 04 66 76 74 80
🕓 Closed Mon.

Les Arènes
✉ Place des Arènes
💲 $$

Note: The Nîmes Romaine combination ticket ($$) provides reduced admission to Les Arènes, La Maison Carrée, and Tour Magne.

The Maison Carrée once stood among other important buildings on Nîmes's ancient Roman forum.

NÎMES'S HISTORIC CORE, BUSTLING WITH CHIC BOUTIQUES and cafés, provides a taste of urban Provence, though most people come here for its ancient history. The Romans established a colony here in 30 B.C., naming it after their river god, Nemausus. With the help of Caesar Augustus (27 B.C.–A.D. 14), the city flourished as an important trading center. Nîmes (pronounced NEEM) still has a number of monuments reflecting its past importance, including one of the world's best-preserved Roman amphitheaters, a near-perfect temple, and the world-famous aqueduct, the Pont du Gard (see p. 87).

While Nîmes belongs to the Languedoc-Roussillon province, its ambience is more Provençal, with its brightly colored café tables and languorous air—a touch of Spain added in to spice things up. Festivals of *corridas* (bullfights) are raucous affairs in the ancient amphitheater—the most important event being the Féria on Pentecost weekend. At night, bodegas fill with sangria-drinking patrons listening to the strains of flamenco.

The city can be difficult to negotiate by car. Essentially, the historic district comprises a triangle bounded by boulevard Gambetta, boulevard Victor Hugo, and boulevard de la Libération/boulevard Amiral Courbet. Follow signs for the Arènes and park in the garage beneath. From here you can explore the old town by foot.

Few sites offer detailed interpretation or historical context. As such, a good first stop is the **Musée Archéologique,** which provides insight into the Roman (and medieval) past with locally excavated statues, sarcophagi, coins, mosaics, and pottery.

Otherwise, you will likely be drawn first to the magnificent, imposing **Arènes** lording over the historic center's southern edge. Built in the first century A.D., this is where gladiators and animals faced each other in bitter combat. The

floor, or arena (which means "sand," used to soak up the blood), covered passages from which wild bears, bulls, and tigers were raised

on an elevator to face the gladiator. The man rarely lost.

Built without mortar, Nîmes arena is in such good condition that it's still used for cultural, musical, and sporting events; bullfights are one of the main attractions—both the traditional Spanish corrida, where the bull is killed, and the Provençal *course Carmarguaise,* where it is not (see feature pp. 90–91).

Two levels of 60 arches each compose the arena's facade, with an additional attic level, of which only traces remain. Romans were preoccupied with the concept of spectator flow pattern, and they perfected

it here with a complicated system of corridors and stairs so that the entire place—23,000 to 24,000 people in 34 tiers of seats—could be emptied in minutes. Climb to the top for the best view—in former times reserved for the prostitutes and other low-life society members. During periods of excessive heat, a canopy was stretched over the seats to shade the spectators.

Another Roman monument stands a couple hundred yards away, at the end of the rue de l'Horloge: the elegant **Maison Carrée** (Square House). Built from local stones between A.D. 3

Maison Carrée
- ✉ Place de la Maison Carrée
- 💲 $

**Carré d'Art—
Musée d'Art
Contemporain**
- Place de la Maison Carrée
- ☎ 04 66 76 35 70
- Closed Mon.
- $$

**Jardins de la
Fontaine**
- Quai de la Fontaine

**Cathédrale
Notre-Dame et
St.-Castor**
- Place aux Herbes

**Musée du Vieux
Nîmes**
- Place aux Herbes
- ☎ 04 66 76 73 70
- Closed Mon. Guided visits Sat. 3 p.m. (French only)

Jeans de Nîmes

Denim, the all-American fabric, originated in France—in Nîmes, to be precise; hence, its name: de Nîmes, "from Nîmes." It all started in the 18th century, when Nîmes had a large Protestant middle class. Banned from government posts, they turned to trade and manufacturing. Among the different products they produced was a twilled silk and wool fabric called *serge*, popular among workers and fishermen for its sturdy, flexible quality. Serge made its way across the Atlantic, where it was used in slave clothing. When Bavarian immigrant Levi-Strauss opened up a dry goods store in San Francisco in the mid-1800s to supply gold miners, he and a pal came up with the idea of making work coveralls from the fabric from Nîmes that would endure the stress of mining. A new fashion trend was thus born. ∎

and 5 and modeled after the Temple of Apollo near Rome, this Corinthian temple is the only entirely preserved building of the forum that once stood here. It's surrounded by columns, six on the short sides, 11 on the long (so it's actually a rectangle, not a square). Inside, panels in French and English describe the temple's history. A handful of ancient artworks include a mosaic of black waves dating from the first century B.C. and several Roman statues found on the road to Beaucaire.

While you're in the area, peek into the **Carré d'Art,** a museum of contemporary art often referred to as the Pompidou Center of southern France.

The Romans established their city around a sacred spring, where they built a sanctuary that included a temple, theater, and baths. Vestiges were discovered when the **Jardins de la Fontaine** (Fountain Garden), northwest of the historic center, was built in 1745. Today you can stroll beneath pines and cedars, among green pools surrounding fountains dotted with marble nymphs. At the garden's south end is the **Temple of Diana,** probably built in the second century A.D. On the garden's north side stands the city's oldest Roman monument, the **Tour Magne** *($)* atop Mont Cavalier, part of the city's ancient ramparts.

Other Roman remains include two imposing gates from the fortified wall that surrounded the ancient city: the **Porte de France,** the exit toward Spain along the Via Domitia; and the **Porte d'Auguste** *(blvd. Amiral Courbet),* where the Via Domitia entered town.

OLD TOWN
The old quarter is a picturesque maze of pedestrian streets, cozy squares, fountains, and historic houses now holding cafés, restaurants, and boutiques. If you amble up Grande Rue you'll come to the **Cathédrale Notre-Dame et St.-Castor** (also called Cathédrale de Nîmes). Consecrated in 1096 by Pope Urban III, it is a composite of styles. During the 16th-century Wars of Religion, Protestants killed eight priests out front.

Next door is the small but interesting **Musée du Vieux Nîmes,** recounting the city's history since the Middle Ages. It's installed in the former Episcopal palace from the late 1600s, with a couple of period rooms reconstructing the interior of Nîmois houses. A surprise is the room devoted entirely to the development of the famous blue-jean fabric—a local specialty (see sidebar this page). ∎

Pont du Gard

NEWLY URBANIZED NÎMES DID NOT HAVE AN ADEQUATE water source, so the Romans built a 31-mile-long (50 km) system of canals that brought fresh water from the springs at Uzès, 15 miles (25 km) away. One of the most amazing aspects of this complex system was the Pont du Gard. The Romans themselves considered the aqueduct the best testimony of their empire—what would they think if they knew their work would last 2,000 years in such majestic totality?

The 900-foot-long (275 m) Pont du Gard comprises three levels of arches: six crossing the River Gard; 11 in the middle tier; and 35 smaller arches carrying the water duct above. Imagine the work it took to hoist limestone blocks weighing up to six tons into place and fitting them together—a thankless job accomplished by thousands of soldiers, craftsmen, and slaves during the reign of Emperor Claudius (R. A.D. 41–54).

Park at the lot on the river's left bank and stroll along the River Gard. The aqueduct soon comes into view. You can walk across the structure's bottom tier, which has been used as a thoroughfare for centuries—in 1285 the bishop of Uzès ordered a toll be collected from all travelers crossing the bridge.

There's an **interpretive cen-** ter on the left bank. The quarry that supplied the *pont's* stone is also open. At the **Concession Pont du Gard,** a museum *($$),* short film *($),* and children's center *($$)* provide further insight into the Romans and their legacy.

Trails lace the forested site. On hot days, swim in the river, or rent a kayak or canoe and skim across a reflection of the ancient aqueduct, towering 158 feet (48 m) above. ∎

Floods

The feisty River Gard has flooded through the centuries, the most recent devastation occurring in 2002—destroying the museum and cafeteria, as well as devastating the riverbank. The 2,000-year-old aqueduct, however, has remained standing every time. ∎

The Pont du Gard carried 9.2 million gallons (34.8 million L) of water a day across the River Gard for Nîmes's ancient citizens. Now it funnels euros into Nîmes as one of France's most popular tourist attractions.

Pont du Gard
🏔 82 C4
Visitor information
✉ Office de Tourisme du Pont du Gard, place des Grands Jours, Remoulins
☎ 04 66 37 22 34

Site du Pont du Gard
✉ Rte. du Pont du Gard
☎ 08 20 90 33 30
www.pontdugard.fr
💲 Parking: $$

Surrounded by
lagoons and
marshlands, the
**Phare (lighthouse)
de Faraman,** in the
Camargue's
southeast, was
built in 1892.

The Camargue
A 82 C1–C2
**Visitor
information**
✉ Esplanade Charles
de Gaulle, Arles
☎ 04 90 18 41 20
www.tourisme.ville-
arles.fr

The Camargue

LONG-HORNED BULLS AND WHITE HORSES WITH FLOWING
manes run semifree throughout the Camargue, a marshland frontier
south of the ancient city of Arles. The Camarguian gardian (cowboy) is alive and well, showing up at tourist events and *courses de taureaux* (bull games) when real work isn't going on. The Camargue is
also a supreme bird preserve—home to more than 300 species, its
most famous denizen being the great flamingo. To watch these lanky
pink birds gliding effortlessly in the pure blue sky, whole flocks of
them, is one of Provence's most memorable sights.

At Arles, the great River Rhône
divides into two, its main arm, the
Grand Rhône, taking a direct route
to the Mediterranean, while the

Petit Rhône meanders west.
Between the two, in the rough
shape of a triangle, is the Rhône
River Delta—the Camargue—a

marshy soup of wetlands, pastures, dunes, and salt flats, with the large Étang de Vaccarès (Vaccares Lagoon) in the middle.

For centuries, humans have inhabited this land with a wary eye toward the sea and river, whose efforts to dominate are ceaseless. It was not until the 19th century that dikes and embankments were built, so that human domination was finally secured and farmlands could be extended to feed a growing population.

A wildlife preserve was created in 1927 and the government established the Parc Naturel Régional de Camargue in 1970. The park preserves 328 square miles (85,000 ha) of this thriving ecosystem; its excellent trails and information stations make visiting easy.

The D570 roughly follows the Petit Rhône's route from Arles to Les-Stes.-Maries-de-la-Mer, the Camargue's main town, while the D36 cuts down along the Grand Rhône to Salin-de-Giraud. In between is the bird-rich Étang des Vaccarès—accessible via smaller roads.

DOWN TO LES-SAINTES-MARIES-DE-LA-MER

About 6 miles (10 km) south of Arles on the D570 is the award-winning **Musée de la Camargue** *(Mas du Pont de Rousty, Albaron, tel 04 90 97 10 82, closed Sun.–Tues., $$),* which provides a thorough introduction into regional history and culture. The museum is housed in a *bergerie* (sheepfold) of the Mas du Pont de Rousty, built in 1812. In the dimly lit space, the imaginative exhibits go into fine detail about the area's geological and human history, with the most interesting part focusing on Camargue life and tradition. Outside, a 2.2-mile (3.5 km) nature trail takes you into the heart of the Camargue's landscape, with wild bulls and lots of birds to see along the way.

The 18th-century **Château d'Avignon,** farther south off the D570, is furnished just as it was in the 1890s, when a wealthy Marseille merchant used it as a hunting lodge.

Farther south is the **Maison du Parc Naturel Régional de Camargue,** a favorite spot for bird-watchers. It's the park's main information center, with an exhibit of mounted birds helping to identify the live ones you can see outside the giant picture windows overlooking the Étang de Ginès (Gines Marsh).

(continued on p. 92)

Château d'Avignon
- ✉ Domaine du Château d'Avignon, rte. d'Arles
- ☎ 04 90 97 58 58
- 🕐 Closed Tues. Dec.–March, Sat.–Thurs. rest of year
- 💲 $

Maison du Parc Naturel Régional de Camargue
- ✉ Mas du Pont de Rousty/RD 570, Pont de Gau
- ☎ 04 90 97 86 32
- www.parc-camargue.fr

Parc Ornithologique de Pont de Gau
- ✉ D570, 2.5 miles (4 km) N of Les-Stes.-Maries-de-la-Mer
- ☎ 04 90 97 82 62
- www.parc ornithologique.com
- 💲 $$

Les-Stes.-Maries-de-la-Mer
- ⚑ 82 B1
- **Visitor information**
- ✉ Office de Tourisme, 5 ave. van Gogh
- ☎ 04 90 97 82 55
- www.saintesmaries delamer.com

Centre d'Information Nature, La Capelière
- ✉ D36B, Réserve Nationale de Camargue
- ☎ 04 90 97 00 97
- 🕐 Closed Tues. mid-Oct.–Easter
- 💲 $

Wild, wild Camargue

On a summer Sunday in Les-Stes.-Maries-de-la-Mer, you might wonder why the main street has suddenly cleared. People crowd along its shoulders, craning to look down the empty road, anticipation filling the air. Then a shout, and everyone cheers, as six bronzed men in black felt hats gallop past on sturdy white stallions with long billowing tails. Among them is the reason for this *abrivado:* a sextet of snorting black bulls destined for the bull ring that evening. People try their best to encourage the bulls to escape—the excitement has begun.

With its vast, undeveloped marshlands, wild longhorn bulls, white stallions, and true-to-life cowboys—called *gardians* here—the Camargue is about as close to the Wild West as France gets. It's a tradition that goes back to the 16th century, when the first gardians established ranch houses—*manades*—to cultivate the native cattle and horses. What has evolved is a singular way of life, one of hard work and independence and freedom.

Small, nimble, known for their intelligence and agility, the horses descend from prehistoric animals. Indeed, they resemble the horses painted on the walls of Lascaux, dating back some 15,000 years. They roam the Camargue part of the year, grazing on stunted reed beds, and marsh and field grasses. Once a year, the gardians round them up. Instead of six-shooters in their holsters, these cowboys use three-forked prongs called *ficherouns* and horsehair lassos that, according to legend, were brought by Buffalo Bill himself. Inferior three-year-old males are removed and gelded. The others are broken and tamed for farm work and, these days, to give trail rides to tourists.

No one knows exactly where the wild bulls came from. Some say it's Attila the Hun who brought their ancestors from Asia Minor, which were then crossbred with the Spanish Navarre bull. Small in stature with lyre-shaped horns, spirited, cunning, and rebellious, these dark, rough-haired beasts are not conducive to farm work. Instead, they roam the Camargue as they please until the bullfight season, when they are rounded up.

In spring, the *ferrada* takes place—the traditional branding of the cattle. In olden days (and still today), it's a time when families from far-off farms gathered and socialized. Year-old calves are branded with an iron stamped on their rump, their ears notched.

But the greatest events are the "bull games." Formerly, bulls were brought to farms, or to the village square, where they were released into an arena fashioned out of carts and barrels. There, young boys confronted them—the precursor of today's *courses Camarguaises.*

These bullfights vary greatly from their Spanish cousins. Most notably, the bull is never killed. He may become extremely angry and perturbed and grunt a lot, but most of the risk falls to the bullfighters, who face the bull on equal terms. Also, it's the bull—not the bullfighter—who is the star. People will travel from village to village to follow a champion bull. One of the most famous was Le Sanglier, who has his own mausoleum in Le Cailar.

A *course* typically consists of six bulls from the same ranch—the strongest bulls kept for last, when the *raseteurs* (bullfighters) are most tired. At the sound of a trumpet, a bull is released into the ring, where await 20 young raseteurs dressed in white. Their goal: to unhook "attributes"—including strings and tassels—from the bull's horns with a finger-held rake. Points are awarded for retrieving different ones (and the bull receives points for avoiding them). It's a game of cat and mouse as the snorting bull charges and the boys spring to safety up and over low safety walls. The excitement comes when the boys take chances, egging on the bull, trying to make him charge. If the pursuing bull bangs the fence, the Toreador overture of *Carmen* is played. If the bull keeps his decorations for 15 minutes, he wins the crowd's respect and the "fight" is over.

The most prestigious bull games—the Cocarde d'Or—take place in Arles in July, where the best bulls and raseteurs compete for prizes. You can also see courses Camarguaises in Nîmes, Tarascon, and Les-Stes.-Maries-de-la-Mer. ∎

A Camargue tradition: the *roussataio*—the releasing of horses and mares into city streets

Sheep still inhabit the 19th-century *bergerie* de Favouillane, one of the last traditional sheepfolds in the Camargue.

Domaine de la Palissade
✉ BP5, Salin-de-Giraud
☎ 04 42 86 81 28
💲 $

Musée du Riz de Camargue
✉ Rte. de Salin-de-Giraud, Le Sambuc
☎ 04 90 97 29 44
🕐 Open Fri.—Mon., by appt. only Sat.—Sun.
💲 $

(continued from p. 89)
Next door awaits one of the area's major attractions, the **Parc Ornithologique de Pont de Gau,** where you'll probably get your closest look at the area's *flamants roses*—great flamingos. This is the only site in Europe where flamingos breed regularly—on average between 10,000 and 13,000 pairs a year. A 2.8-mile (4.5 km) trail takes you through 148 acres (60 ha) of marshland. Other denizens: white storks, rollers, hoopoes, and Egyptian vultures (if you're lucky).

Next stop, **Les-Saintes-Maries-de-la-Mer,** full of Spanish charm with its tile roofs and devotion to bulls. The popular beach, boardwalk, and souvenir shops give it a Coney Island feel as well. The tallest thing around for miles is the Romanesque **Église des Stes.-Maries** *(place de l'Église),* with its single, upright nave, built in the 12th and 15th centuries. Somber and cavelike, the interior has a crypt beneath the altar lit with hundreds of votives. Here are preserved the relics of the Sts. Mary—Mary Salomé, mother of the apostles James and John; and Mary Jacobé,

the Virgin Mary's sister. Upon Jesus's crucifixion, they, along with Mary Magdalene, Lazarus, and other biblical figures, were shoved out to sea without sails or oars, finally washing ashore here. A statue of their Egyptian servant Sara, the gypsies' highly revered patron saint, is also preserved in the crypt, covered with a huge layer of dresses provided as offerings. On May 24 and 25, thousands of gypsies pilgrimage here to worship the Marys and Sara. Be sure to climb the narrow spiral steps to the **Terrasse de l'Eglise** *($),* the rooftop terrace surrounded by a parapet with battlements and machicolation—hinting at the church's onetime role as a fortress against Saracen, Arab, and pirate attacks.

If the loudspeakers are blaring near the beach, it's a probable sign that a *course de taureaux* is taking place at the Arènes, near the Office de Tourisme. Inquire at the tourist office for a schedule and ticket information.

TO THE OTHER SIDE OF ÉTANG DE VACCARÈS
From Les-Stes.-Maries-de-la-Mer, backtrack 14.3 miles (23 km) north

to the turnoff for the D37, which brings you around the northern edge of Étang de Vaccarès.

Farther on at Villeneuve, the D36B sidles next to the water along the lagoon's east side, with observation towers along the way to birdwatch. The **Centre d'Information Nature,** in the hamlet of La Capelière, has exhibits on flora and fauna, plus trails to wander.

Follow signs to industrial **Salin-de-Giraud,** where the landscape changes dramatically. The enormous saltworks here have been in production since the 19th century. You can see pyramids of the white stuff from an overlook just south of town on the D36D (there's a snack shop here, too).

A few miles farther south on the D36D is the **Domaine de la Palissade,** interesting in that it's only 2.5 miles (4 km) from the Great Rhône's mouth and the only area outside the dike system that protects the rest of the region from flooding. Four short tracks help discover what the delta originally looked like.

North on the D36, the **Musée du Riz** (Museum of Rice; *reservations required*) tells you everything about the Camargue's famed rice. ■

The wild side

Outdoor activities in the Camargue include horseback riding, biking, hiking, and bird-watching. You can also take a boat trip *(promenade en bateau)* along the Petit Rhône to see birds, horses, and bulls; take a 4WD "safari" to see the same animals; and horseback ride or bike into the outback. There is no shortage of outfitters in Les-Stes.-Maries-de-la-Mer (see Activities pp. 232–234).

During the annual gypsy pilgrimage to Les-Stes.-Maries-de-la-Mer, festivities include a procession down to the beach, where a priest blesses the sea and people from an offshore boat.

Arles

Market days
Sat.: blvd. des Lices & blvd. Clemenceau
Wed.: blvd. Émile Combes

Arles
🅰 82 C3
Visitor information
✉ Esplanade Charles de Gaulle
☎ 04 90 18 41 20
www.tourisme.ville-arles.fr

ARLESIENS HAVE LONG EXALTED IN THEIR PANOPLY OF Roman treasures—indeed, the amphitheater, arena, public baths, and *cryptoportiques* are some of the monuments still standing since Julius Caesar first granted Arles capital status for its help in defeating Marseille. Arles is just as famous for its connection to van Gogh—he painted many of his most famous paintings on Arles's streets, and this is where he chopped off his earlobe. Here, too, Provençal poet Frédéric Mistral built a museum memorializing his beloved Arlesiens. Everywhere you look, you come across relics of the town's past.

Accessed via different gates, Arles's historic core is encircled by a wall bounded by blvd. Émile Combes, boulevard des Lices, rue Gambetta, and the Grand Rhône.

A good place to begin a visit is outside the walls at the **Musée de l'Arles Antiques,** a modern,

airy museum built adjacent to the vestiges of a 1,476-foot-long (450 m) Roman chariot race track. Detailing Arles's classical past, its excellent exhibits provide a good preface for the ruins that you will see in town.

The museum is arranged chronologically, beginning with Arles's prehistory and progressing through the Iron Age and, finally, the Roman period—in which various subjects are explored, including the coming of the Romans, the economic prosperity of Roman Arles, and everyday life.

One of the museum's strengths

is its 11 detailed models of Roman and other landmarks—including the theater, chariot-racing circus, and amphitheater—which now lay in ruin in the old town. Related artifacts—a rich assemblage of sculpture, mosaics, vases, jewelry, and inscriptions—complement them.

Among a large display of mosaics is one that once adorned a dining room at Trinquetaille. The exhibits end with a walk through an alley of Roman Christian sargophagi from Les Alyscamps (see pp. 96–97), comprising one of the world's most famous collections.

ROMAN ARLES

The most dramatic Roman landmark is **Les Arènes,** the arena built for gladiator standoffs. Most of the walls remain of the two-level structure, each with 60 arches. It could seat 20,000 spectators, all of whom could disperse within minutes through 180 exits. The first bullfight took place here in 1830 to celebrate the taking of Algiers; bullfights are still hosted in early summer. For a good view, climb the three towers that remain from medieval times, when the amphitheater was turned into a fortress; then, houses invaded the perimeter, with most being dismantled between 1826 and 1830.

Precious little remains of the nearby **Théâtre Antique,** the Roman theater—only twin Corinthian columns and a jumble of ruins. Built at the end of the first century B.C., it is one of the earliest freestanding theaters using radiating walls and galleries. Originally, 10,000 to 15,000 spectators could sit here. The exquisite Venus of Arles was found here in 1651, armless and broken into three pieces; it probably decorated the stage wall. The original is now in the Louvre,

Museum pass
The Pass Monuments covers entry to all sites for $$$; available at the sites and at the tourist office.

Musée de l'Arles et de la Provence Antiques
🅐 Map p. 99
✉ Presqu'île du Cirque Romain/BP205
☎ 04 90 18 88 88
www.arles-antique.cg13.fr
$ $$

Les Arènes Romaines
🅐 Map p. 99
✉ Rond-point des Arènes
☎ 04 90 96 03 70
$ $$

Théâtre Antique
🅐 Map p. 99
✉ Rue de la Calade
☎ 04 90 96 93 30
$ $

Cryptoportiques de Forum
🅐 Map p. 99
✉ Rue Balze
☎ 04 90 49 36 36
🕓 Closed for renovation

Thermes de Constantin
🅐 Map p. 99
✉ Rue Dominique Maïsto
☎ 04 90 49 36 36
$ Included with entrance to Les Arènes

A Fête de Gardian— cowboy festival— in Arles

Museon Arlaten
- 🗺 Map p. 99
- ✉ 29 rue de la République
- ☎ 04 90 93 58 11
- 🕐 Closed Mon. Oct.–June
- 💲 $

Église St.-Trophime
- 🗺 Map p. 98
- ✉ E side of place de la République
- ☎ 04 90 96 07 38

Cloître St.-Trophime
- 🗺 Map p. 98
- ✉ Place de la République
- ☎ 04 90 49 36 36
- 💲 $

Musée Réattu
- 🗺 Map p. 98
- ✉ 10 rue du Grand Prieuré
- ☎ 04 90 96 37 68
- 💲 $

Les Alyscamps
- 🗺 Map p. 98
- ✉ Rue Pierre-Rendudel at ave. des Alyscamps
- ☎ 04 90 49 36 36
- 💲 $

though you can see a copy at the Musée d'Arles Antiques.

Nothing remains of the Roman forum, the typical monumental center of a Roman city, where people met, conducted business, and worshiped god, emperor, and notables. In Arles the forum was located where the place du forum now stands. You can, however, get a rare glimpse *inside* the forum. Since it was built to slope down to the river, a strong foundation was needed underground. The solution: underground galleries called **cryptoportiques,** built at the end of the first century B.C. Later, during World War II, residents and Résistance leaders hid out here. Note that they were closed at the present time for renovations; be sure to ask the tourist office for an update.

Around the corner and up rue de l'Hôtel de Ville, the **Thermes de Constantin**—the Roman public baths—remain in crumbling brick-marble-and-mortar glory. What you see represents only a small part of the once grand Palais Constantin, probably the largest baths in Provincia Romana, built in the fourth century. Note the underfloor heating system.

MORE SIGHTS

For a better understanding of the region's Arlesian side, the **Museon Arlaten** is a meticulously detailed, seemingly bottomless collection of all things Provençal: room after room of Arlesian costumes, household wares, Provençal furniture, santons, religious medals, and tools belonging to different trades, including silk-weaving looms and wheat-chafing implements. Nobel Prize–winning Provençal poet Frédéric Mistral (see sidebar p. 38) founded the museum in 1896 in an effort to revive his beloved culture and language.

On the east side of the place de la République, the former **Église St.-Trophime** is named for the third-century bishop of Arles. St.-Hilaire built the original church in the fifth century, but it was much altered in the 11th and 15th centuries in Romanesque style. It was here that St.-Augustine was consecrated the first bishop of Canterbury in the sixth century. The church's long, narrow nave features a series of chapels filled with treasures. In the **Chapelle des Reliques,** little boxes contain saint relics, including those of St.- Étienne, the first Christian martyr, and St.-Trophime. A paleo-Christian sargophagus in the Chapelle St.-Genest shows the parting of the Red Sea. Don't miss the outstanding sculpture group of the Last Judgment on the tympanum of the West Grand Portal, dating from the 12th century.

To see the delightful **cloisters,** considered Provence's finest, exit the church and turn left, then left again at the sign. The masters of St.-Gilles carved this elaborate, two-tiered structure in both Gothic and Romanesque styles.

Nearby, the small **Musée Réattu** features a solid collection of fine art, including numerous paintings by Arlesian Jacques Réattu (1760–1833) himself. There's a special emphasis on modern and contemporary artists, with the most significant works being 57 drawings by Picasso.

One last sight worth a peek is **Les Alyscamps,** in the town's southeast corner. A necropolis founded by Romans, it gained fame when a Roman civil servant, beheaded for his Christian beliefs and made a saint, was buried here and miracles began to happen. Then *everyone* wanted to be buried here; coffins were shipped

Van Gogh's Arles

Vincent van Gogh came to Arles in February 1888 during a snowstorm. After the streets cleared, he saw a shabby city confronting the new reality of the industrial age: river embankments that cut the city off from the Rhône, a new railroad line whose Belgian workers were housed in dilapidated dwellings. But van Gogh detected something special here. He took a room in a poor neighborhood by the station and painted his heart away. "Café de Nuit," "La Maison Jaune," and "Le Pont de Langlois" are just some of his most famous works created during this period.

While van Gogh left an indelible print of Arles in his paintings, there are not many van Gogh sites left to see. The famous bridge, the

yellow house, and the café were destroyed by American bombers during World War II or after. The Hôtel Dieu, one of van Gogh's subjects, has been converted to a media center and multimedia gallery called the **Éspace Van Gogh.**

At the **Fondation Vincent Van Gogh,** facing the Arènes, the greatest international artists— Arman, Lichtenstein, Botero, César—pay tribute to van Gogh in special exhibitions.

The tourist bureau has placed a number of plaques depicting copies of paintings on the spots where van Gogh once stood with his easel. You can obtain a brochure that lists them, or join a guided tour. ■

Arles's Pont Van Gogh typifies the scenery and architecture that inspired some of van Gogh's greatest paintings.

Éspace Van Gogh
- Map p. 98
- Place Félix Rey
- 04 90 49 39 39

Fondation Vincent Van Gogh
- Map p. 98
- Palais de Luppé, 24 bis rond-point des Arènes
- 04 90 49 94 04
- www.fondationvan gogh-arles.org
- Closed Mon. Oct.–March
- $$

down the Rhône and, by the tenth century, word spread that even the heroes of Roncevaux— Roland and Olivier—were laid to rest here. At its peak in the Middle Ages, Les Alyscamps stretched for 1.5 miles (2.5 km) and contained 19 chapels and several thousand tombs, many

packed five bodies deep. Today, poplar-shaded **Allée des Sarcophages** is a beautiful place to promenade past empty sargophagi (the best have been removed to various churches and museums in Arles), a scene vividly depicted by Paul Gauguin and van Gogh. ■

A walk around Arles

This walk takes in the heart of Arles, its museums and monuments standing grandly amid bustling restaurants, boutiques, and souvenir shops.

Little Rome on the Rhône has gone about its business since the sixth century B.C.

Begin at the lively **place du Forum** ❶, buzzing with cafés (serving mediocre food). This square was once the site of the Roman forum, the central political, religious, and administrative meeting place. The **Grand Hôtel Nord-Pinus,** on the southern side, is one of Arles's finest places to rest your head (see Travelwise p. 215). The **Café La Nuit** is reminiscent of the café van Gogh immortalized in his 1888 "The Cafe Terrace on the Place du Forum at Night, Arles"; American bombers destroyed the original building during World War II. Lording over the square is a statue of

Provençal poet Frédéric Mistral, leaning on a walking stick as if waiting for a train, as he himself complained when it was unveiled.

Walk up rue des Arènes, past ancient, elegant facades. On the left rises the **Hôtel Quiqueran de Beaujeu,** a lovely 18th-century *hôtel particulier (closed to visitors).* The lane narrows to a ruelle, and then you're funneled into the carnival atmosphere of **Les Arènes** ❷ (see p. 95)— shops, restaurants, peddlers all plying for your business, probably exactly the same as when the Romans were here. Visit the arena, then seek out the **Fondation Vincent Van Gogh** on its western side, where famous artists pay tribute to van Gogh through various expositions (see p. 97).

Exiting the Fondation Van Gogh to the right, go right on rue Diderot (Ancienne Rue des Cordeliers). At the next corner, rue de la Bastille (no sign), turn left. The **Théâtre Antique** ❸ (see p. 95) is straight ahead.

After visiting the theater, go right from the exit, arcing around little place Henri de Bornier. Go down rue Porte de Laure (unsigned), the busy lane in front of you. When you reach **Jardin d'Été** ❹, go down the stairs (a sign indicates this is montée Vauban). Down the steps to the right is an entrance to the park; go inside. Right away you'll spot one of the many panels scattered about town indicating that van Gogh painted here—"L'Entrée du Parc Publique" (1888).

On the park's other side awaits boulevard des Lices—another favorite van Gogh subject, with its great rows of plane trees and onetime Arlesian beauties. Turn right; a block past bustling cafés, turn right again, on cours Jean Jaurès. This will lead you to the classical **place de la République** ❺, dominated by an obelisk that once stood in the center of Arles's Roman circus. On the western side stands **Ste.-Anne,** built in the Middle Ages before **St.-Trophime** (see p. 96), the grand cathedral across the way.

Now walk through the **Hôtel de Ville** ❻ (Town Hall) on the square's north side, admiring its Versailles-style facade and, inside, the splendid vestibule vaulting.

Exiting on the other side, turn left on **rue du plan de la Cour,** a small medieval square. Continue straight, on rue Balze, to the **Chapelle des Jésuites** ❼. In 1648

> 🗺 See area map p. 82
> ▶ Place du Forum
> ◀ 1 mile (1,600 m)
> 🕐 2 hours (more with stops)
> ▶ Place du Forum
>
> **NOT TO BE MISSED**
> - Place du Forum
> - Les Arènes
> - Museon Arlaten

Jesuits installed a college in the Théâtre Antique but subsequently moved it here, to the 15th-century Palais Laval-Castellane. The entrance leads to the **cryptoportiques** (see p. 96; *closed for renovations*).

Exiting the chapel, turn left on rue Balze and proceed to the corner; turn left at the first street (unsigned), then left again on rue de la République, to the entrance of the **Museon Arlaten** ❽ (see p. 96). After taking in this world of local culture, return to place du Forum by retracing your steps, going right on the unmarked road, right on rue Balze, and left on the next unmarked road to the square. If you have more energy, consider continuing on rue de l'Hôtel de Ville to the **Thermes de Constantin** (see p. 96) and, around the corner, to the **Musée Réattu** (see p. 96). ∎

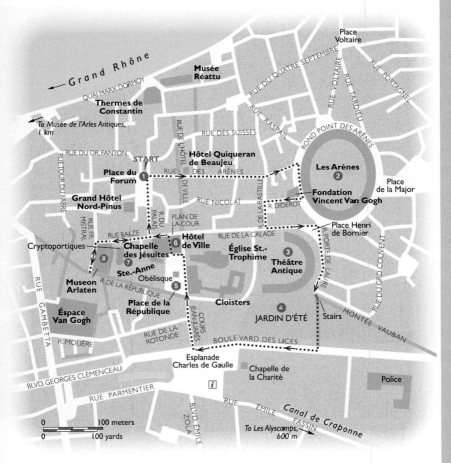

Les Baux-de-Provence

Les Baux
🅰 82 D3
Visitor information
✉ Office de Tourisme, Maison du Roy, Les Baux
☎ 04 90 54 34 39
www.lesbauxde provence.com

Musée des Santons des Baux
✉ Place Louis Jou

THE SETTING IS GRIMLY MEDIEVAL, THE REMAINS OF AN enormous stone citadel rising out of a shadowy, windswept massif high above the southern Alpilles. This is the ancient stronghold of the seigneurs of Les Baux, a rebel fiefdom that terrorized southern Provence. Today it is France's No. 2 tourist sight, attracting more than two million visitors a year—visit early or late in the day, or off-season.

The lords of Les Baux ruled in the Middle Ages, perhaps building their fortress as long ago as the ninth century. Claiming to be descended from Balthazar, one of the Three Kings, they did not acknowledge the French king, nor the emperors—they didn't have to, given their protective mountain setting. When Raymond de Turenne, a blood-thirsty distant relative, took over in 1372, he sent men throughout the land to kidnap people who, if their families couldn't pay the ransom, were forced to walk over the cliff's edge. But it was also at Les Baux that the most famous troubadours sang songs of courtly love.

Les Baux was integrated into the county of Provence, then

became a part of France, with Provence, in 1481. Upon this integration, the population revolted, to which Louis XIII responded by ordering the castle destroyed in 1632. It's thanks to Provençal poets, including Frédéric Mistral, that the place was not forgotten.

The site comprises two parts—the "living city," a pedestrian-only village in the lower town, and the "dead city," or *ville morte*—the ruined castle complex.

LIVING CITY

The lower town has been painstakingly restored, its beautiful, ivy-clad Renaissance facades, churches, and hôtels particuliers now holding shops, shops, and more shops.

Among the handful of sights is the **Musée des Santons,** which has a display of clay figurines dating from the 18th and 19th centuries. Up the street, beyond the ramparts, the **Porte d'Eyguières** was, until the 18th century, the city's only entrance. The **Église St.-Vincent,** on place de l'Église, encloses three chapels from the tenth century, with stained-glass windows by Max Ingrand, presented by Prince Rainier of Monaco in 1960. On the same square, the **Musée Yves Brayer** displays some of this well-known local figurative painter's works—a sample of which you can see opposite, in the 17th-century **Chapelle des Pénitents Blancs.** Brayer decorated its walls in 1974 with colorful scenes of a shepherd's Noël.

DEAD CITY

Windswept, rocky, with breathtaking views over the Alpilles, it's hard to believe that hundreds of years ago, 6,000 inhabitants once resided on this forlorn plateau. With audioguide in hand highlighting points of interest, follow the path through this dead city. At the entrance, a small museum provides a historical primer.

Several reproductions of medieval warfare are on display, including a catapult and battering ram. The ruined château dominates the plateau, its fragments of towers and walls sticking out of the bare rock. The only intact part is the *donjon,* atop which you are treated to views over the valley beyond.

Back toward the exit, stop by the 12th-century **Chapelle St.-Blaise,** used as a meeting place until the 18th century by the Guild of Wool Combers and Weavers. Inside, a film describes the Baux of the artists—van Gogh, Cézanne, Gauguin … ■

Musée Yves Brayer
- ✉ Hôtel des Porcelet, place de l'Église
- ☎ 04 90 54 36 99 www.yvesbrayer.com
- 🕐 Closed Tues. Oct.–March & Jan.–mid-Feb.
- 💲 $

Musée d'Histoire des Baux
- ✉ Château des Baux de Provence
- ☎ 04 90 54 55 56 www.chateau-baux-provence.com
- 💲 $$

Bloodthirsty warlords—distant relations of Monaco's ruling royal Grimaldi family—once terrorized from Les Baux, now a popular tourist draw.

La Montagnette
🗺 82 C2–D3

Visitor information

✉ Office de Tourisme,
16 blvd. Itam,
Tarascon

☎ 04 90 91 03 52
www.tarascon.org

Boulbon's *carreto ramado,* **in which decorated horses pull a chariot through the streets**

La Montagnette

SCENTED WITH THYME AND ROSEMARY, A PARADISE FOR walkers and mushroom gatherers, this untraveled "little mountain" north of Tarascon and south of Avignon offers a cluster of delights—including an abbey, a château, and pastoral views all around.

The remains of a 12th-century feudal castle dominates sleepy **Boulbon,** about 5 miles (8 km) north of Tarascon on the D35. Leaving place de la Mairie at the village's entrance, you will pass through the fortified **Porte**

Loriol to **Grand'rue,** a street lined with flower-draped old houses. Near the château, **Église Ste.-Anne** was built in 1626.

About 4 miles (6.5 km) farther north on D35 is the medieval village of **Barbentane,** overlooking market gardens along the Rhône. Its elegant, 17th-century **château** (*1 rue du Château, tel 04 90 95 51 07, closed Wed. mid-April–June & Oct., & Nov.–mid-April, $$*), the home of Barbentane marquesses since 1674, is built in classical style. Through the village's medieval gates, tiny lanes harbor ancient houses, including the **Maison des Chevaliers,** a seigniorial house from the 12th century with 16th-century additions. Atop the hill is the medieval **Tour Anglica,** crowned by a round turret. Built in 1385 as the *donjon* of Barbentane's original castle, it was sung by Frédéric Mistral in the "Iscles d'Or."

Leaving the D35 via the D35E brings you up through sweet-scented forest to the neo-Gothic **Abbaye St.-Michel-de-Frigolet** (*tel 04 90 95 70 07, closed Tues.–Wed. Oct.–March*), founded in 1133. Its name derives from the Provençal word for "place where thyme grows abundantly"— *ferigoulo* or *ferigoulet*. The thyme-related elixir produced here is celebrated for its curative powers. You are free to wander the peaceful grounds and peek into some of the buildings. The abbey restaurant (*tel 04 90 90 52 70*) offers meals, and the Hôtellerie St.-Michel (*tel 04 90 90 52 70*) has rooms overlooking the gardens. ∎

St.-Rémy-de-Provence

NESTLED AT THE FOOT OF THE ALPILLES, SURROUNDED BY fields of wheat and red poppies, St.-Rémy is a peaceful market town of winding lanes behind vestiges of ancient walls. Nostradamus was born here in 1503, and in 1922 Gertrude Stein and Alice B. Toklas found St.-Rémy after "wandering around everywhere a bit." But St.-Rémy is most associated with Vincent van Gogh. After cutting off his earlobe in 1888, the tortured artist committed himself to an asylum here, during which time he captured olive trees, irises, and the nearby bleach-white Alpilles on more than 150 canvases.

Early on, the Romans built a city here on the Via Domitia, the road linking Italy and Spain. The ruins have been excavated and can be visited just south of St.-Rémy on the D5, at Glanum, one of Europe's most famous Roman sites. The **Site Archéologique de Glanum** comprises two parts: Les Antiques and, across the road, Glanum. Archaeologists believe that the excavated ruins represent only a sixth of the city's original size.

At **Les Antiques**, the **Arc de Triomphe** dates from the reign of Augustus (63 B.C.–A.D. 14). Marking the entry road to the Roman city, it is decorated with reliefs illustrating Caesar's conquest of Gaul. The elegant, three-tiered **Mausolée des Jules** is the best preserved mausoleum of the Roman world, dating from 30 to 20 B.C. Raised by an important Roman family to honor their father and grandfather, its podium base is adorned on all sides with bas-reliefs depicting battle and hunting scenes.

Just up the road is the main sight of **Glanum.** The Romans used a layout characteristic of all their great cities—a low town with thermal baths and lavish villas; a middle town

Sheep rumble through St.-Rémy in the age-old tradition of transhumance, the seasonal migration to greener pastures.

Market day
Wed.

St.-Rémy-de-Provence
🅰 82 D3
Visitor information
✉ Office de Tourisme, place Jean Jaurès
☎ 04 90 92 05 22
www.saintremy-de-provence.com

**Site
Archéologique
de Glanum**
🅰 82 D3
✉ Rte. des Baux-de-
Provence
☎ 04 90 92 23 79
www.monum.fr
🕐 Closed Mon.
Sept.–March
💲 Les Antiques: free.
Glanum: $$

**St.-Paul-de-
Mausole**
✉ Route des Baux-
de-Provence/Ave.
Van Gogh
☎ 04 90 92 77 00
💲 $

**Musée
Archéologique/
Hôtel de Sade**
✉ I rue du Parage
☎ 04 90 92 64 04
www.monum.fr
🕐 Closed for
renovations at
press time

**Musée des
Alpilles**
✉ Hôtel Mistral de
Mondragon,
I Place Favier
☎ 04 90 92 68 24
🕐 Closed Sun.–Mon.
💲 $

with a basilica and temples; and a narrow high town, with walls guarding the town entrance. Among the treasures are the houses along both sides of the rue des Thermes, abandoned in the third century; the remains of a fountain; thermal baths; a *palestra* (exercise yard); and a *piscina* (pool). There are also sewers, a forum, and a nymphaem. For a better understanding of Roman history, visit the Hôtel de Sade in St.-Rémy, which holds the Musée Archéologique (see below).

Just down the road stands the Romanesque church and chapel of **St.-Paul-de-Mausole,** lovely in its own right but best known for its association with van Gogh. The artist chose St.-Paul as a place of refuge between May 1889 and May 1890—after he cut off his ear. This year was his most intense, and most prolific, during which time he produced some of his most famous works, including "Nuit Etoilée" ("Starry Night") and "Les Blés Jaunes" ("Cornfield and Cypress Trees"). His "Les Oliviers" and "Ciel Jaune et Soleil Resplendissant" were painted along the driveway leading to the complex.

Founded in the 900s and much rebuilt in the 11th and 12th centuries, the St.-Paul site retains its Romanesque church and cloister. In 1810 the monastery buildings were purchased for use as a private hospital, and it remains an art therapy hospital, though van Gogh's room is open to the public. The serenity is striking, and visits are tolerated only if it is respected.

You walk past the peaceful cloister and up stone steps to van Gogh's room, a tiny space with a green metal bed, a couple of chairs, a tiny wooden desk, and a view onto flower-dotted fields and a stone wall (a scene

that also appears in many of van Gogh's paintings). This cell was later occupied by an interned German during World War I—Albert Schweitzer.

The tourist office has included in its tourist brochure a walking tour that takes in the world of van Gogh—starting from the entrance of Glanum and going to the heart of St.-Rémy, 21 panels portray reproductions of van Gogh's works on the precise spots he painted them.

CENTRE VILLE
Surrounded by plane-tree-shaded boulevards, the *centre ville* is filled with sophisticated boutiques, old fountains, and shady squares. Plaques denote historical sites, including the birthplace of physician and astronomer Nostradamus *(rue Hoche).* The **Hôtel de Sade** on rue du Parage, currently undergoing restoration, is housed in a beautiful 15th-century town house. Built on the remains of a Gallo-Roman monument, it contains the town's archaeological museum: Roman findings from Glanum include sculptures, pottery, coins, and jewelry.

Nearby, in the Hôtel Mistral de Mondragon, the **Musée des Alpilles** is a popular and rural art museum. It explains the natural and man-made landscapes of the Alpilles, including flora and fauna; centuries-old farming and trading traditions (including olive oil, sheep, and vines); and traditional costumes and celebrations.

Relating to van Gogh, the **Centre d'Art Présence Vincent Van Gogh** *(8 rue Lucien Estrine),* located in the handsome Hôtel Estrine, features reproductions and slide shows on different themes related to the artist. Contemporary artists are featured on the upper floors. ∎

More places to visit south along the Rhône

Beaucaire's quiet harbor anchors a working city best known for the remains of its 11th-century castle.

ABBAYE DE MONTMAJOUR

Looming above marshlands on Mont Majour ("big mountain"), the stark medieval abbey is a shadow of its former thriving self. Founded in 948 by Benedictine monks, who lived here until 1790, it was even a papal retreat (circa 950). The abbey is vacant now, and the self-guided tour is a little hard to follow, even with the English-language pamphlet. Nonetheless, what you take away from this brooding monstrosity is a sense of peace and quietude. You nearly expect a monk to greet you around the next corner.
🅰 82 C3 ✉ Rte. de Fontvieille ☎ 04 90 54 64 17, www.monum.fr 🕓 Closed Mon. Oct.–March 💲 $$

AIGUES-MORTES

A gateway to the Camargue, Aigues-Mortes is most interesting for its history. In 1248 Louis IX (St.-Louis) and his 1,500 knight-filled ships left from here on the Seventh Crusade to the Holy Land. His successor, Philip III, added the walls to town, and by the 13th century, it was flourishing as France's only Mediterranean port (Marseille was then part of Provence). Victim of the delta's mercurial ways, the sea deserted Aigues-Mortes so

that, despite attempts to dredge the harbor, it fell into decline after 1350. Today its narrow streets are filled with tourists who come to see the mile-long walls; the **Tour de Constance** (tel 04 66 53 61 55, $$), the enormous defense tower; and the church from which St.-Louis left—but mostly to browse souvenir shops and sit at sunny cafés. ✉ 82 B2 **Office de Tourisme** ✉ Porte de la Gardette ☎ 04 66 53 73 00, www.ot-aiguesmortes.fr

CATHÉDRALE DES IMAGES

Images are projected from 48 different sources onto the floor and 65-foot-high (20 m) walls of this disused bauxite quarry. Top photographers regularly put together new shows on different themes, accompanied by specially composed music. ✉ 82 D3 ✉ Rte. de Maillane, Val d'Enfer (0.3 mile/0.5 km N of Les Baux) ☎ 04 90 54 38 65, www.cathedrale-images.com 💲 $$

FONTVIEILLE

This charming, low-key village is famous for the windmill that inspired Alphonse Daudet to write his collection of short stories, *Lettres de Mon Moulin (Letters from My Windmill)* in 1869. While **Le Moulin de Daudet** (allée des

Pins, tel 04 90 54 60 78, closed Jan., $) houses a small museum commemorating this great Provençal writer, it is not *the* windmill. To see that, you'll have to stroll along the 1.5-hour trail that circles past Moulin Ramet to the **Moulin Tissot-Avon**—*voilà*, Daudet's former haunt. The trail continues past the **Château de Montauban**, where Daudet resided with his cousins during his stay in town. Just outside town, in the direction of Arles, are the remains of a Roman aqueduct. ✉ 82 C3 **Office de Tourisme de Fontvieille** ☎ 04 90 54 67 49

MAILLANE

Provençal poet Frédéric Mistral was born in a farmhouse on Maillane's outskirts in 1830. Upon his father's death, he and his mother moved into the small, pleasant town and, when marrying at the age of 46, he and his bride moved next door. Today, their home is the well-presented **Musée Frédéric Mistral,** with books, paintings, photos, and souvenirs the poet collected over the years. He is buried in the village cemetery. ✉ 82 D3 **Musée Frédéric Mistral** ✉ Ave. Lamartine ☎ 04 90 95 84 19 🕐 Closed Mon. 🛈 $

MAS DES TOURELLES & LE VIEUX MAS

At the reproduction of the ancient Mas des Tourelles winery, you learn how Romans produced wines. The intriguing visit takes in a film, exhibits, and the tasting of wines based on 2,000-year-old recipes. Various ingredients used for preservation included cinnamon, honey, and seawater. Nearby, Le Vieux Mas is the re-creation of a traditional working farm from the 1900s, showcasing farm animals and equipment. ✉ 82 C3 **Mas des Tourelles** ✉ 2.5 miles (4 km) SW of Beaucaire, on the D38 ☎ 04 66 59 19 72, www.tourelles.com 🕐 Open daily April–Oct., Sat. p.m. Nov.–March. Closed Jan. 🛈 $ **Le Vieux Mas** ✉ Route de Fourques (D15), 3.7 miles (6 km) S of Beaucaire ☎ 04 66 59 60 13 🕐 Open daily April–Sept., & Wed., Sat.–Sun. rest of year. Closed all Jan. 🛈 $$

ROUTE À L'OLIVIER

The picturesque lands south of St.-Rémy harbor some of Provence's best olive-growing orchards. From St.-Rémy, the D5 brings you into the region's heart. Farms and olive mills are especially abundant along routes D78 and D17. Among the many olive mills *(moulins à olives)* to stop at: **Château d'Estoublon** *(rte. de Maussane à Fontvieille, tel 04 90 54 64 00, www.estoublon.com)* and **Moulin Jean-Marie Cornille** *(13520 Maussane les Alpilles, tel 04 90 54 32 37).* ✉ 82 D3

TARASCON & BEAUCAIRE CASTLES

Louis II built Tarascon Castle on the Rhône's east bank in the 15th century to defend the border. A storybook feudal fortress, complete with crenellations and a moat, the castle was actually quite luxurious inside thanks to the Good King René, Louis II's son, who loved the good life. His last ten years were spent here in the company of poets and artists. Today, the structure is empty, save for ten 17th-century tapestries depicting the life of Scipio and some 18th-century pharmaceutical pots. Graffiti left by British sailors recall the castle's later use as a prison, between 1754 and 1778.

Across the river, Beaucaire Castle was a powerful citadel during the reign of St.-Louis and has dominated the town since the 11th century. Today it lies in ruins—only the round tower and chapel remain. The castle is open only for falconry displays, with falconers in Roman costume. ✉ 82 C3 **Château de Tarascon** ✉ Blvd. du Roi René, Tarascon ☎ 04 90 91 01 93 🕐 Closed Mon. Oct.–March 🛈 $$ **Château de Beaucaire** ✉ Place du Château, Beaucaire ☎ 04 66 59 26 72, www.aigles-de-beaucaire.com 🛈 $$ ∎

Poised between the land and the sea, this forested realm features dignified Aix, revitalizing Marseille, star-struck St.-Tropez, and plenty of rugged mountain-scapes in between.

Aix, Marseille, & the Var

The bounty of Aix's daily market at place Richelme

Aix, Marseille, & the Var

PROVENCE TAKES ON A MODERN, SOPHISTICATED FEEL IN THIS VARIED region centered around Marseille, Aix-en-Provence, and St.-Tropez. Inland, the Var's forested Vallée Intérieure provides a bucolic escape into a lesser traveled realm.

Provence's ancient capital, Aix-en-Provence, gained its polished panache in the 17th and 18th centuries, when noble families funded a rash of *hôtel-particulier* building. Cours Mirabeau shines as one of France's most elegant boulevards, with its giant elms, venerable cafés, and 18th-century fountains. Paul Cézanne was born here in 1839, immortalizing nearby Mont Ste.-Victoire in more than a hundred paintings—thereby kick-starting cubism.

It's an exciting time for Marseille, only 15 miles (25 km) south, whose growth spurt is

unprecedented since the Phocaeans first set foot here 2,600 years ago. Its grimy image is slowly being transformed as millions of euros are being poured into its economy as part of the Euroméditerranée project, aimed at turning Marseille into the Mediterranean's most important port by 2010. Important museums include the Musée d'Archéologie Méditerranéenne at La Vieille Charité and Musée Cantini, full of 20th-century art. But nothing beats sitting by the old port, sipping an authentic bowl

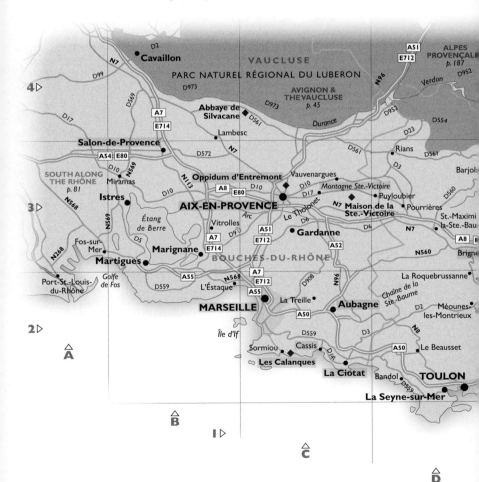

of bouillabaisse at one of the outdoor cafés.

East of Marseille, *calanques*—limestone cliffs that plunge deep into azure waters—riffle the coast. A good base is the warm-hued fishing village of Cassis, famed for its crisp white wine. Hyères is an elegant, palm-shaded town, with the eucalyptus-scented Îles des Pourquerolles beckoning just offshore.

Farther east, St.-Tropez's reputation for its high life precedes it. Even if you're not rich and/or famous, you can admire the mega-yachts in the port, window-shop at chic boutiques along hilly, cobbled streets, and watch for incognito stars.

Inland, in the Vallée Intérieure, tiny lanes wind past vineyards, medieval towns, and one of Provence's trio of Cistercian abbeys, making for an idyllic drive. ■

Le mistral

The dry, cold mistral wind rages down from the north up to 100 days a year. Some say it's the north's revenge on the south's otherwise idyllic weather. Its entrée is the River Rhône valley, gusting up to 60 mph (97 kmph) and brutalizing Avignon and Arles the worst but affecting most corners of the province. It's said to last in multiples of three—3, 6, or 9 days … enough to drive you crazy. Indeed, an accusation of crime might very well be dropped if it is proven to have happened during the mistral. ■

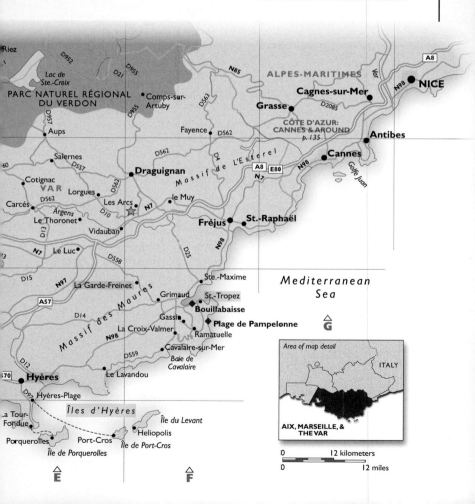

Aix-en-Provence

AT DUSK, A GOLDEN LIGHT WARMS THE HONEY-HUED
buildings of this magical Midi town, as well-heeled Aixois sip apéritifs
at one of dozens of plane-tree-shaded squares, musical fountains
playing a soft serenade. This is aristocratic, refined Aix, one of the
most beautiful towns in the south of France. For what it lacks in
major museums and historical sights, the old capital of Provence
makes up in culture and ambience.

More than 2,000 years ago, the war-
waging Salyens, a Celto-Ligurian
tribe, built their fortified town on
the strategic plateau of Entremont
(see p. 134), just north of Aix's present location. The Romans sacked
the town in 123 B.C., and the
Roman consul Sextius set up his
own community around a thermal
spring (which still flows), calling it
Aquae Sextiae, the waters of
Sextius, thereby creating Gaul's first
Roman settlement. As the Roman
Empire fell in A.D. 476, Visigoths
destroyed much of the city. Unlike
many other Provençal towns, few
traces of the Roman settlement
remain; one of the principal

gateways has been worked into
the 16th-century clock tower in
place de l'Hôtel de Ville, and the
Thermes Sextius (Sextius Baths;
55 cours Sextius) sit behind glass
next to a new, state-of-the-art spa.

In the Middle Ages, the counts
of Provence took up residence in
Aix, the most famous of whom was
Bon Roi René (Good King René;
1409–1480). A royal patron of the
arts, he founded many popular festivals and made Aix into a cultural
center comparable to Avignon. In
1486 Provence was annexed to
France, but until 1790 remained
relatively autonomous. Aix was kept
on as capital of Provence and

became, beginning in 1501, the seat of the Supreme Court of Justice, otherwise known as the Parliament of Provence. Aix entered its golden age, with noble families building more than 160 hôtels particuliers in the Italian baroque style, complete with elaborate carvings and wrought ironwork. It is these buildings above all that give Aix its dignified appearance. During the Revolution, Aix's aristocrats fled, leaving the town to slumber until its recent revival as an arts town.

VISITING AIX
Elm-shaded **Cours Mirabeau** is Aix's main artery, created in 1650 for carriages but soon after becoming the local promenade of choice. With its elegant hôtels particuliers lining either side and its procession of fountains, the cours is arguably the most beautiful street in the south of France. Café tables spill out onto the sidewalk, where locals and tourists alike enjoy a respite. Probably the most famous is **Les Deux Garçons** (*53 cours Mirabeau, tel 04 42 26 00 51*), a former intellectual hangout with a spectacular interior dating from 1792. It remains the place to see and be seen.

When the plague contaminated city waters in 1720, lovely fountains were built to receive new sources of water—thereby earning Aix the moniker City of a Thousand Fountains (though the count is closer to one hundred). Four of the most beautiful grace the cours, beginning with the most spectacular, the black-and-white marble **Fontaine de la Rotonde** in place du Général de Gaulle. Designed by Napoléon III's chief civil engineer in 1860 at the former Porte Royale—for centuries the main entrance to the city—its three graceful marble statues represent Justice (facing Aix), the Arts

(facing Avignon), and Agriculture (facing Marseille).

Resembling a mossy stump, the 17th-century **Fontaine des Neuf Canons** replaced a watering place where flocks of sheep came to drink during the transhumance. Farther up the cours, another mossy stump, the 17th-century **Fontaine Moussue,** is fed by hot water brought by underground channels and aqueducts from the Fontaine des Bagniers (*place des Chapeliers*). At the top of the cours stands the 19th-century **Fontaine du Roi René;** note the cluster of grapes in the statue's hand—above other pursuits, the king introduced the muscat grape to Provence.

BOURG ST.-SAUVEUR
To the north of Cours Mirabeau, the old village of St.-Sauveur runs between the old ramparts and the Tourreluque watchtower, the last vestiges of the medieval fortifications. In its heart rises the **Cathédrale St.-Sauveur,** which comprises a curious hybrid of religious architectural styles both old and new: Roman foundations from the earliest days of the Christian era, a Merovingian baptistery from the fifth century, a Romanesque nave (into which you enter the structure), and a Gothic nave (to the left as you enter). Inside you'll find several Provençal primitive works of art, the most famous of which is "Le Buisson Ardent" ("Burning Bush"), a minutely observed triptych attributed to Nicolas Froment and commissioned by Bon Roi René in 1475. The intricately carved wooden doors of its western facade, carved by Toulon artist Jean Guiramand in 1508 to 1510 and normally protected behind shutters, are decorated with statues of the four great prophets and the 12 pagan sibyls.

The small, light-filled **cloître** (cloister), dating from the late 12th

Cathédrale St.-Sauveur
- Map p. 115
- 34 place de l'Université
- www.monum.fr

Cloître St. Sauveur
- Map p. 115
- 34 place de l'Université
- 04 42 23 45 65
- Closed Sun.

Musée des Tapisseries
- Map p. 115
- Palais de l'Archevêché, 28 place des Martyrs de la Résistance
- 04 42 23 09 91
- Closed Tues.
- $

Musée du Vieil Aix
- Map p. 115
- Hôtel Éstienne de St.-Jean, 17 rue Gaston de Saporta
- 04 42 21 43 55
- Closed Mon.
- $

Pavillon Vendôme
- Map p. 115
- 32 rue Célony
- 04 42 21 05 78
- Closed Tues. & Nov.–mid-April a.m.
- $

Musée Paul Arbaud
- Map p. 115
- 2a rue du 4 Septembre
- 04 42 38 38 95
- musee.arbaud.free.fr
- Closed Sun.
- $

Musée Granet
- Map p. 115
- Place St.-Jean-de-Malte
- 04 42 52 88 32
- www.museegranet-aixenprovence.fr
- Closed a.m. Sun.–Mon.
- $

century, is open only by guided tour. Its four charming galleries represent, in turn, the Old Testament, the life of Christ, the Judgment, and Nature. What's interesting is that much of the material was taken from other sources, including pillars from hôtels particuliers for columns, and gravestones that were worked into the base.

Nearby, on place des Martyrs de la Résistance, the small **Musée des Tapisseries** (Tapestry Museum) is housed on the first floor of the Ancien Archevêché, the former archbishops' palace (1650–1730). The meager collection of Beauvais tapestries includes a series on the life of Don Quixote after cartoons by Natoire, collected by the archbishops to decorate the palace. Rare 17th- and 18th-century furnishings are also displayed.

Down rue Gaston de Saporta, the small **Musée du Vieil Aix** is installed in the elegant Hôtel de St.-Jean, built in the 17th century and featuring high fluted pilasters, Corinthian capitals, and main doors with sculptured arches. The museum is rich in local souvenirs from Aix's past, including objets d'art, furniture, costumes, santons, and faïence. There is a splendid collection of masks and other items related to the annual Corpus Christi or Fête Dieu celebration, which was instigated by Bon Roi René in 1462 and involved a huge public procession of figures acting out scenes from the Bible. A Fête Dieu celebration is portrayed on an enormous, exquisitely painted 18th-century screen. Also seek out the "talking crib," a marionette theater in which the Provençal mystery plays were performed. Upstairs you'll find two more small rooms of exhibits. The back room is perhaps the most interesting, with its model of the long-since-demolished old counts of Provence palace.

The **Pavillon Vendôme,** near the thermal baths, was built in 1665 by Pierre Pavillon for the duke of Vendôme, the scene of the latter's secret love affairs. The pavilion today houses a collection of Provençal furniture and paintings from the 17th and 18th centuries.

QUARTIER MAZARIN
South of Cours Mirabeau, the Mazarin Quarter shelters a collection of aristocratic 17th-century town houses, built in a grid plan during the reign of Louis XIV. Among the prettiest streets are rue Mazarine and place des Quatre Dauphins, with its fountain of four dolphins. The **Musée Paul Arbaud,** housed in the 18th-century Hôtel d'Arbaud, has a remarkable collection of Provençal faïence.

The coup de grâce of all Aix museums is the **Musée Granet,** an art and archaeological museum housed in a 17th-century priory of the Knights of Malta. A recent five-year renovation has improved and enlarged the layout, showcasing its impressive current permanent collection to perfection. Among the highlights are Italian school works from the 17th and 18th centuries (most notably, a *modello* by Guercino for his Exhumations of St. Petronilla in the Vatican collections); Flemish school works (including a 15th-century Virgin in Glory attributed to Campin and several good portraits by Rubens); excellent Dutch paintings (self-portrait by Rembrandt, ca 1665); and French paintings from the 16th to 20th centuries (fine portraits by Hyacinthe Rigaud and Jean Van Loo). One of Ingrès's greatest portraits is also here, his portrayal of Provençal painter François-Marius Granet (1775–1849), posed against a severely painted background featuring the Villa Medici in Rome.

Granet, who is best known for his dark and atmospheric scenes of monastic life, founded the museum in the 19th century and most of his works are here. Despite the fact that an early director declared that the walls of this museum "would never be sullied by a Cézanne," the museum also owns eight of the

lonely, the artist was also a very meticulous man who numbered every single prop, and his atelier is just as he left it: the gray-blue walls of the upstairs; window-lit studio (over whose exact color he wrestled for five weeks); the old bottles; milk cans; plates; cloths; and fruit (replaced daily—or weekly). Tour

Along Cours Mirabeau, Aix's fashionable main boulevard

local artist's paintings (none major) and kicked off its reopening gala in 2006 with a 150-piece lineup of his most famous works. The museum also holds an archaeology room with artifacts from ancient Aix, including Celto-Ligurian statues, and unique pieces of Celtic art found at Oppidum of Entremont.

ATELIER CÉZANNE

Cézanne bought this cottage and garden, called Les Lauves, in 1901, where he painted for the last years of his life. Stubborn, ill-tempered,

guides will show you copies of his paintings containing these very props. Cézanne's coat and beret still hang on the wall, and an easel with an unfinished picture daubed with paint wait for the master to return.

The most famous painting created here was "Les Grandes Baigneuses." After realizing the giant canvas couldn't fit down the stairs, Cézanne had an opening cut in the wall alongside a window so he could easily move it outside to paint. You can still see the poorly patched hole. ■

Atelier Cézanne

🅰 Map p. 115

✉ 9 ave. Paul Cézanne

☎ 04 42 21 06 53, www.ateliercezanne.com

💲 $$

Above: Cathédrale St.-Sauveur. Below: A door knocker, Hôtel de Ville

Exploring old Aix

This delightful promenade takes in some of Aix's most charming—and historic—streets in the jumbled labyrinth of its old town.

Begin at **La Rotonde ①** (see p. 111), the fountain on the former site of the city's main gate, at the foot of elegant **Cours Mirabeau.** Walk up the cours, admiring the cafés, hôtels particuliers, and fountains. Two of the largest town houses are No. 20, the 17th-century **Hôtel de Forbin,** and No. 28, the 18th-century **Hôtel du Chevalier Hancy.**

At **Fontaine des Neuf Canons ②,** take a left at rue Nazareth and, at rue Espariat, go right, past rue Aude, to **place d'Albertas ③,** full of Parisian elegance. Rococo facades front three sides of the secluded square, and the base of the fountain dates from 1912. Open-air concerts are sometimes held here.

Backtrack to rue Aude and go right. At the junction, keep going straight, on rue Maréchal Foch, to **place de l'Hôtel de Ville,** dominated by the **Tour de l'Horloge.** The clock tower has two clock faces: a typical one and, below that, an astronomical clock from 1661. On the latter, four statues, each representing a season, are shown in turn. The adjoining **Hôtel de Ville ④** (Town Hall), with its Italianate facade and sculptured wood doors, was built between 1655 and 1670 by Pierre Pavillon.

On the square's south side, the **Ancienne Halle aux Grains** (former Wheat Exchange), built between 1759 and 1761, reflects the importance of wheat at the time. Topping the north facade is an allegorical pediment featuring the two important sources of water for farmers: the strong, steady Rhône, represented by a rough-looking man, and the temperamental, flood-prone Durance, symbolized by a woman half jumping out of the sculpture. On the square's south side is another square, **place Richelme,** site of a daily fruit and vegetable market.

Pass through the clock tower and proceed up rue Gaston de Saporta. You'll pass by the **Musée du Vieil Aix** on the left (see p. 112) and, just beyond, also on the left, will be the **Hôtel de Châteaurenard** ❺. A splendid town house built in the mid-1600s by Pierre Pavillon, it's a cultural center now. Peek inside to see the trompe l'oeil painted up the staircase, the 1660 work of Bruxellois Jean Daret, appointed king's painter by Louis XIV. The images rotate around the central figure of Minerva, on the ceiling above, who represents nobility.

Just up rue Gaston de Saporta, at the far eastern end of the place des Martyrs de la Résistance, is the **Palais de l'Archêveché** (1650–1730), the former archbishops' residence, adorned with a Regency door. This is the headquarters for the International Festival of Lyric Art, which takes place every July. Here, too, is the **Musée des Tapisseries** (see p. 112), featuring a collection of Beauvais tapestries.

The walk ends farther up the street at the magnificent **Cathédrale St.-Sauveur** ❻ (see p. 111). Paul Cézanne's studio (see p. 113) is just a half a mile farther up the road, via avenue Pasteur. ∎

🅜 See area map p. 108
▶ La Rotonde
⟷ Half mile (800 m)
🕐 1 hour (more with stops)
▶ Cathédrale St.-Sauveur

NOT TO BE MISSED
- Cours Mirabeau
- Place de l'Hôtel de Ville
- Cathédrale St.-Sauveur

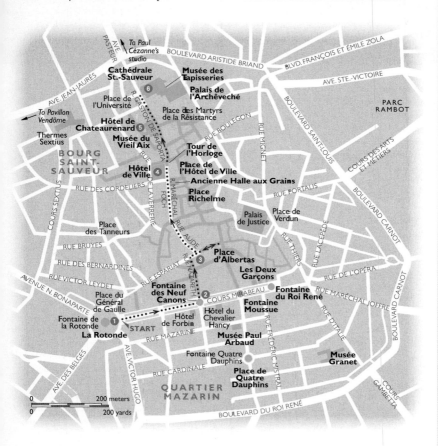

Montagne Ste.-Victoire near Aix provided Paul Cézanne with an ever changing tableau of color and form.

Montagne Ste.-Victoire
🅰 108 C3–C4

Cézanne's Montagne Ste.-Victoire

PAUL CÉZANNE, THE FORERUNNER OF CUBISM WITH HIS blocky use of color, was fixated on painting Mont Ste.-Victoire, determined to get it just right—its colors, its texture, the play of light. In the last ten years of his life he painted it more than a hundred times. You can follow in the artist's footsteps, circling the mountain all around, admiring it from every angle, pausing at places he knew so well. Along the way are pretty villages, vineyards and olive groves, and a famous château.

From Aix, the D17—labeled the Route de Cézanne—heads east. You quickly leave behind suburbia, entering a painter's paradise of woods and hills. Mont Ste.-Victoire, partially hidden by trees and hills, flirts with you as you approach the hamlet of **Le Tholonet,** where Cézanne rented two rooms to store his materials and to be near his beloved landscape. Between 1888 and 1904, he roamed the area in search of subjects that would conform to his vision of seeing in nature the cylinder, the sphere, and the cone; he found them in the **Château Noir**—visible from the D17—and in the Bibémus quarry. Just before town a sign indicates the start of a *sentier de découverte*—a 4.3-mile (7 km), two-hour trail that leads to **Zola Dam,** constructed in 1854 to provide the water supply for Aix.

The trailhead is located across the street from the mustard-colored **Relais Cézanne,** a café-restaurant that Cézanne knew well.

Just ahead, at the cusp of the hill, you get your first wide-angle view of the mountain. For obvious reasons, this was one of the artist's favorite spots to perch his easel—commemorated by a monument. The nearby **Moulin de Cézanne** holds temporary exhibits.

Onward, the mountain looms larger, coming to artistic perfection at the crossroads with the Beaurecueil road. At St.-Antonin, the **Maison de la Ste.-Victoire** offers advice on hiking up the mountain; several trails take off in the vicinity. Here, too, are natural history exhibits.

Proceeding along the D17, you enter a fertile plain carpeted with vineyards and olive groves. A good winery to stop at is **Domaine de St.-Ser,** one of the area's fine Côtes de Provence vineyards. The tiny

village of **Puyloubier** snuggles at the mountain's base.

To continue around the mountain, take the D623 through **Pourrières,** a *vigneron* (winemaking) town. Some say its name comes from *campi porrerias*—fields of leeks. Others suggest that this was the site of Marius's famous victory, and the dead bodies of the Germanic tribes lay here to rot, hence *campi putridi.*

Following the D23, D623, and D10, you squiggle up through impossibly rocky terrain, with exquisite views at every turn. Eventually you come to the **Col des Portes,** with the mountain etched against the distant sky. Hiking trails meander off from here.

Proceed to the little town of **Vauvenargues,** with balcony views to the northern slopes of Mont Ste.-Victoire all along its narrow length. The castle rising in the valley before you, built between the 14th and 17th centuries, has the best view—Pablo Picasso, who greatly admired Cézanne, bought it in 1958 "to own the original." The Catalan artist is buried on the private grounds.

Just beyond the château is one of the easier hikes to the top of the mountain and the **Croix de Provence,** a two-hour trek along the **Sentier des Ventures.** Several parking areas—one in Vauvenargues and a couple of others along the road beyond—lead to trailheads.

From Vauvenargues, it's a quick trip back to modern Aix. ∎

Cézanne's painting satchel

Relais Cézanne
- 108 C3
- Rte. de Cézanne/D17, Le Tholonet
- ☎ 04 42 66 91 91

Moulin de Cézanne
- 108 C3
- Rte. de Cézanne/D17, Le Tholonet
- ☎ 04 42 66 90 41 (town hall)
- 🕒 Closed Oct.–April

Maison de la Ste.-Victoire
- 108 C3
- St.-Antonin-sur-Bayon
- ☎ 04 42 66 84 40

Domaine de St.-Ser
- 108 C3
- Mas de Bramefan/D17, Puyloubier
- ☎ 04 42 66 30 81

Marseille

Marseille

🅼 108 C2

Visitor information

✉ 4 La Canebière

☎ 04 91 13 89 00

www.marseille-
tourisme.com

*After centuries
of grittiness,
Marseille's Vieux
Port (Old Port)
sparkles with
economic renewal.*

ONCE BESIEGED BY GANGSTERS AND SMUGGLERS, REPUTED for its grit and grime, this ancient port town is being rejuvenated. Over the past few years, hundreds of millions of dollars have begun metamorphosing Marseille into an up-and-coming destination. Its dazzling Vieux Port buzzes with trendy restaurants and cafés, and revitalization projects promise to make the place respectable.

HISTORY

For 26 centuries, Marseille has been, in the words of Alexandre Dumas, the "meeting place of the world." Indeed, through the years the city's coffers have overflowed with the trade of exotic riches— cottons, silks, spices, perfumes, leather, and coffee—and a rich mix of immigrants from Greece, Italy,

Spain, Armenia, West Africa, Southeast Asia, and North Africa have synthesized into the population, giving Marseille a mystique all its own.

The Phocaeans (Greeks from Asia Minor) came ashore in 600 B.C., setting up a trading post called Massalia on the site of today's Vieux Port (Old Port). After the Persians destroyed Phocaea in 540 B.C., the Athenian Greeks took over. The city flourished culturally and legally, the port reigning as a major trading center. After Rome occupied most of Provence, the Greeks retained Massalia as an independent republic, allied to Rome. All was fine, until the Greeks sided with the wrong Roman during the 49 B.C. civil war—backing Pompey rather than Caesar. A vengeful Caesar stripped Massalia of its treasures, and its fleet and trade were dispersed to Arles, Fréjus, and Narbonne. Nevertheless, it remained a free city, its excellent Greek university being the last place in the West where courses were taught in Greek. The city did not

Market days
Fish market: daily a.m.
General & flea markets: Tues.–Sun.

City Pass
The City Pass, available at the tourism office, offers one ($$$$) or two ($$$$$) consecutive days and covers admission to all city museums, unlimited use of public transportation, free guided city tours, a boat trip to the Île d'If, and rides on the tourist trains.

Musée des Civilisations de l'Europe et de la Méditerranée
- ⊠ Fort St.-Jean, esplanade St.-Jean, 2e
- ☎ 04 96 13 80 96
- ⊕ Closed Tues. & a.m.
- $ $
- 🚇 Metro: Vieux Port

Hôtel de Ville
- 🅰 Map p. 121
- ⊠ Quai du Port

Musée du Vieux Marseille
- 🅰 Map p. 121
- ⊠ 2 rue de la Prison, 2e
- ☎ 04 91 55 28 68
- ⊕ Closed Mon.
- $ $
- 🚇 Metro: Vieux Port

**Musée des
Docks Romains**

<table>
<tr><td>⬛</td><td>Map p. 121</td></tr>
<tr><td>✉</td><td>Place du Vivaux, 2e</td></tr>
<tr><td>☎</td><td>04 91 91 24 62</td></tr>
<tr><td>🕐</td><td>Closed Mon.</td></tr>
<tr><td>🕐</td><td>$</td></tr>
<tr><td>🚇</td><td>Metro: Vieux Port</td></tr>
</table>

**Ancient lanes
typify Marseille's
Le Panier, an
increasingly
trendy quarter.**

regain any major significance until the Crusades, when, as an independent republic, it supplied ships headed to the Middle East. It grew richer still under French rule, when its vast entrepôt of docks, shipyards, and warehouses processed raw goods from the far-flung colonies. During World War II, bombing destroyed much of the city.

Marseille's tough seaport reputation comes deserved. When law enforcement agencies cracked down in the early 1970s, they exposed the city's gangster-powered underworld of drug trafficking, prostitution, and racketeering. Political and financial corruption was also rampant. Slowly, Marseille's character is turning, the most prominent impetus being the uroméditerranée project. Marseille has been chosen to be the central hub of this interna-tional economic initiative of all Mediterranean countries and will receive three billion euros to transform the city into a booming business center and tourist attraction.

VIEUX PORT & LA CANEBIÈRE

Everything begins at Marseille's U-shaped Old Port in the city's heart, where ships have docked continually for 2,600 years. The commercial docks were transferred to La Joliette beyond the city's headland in the 1840s—the ancient port is more pleasure marina these days than working port, with pleasure yachts, small fishing boats, and sailboats filling more than 10,000 slips. Ferries chug across the harbor, transporting passengers from one side to the other, as well as to the nearby Château d'If (see p. 125). Around the port, fishermen mend nets on wide quays and seamen lounge on benches, reading newspapers in Greek and Arabic, while cafés and restaurants serve up savory seafood.

Guarding the port's entrance are the 17th-century **Fort St.-Nicolas** *(on the south end)*, its cannon turned facing the city, to keep the rebellious population in line; and **Fort St.-Jean** *(across the water on the north end)*, dating from the 12th century. The new **Musée des Civilisations de l'Europe et de la Méditerranée** (Museum of European and Mediterranean Civilizations) inside St.-Jean is already holding temporary exhibitions with the official opening set for 2010.

Along the quai du Port, on the

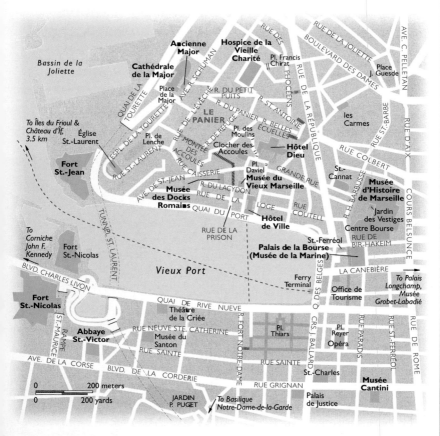

port's north side, rises the impressive 17th-century **Hôtel de Ville** (Town Hall), with its statue of Louis XIV. The nearby **Musée du Vieux Marseille** (Museum of Old Marseille), created at the end of the 19th century under the initiative of Provençal poet Frédéric Mistral and newly renovated, is devoted to all things Provençal. Its vast inventory of exhibits includes beautifully carved furniture, traditional-style costumes, santons, and paintings and photographs from the 17th through 20th centuries. Of special interest is the collection of locally made playing cards; Marseille was one of the medieval ports of entry for this innovation from the East. The museum occupies the mannerist-style **Maison**

Diamantée, a diamond-beveled facade constructed in 1570 by wealthy merchant Pierre Gardiolle.

For such a historic city, few vestiges remain from its earliest days. One exception is found nearby at the modest **Musée des Docks Romains.** Here a portion of the first century A.D. Roman quay—where oil- and wine-filled *dolia* (jugs) were stored—has been uncovered and left in its natural setting. Surrounding exhibits showcase items discovered in shipwrecks, mostly terra-cotta jars, *amphorae,* and coins, that help catalog the ancient importance of trade.

It's a little surprising to find the Roman treasures of the **Musée d'Histoire de Marseille** (Marseille History Museum) on

Musée d'Histoire de Marseille

🔼 Map p. 121

✉ Ground floor, Centre Bourse shopping center, place Belsunce, 1er

☎ 04 91 90 42 22

🕐 Closed Sun.

💲 $

🚇 Metro: Vieux Port

Musée de la Marine et de l'Économie de Marseille

✉ Palais de la Bourse, 9 La Canebière, 1er

☎ 04 91 39 33 21

💲 $

🚇 Metro: Vieux Port

Musée d'Histoire Naturelle

✉ Palais Longchamp, blvd. Philippon, 4e

☎ 04 91 14 59 50

⊕ Closed Mon.

$ $

Ⓜ Metro: Longchamp-Cinq Aves.

the ground floor of a shopping center. (The ruins here were exposed during excavation for the mall, so the mall had first rights to stay.) Groupings of archaeological finds illuminate Marseille's history, beginning with Celto-Ligurian times and proceeding through the Greeks and medieval Marseille all

eel, sea urchins, perhaps a squirming octopus or two. From here, **La Canebière**—the city's main thoroughfare—was laid out in Louis XIV's expansion scheme of 1666 between the port and the ropemakers' quarter (the word *canèbe* is Provençal for "hemp"). The once grand promenade has

Religious procession at the Cathédrale de la Major

Musée Grobet-Labadié

Ⓜ Map p. 121

✉ 140 blvd. Longchamp

☎ 04 91 62 21 82

⊕ Closed Mon.

$ $

Ⓜ Metro: Longchamp-Cinq Aves.

the way to the 17th and 18th centuries, when the port of Marseille flourished with the trade of Oriental riches. Most intriguing are the amazingly preserved fragments of a Roman cargo boat from the third century and the hull of a fourth-century Greek boat. Your ticket also includes admission to the adjacent **Jardin des Vestiges,** where excavations have uncovered the remains of the original Greek walls and a corner of the Roman port in a parklike setting.

At the head of the port, the **quai des Belges** is the site of a daily morning fish market, with its makeshift trays stacked with squid,

faded a bit since the fall of the French Empire; it's now dominated by chain stores, banks, and airline offices.

Near the foot of the boulevard looms the glorious **Palais de la Bourse,** France's oldest stock exchange, built in 1860 by Napoléon III. On its ground floor you'll find the excellent **Musée de la Marine et de l'Économie de Marseille,** a fascinating collection of ship models, engravings, and paintings that chart Marseille's growth as a port from the 17th century on.

Just west of La Canebière is **Belsunce,** Marseille's North African neighborhood, with shop windows displaying an eclectic mix of chandeliers, honey-dripped pastries, and couscous dishes. The area around **rue du Bon Pasteur** and **rue d'Auburne** is the Arab quarter, where the **Attaqua mosque** calls so many worshipers to prayer that some must lay out their prayer rugs in the street.

La Canebière splits, with boulevard Longchamp extending to the lovely **Palais Longchamp,** a pastiche of pools, fountains, and cascades built in the late 19th century as the grand conclusion to an aqueduct that brought water from the Provence Canal. In the palace's north wing is the **Musée des Beaux Arts** (tel 04 91 14 59 30, closed for renovation through 2010), which centers around art "acquired" by Napoléon's army. The south wing contains the **Musée d'Histoire Naturelle,** established in 1815 to classify more than 200,000 species.

Across the street in a late 19th-century building, the **Musée Grobet-Labadié** houses the private collections of affluent Marseille merchants Louis Grobet and Marie-Louise Labadié. Spanning the 13th to the 18th centuries, the luxuriant objets d'art include paintings, furniture, ironwork, and porcelain.

On La Canebiére's south side is hip **Cours Julien,** full of designer clothing stores, restaurants, cabarets, cafés, and fringe theaters. With 22 bookstores, it's also known as Le Quartier du Livre, the Book Quarter.

Nearby, the **Musée Cantini** is tucked away on the shop-filled rue Grignan. This fairly tiny space of modern and contemporary art shelters some big names—including Raoul Dufy ("Usine à Estaque," 1908), Paul Signac ("L'entrée du Port de Marseille," 1908), and, on the first floor, André Masson ("L'Âme de Napoleon," 1967), Joan Mirò ("Peinture," 1930), and

one Picasso ("Tête de Femme Souriante," 1943), done in black and white. Many of the paintings depict local scenes.

South of the Vieux Port is the **Musée du Santon,** which holds a private collection of santons (terracotta figurines) dating back to the French Revolution, as well as offering tours of their own workshops.

Just beyond, the medieval **Abbaye St.-Victor** pokes up from the hillside, fortresslike in appearance with its crenellated towers and crudely peaked windows. Founded by Jean Cassien in the fifth century and built on the site of an ancient necropolis, the original structure was destroyed by Saracens in the 11th century and rebuilt and fortified in the 14th century. The Saracens didn't get the crypts ($), however, which contain ancient sarcophagi, including that of martyr St.-Victor. A Roman officer, he was tortured and beheaded for his Christian beliefs at the end of the second century. Some of his relics are located to the right of the altar in the main church, a dark, somber space inviting reflection.

LE PANIER

Le Panier quarter—the breadbasket—is named after a popular 17th-century cabaret, though the quarter's cobbled, hilly lanes, snaking up from the quai du Port, date from the days of the Greeks. One of the city's oldest sections, Le Panier represents only a fraction of what used to exist before Hitler dynamited it during World War II to flush out the Jews and Résistance fighters hiding out there. Up until the 1970s, it was a center for the purification of heroin that Marseille exported to Europe and the United States (hence the "French connection" depicted in the 1971 movie). Today, there's a certain authenticity about the

Musée Cantini
- Map p. 121
- 19 rue Grignan, 6e
- 04 91 54 77 75
- Closed Mon.
- $
- Metro: Estrangin-Préfecture

An 18th-century dive suit, Musée de la Marine et de l'Économie de Marseille

Musée du Santon
- Map p. 121
- 47 rue Neuve Ste.-Catherine, 7e
- 04 91 54 26 58
- Closed Mon.
- Metro: Vieux Port

Abbaye St.-Victor
- Map p. 121
- 3 rue de l'Abbaye, 7e
- 04 96 11 22 60
- Crypt: $
- Metro: Vieux Port

Église St.-Laurent

- Map p. 121
- Esplanade de la Tourette
- 04 91 90 52 87

Hospice de la Vieille Charité

- Map p. 121
- 2 rue de la Vieille Charité, 2e
- 04 91 14 58 80
- Closed Mon.

Musée d'Archéologie Méditerranéenne

- 04 91 14 58 80
- $

Musée d'Arts Africains, Océaniens, et Amérindiens

- 04 91 14 58 38
- $

Basilique Notre-Dame-de-la-Garde

- Map p. 121
- Place Colonel Edon, 6e
- 04 91 13 40 80
- Metro: Estrangin-Préfecture. Bus: No. 60 from the port at Cours Jean Ballard. Tourist Train ($$) from the port.

Bouillabaisse

Bouillabaisse is Marseille's supreme contribution to the culinary world. Originally it was a simple fishermen's dish, in which the best fish parts would be sorted out for sale, and the less desirable pieces kept aside to be prepared with a *rouille* sauce and bread crusts rubbed with garlic. Today, there is *the* authentic dish, and there are plenty of second-rate *soupes des pecheurs* and *bouillabaisses à notre façon*. Restaurateurs concerned about protecting and defending the authentic recipe, which requires that precise ingredients be used in a certain way, drew up the Marseille Bouillabaisse Charter in 1980. To be sure you are sampling the real thing, make sure your chosen restaurant is a signatory of the charter. You can be guaranteed the authentic dish at Le Miramar *(12 quai du Port, tel 04 91 91 10 40)* and Le Caribou *(38 place Thiars, tel 04 91 33 22 63)*. ∎

ancient buildings lining picturesque backstreets—kids playing, laundry flapping, people gossiping in the squares or playing *boules*. A number of small, recently opened shops purvey paintings, pottery, and handcrafted soaps, a local tradition.

From the quai du Port, walk up rue de la Prison or rue de la Guilande to the Montée des Accoules; at the top of the stairs, follow signs to **Église St.-Laurent.** The church's esplanade offers fabulous views over the port. Then follow Esplanade de la Tourette to another church, the dark-green-and-white-striped **Cathédrale de la Major** *(place de la Major, 2e, tel 04 91 90 52 87),* constructed on the ruins of the Temple of Diana. The neo-

Byzantine cathedral was built between 1852 and 1893—France's largest church raised since the Middle Ages (450 feet/137 m long, with the main dome rising almost 210 feet/64 m)—complete with domes and cupolas that look more Turkish than French. The large, airy nave is adorned with mosaic floors and red-and-white marble banners. Among the church's treasures is a graceful statue of St. Veronica wiping Christ's face on Cavalry, by Auguste Carli.

Follow signs through the maze of picturesque streets to Le Panier's major draw—**Hospice de la Vieille Charité,** housing two outstanding museums. Built between 1671 and 1745 as a poorhouse, the complex was designed by Nice-born Pierre Puget. Comprising a central courtyard surrounded on all four sides by arcaded buildings, it has been beautifully restored. Entering the complex, you face the central chapel, a pure Roman baroque structure with an elliptical dome that now holds temporary exhibits.

On the first floor of the surrounding buildings, hidden away in various rooms, is the highly touted **Musée d'Archéologie Méditerranéenne.** Its Egyptian collection, second in France only to the Louvre's, is beautifully presented in a tomblike ambience. It represents all aspects of ancient life on the Nile, from the Ancient Empire through to the Coptic Period. Ancient artifacts include tiny bronze rings, mummified ibises used as offerings, and enormous sarcophagi. The prehistoric collection presents ancient artifacts found in Provence, including a magnificent lintel etched with four horses from the Sanctuary of Roquepertuse site, near Aix, abandoned about 125 B.C.

On the second floor, the **Musée d'Arts Africains, Océaniens, et Amérindiens**

is the only French museum outside Paris devoted to tribal art. Artifacts range from vases and jewelry from the Near Orient; to Baoule statuettes from the Ivory Coast; to masks, papier-mâché objects, and *nierikas* (yarn paintings) from Mexico. One of the most bizarre yet tasteful galleries houses the collection of Henri Gastaut, a brain researcher who had a passion for heads and skulls. Here you'll find his collection of human skulls from the South Seas, painted and decorated with feathers and leather, though the shrunken heads of the Jivaros Indians from Ecuador probably make the biggest impression.

As you wander Le Panier, keep an eye out for a couple of sites: The **Hôtel Dieu** *(6 place Daviel),* the former city hospital, dates from the 18th century. The old Greek *agora* (marketplace) stood at **place de Lenche,** while, at the summit of the old town, is ocher-washed **place des Moulins,** where 15 flour mills churned away in the 16th century.

FARTHER OUT
The **Basilique Notre-Dame-de-la-Garde** overlooks nearly every niche of Marseille from its 505-foot-high (154 m) perch atop Colline de la Garde. The domed neo-Byzantine-style structure, designed by Espérandieu, was erected between 1853 and 1864 on the site of a 1214 chapel constructed by St.-Victor. It is topped by a 33-foot-high (10 m) gilded bronze statue of the Madonna, who watches out for the fishermen headed to sea.

The interior is overwrought with gilded mosaics and murals, plus remarkable collections of ex-votos and other works of art, including an "Anunciation" by Lucca della Robbia. Above the altar, mosaics representing creation—plants, fish, birds—surround a silver statue of the Virgin. Outside, a walkway extends around the entire building, providing a 360-

degree panorama overlooking Marseille, the hills behind, and the islands offshore. Look for the wall that bears scars received during Marseille's Battle of Liberation in August 1944.

The **Corniche John F. Kennedy** heads east from the Vieux Port, curving along the cliff-gouged, albeit built-up, coast, interspersed with beaches and centuries-old villas. At the end awaits the **Plage du Prado,** a developed

beach resort. Nearby, **Château Borely** *(134 ave. Clot Bey, tel 04 91 25 26 34, closed for renovation),* surrounded by a park and botanical gardens, has temporary art exhibits; and the **Musée de la Faïence** *(Château Pastré, 157 ave. de Montredon, tel 04 91 72 43 47, $)* showcases earthenware pieces representing Marseille's historic role as a pottery town.

CHÂTEAU D'IF
Alexandre Dumas brought fame to this 16th-century prison-fortress, lording over a tiny island 2 miles (3.5 km) west of the Old Port. In his best-selling 1844 novel *Le Comte de Monte-Cristo,* his legendary fictional count of Monte-Cristo was incarcerated here as Edmond Dantès. Boats leave regularly from behind the fish market on the quai des Belges. ∎

The Château d'If became internationally famous upon its appearance in Alexandre Dumas's 19th-century novel *The Count of Monte-Cristo.*

Château d'If

✉ Marseille harbor

☎ 04 91 59 02 30

🕐 Closed Mon. Oct.–March

💲 $$

🚢 Boats leave from outside Groupement des Armateurs Côtiers Marseillais (GACM) office at Vieux Port (tel 04 91 55 50 09). Round-trip fare: $$$.

Cassis & *les calanques*

BIJOU-LIKE CASSIS, ITS PASTEL-WASHED HOUSES TUMBLING down the steep hillside to the tiny port, has definitely been discovered. Once a coral-fishing harbor, and a favorite subject of the fauvist painters—including Raoul Dufy and Henri Matisse—the seaside village has evolved to become trendy and chic, thankfully without self-regard. The stunning white cliffs that surround the town, called calanques, offer an amazing foray into the natural world.

After perusing boutiques and dining in one of the portside seafood cafés, there's not much to do in Cassis besides sunbathing and splashing in the surf. Of the town's five beaches, the largest is sandy **Plage de la Grande Mer,** on the seaside of the breakwater. The **Plage du Bestouan** is sheltered at the port's western end. Another option is to wander along the **Promenade des Lombards,** linking Grande Mer beach with Lourton Bay and passing by a 13th-century castle.

Don't leave before exploring the calanques, whether by land or water. These indigo-watered inlets are ancient riverbeds cut into massive limestone cliffs and shaped by erosion from rivers, rain, wind, and the sea. A 12.4-mile (20 km) stretch

has been protected as a natural monument since 1975. The cliffs shelter an extraordinary wealth of flora and fauna, including 900 plant species, of which 50 are classified as rare. **Port-Miou** is reachable from town, while **Sormiou** and **Morgiou** can be visited by car. For a short walk, try the well-marked **Route des Calanques,** which leaves from behind the western beach and brings you to pretty **En-Vau,** the farthest calanque.

But most calanques are accessible only by sea. Informal boat tours operate from the port; the little tourism office there sells tickets for trips that take in 3, 7, or 13 calanques (three, composing a 45-minute boat trip, is enough for most). ■

Hyères & Îles d'Hyères

THREE GOLDEN ISLANDS HOVERING JUST OFFSHORE THE palm-shaded city of Hyères offer a quick dip into the Mediterranean's exotic side. Legend states the isles were created from beautiful princesses who, chased by pirates, were turned into islands by gods. Whatever the case, each one has its own distinct personality.

Market day
Sat.

Île de Port-Cros's picturesque port

The monks of Lérins colonized the islands in the fifth century. They were taken over by the Saracens in 1160 and later fortified by François I. During the Renaissance they were called the Golden Isles, or Îles d'Or, for the gilded glow sometimes emanating from the sunlit rocks. For centuries the haunt of pirates and smugglers, only peace and calm await visitors today.

Measuring 4.5 miles long (7 km) and 1.9 miles wide (3 km), the largest and most developed island is **Île de Porquerolles.** It has two forts from the early days: **Fort du Petit Langoustier** and **Fort Ste.-Agathe** (with an underwater archaeological exhibition). The main village, also called **Porquerolles,** centers around café-fringed place d'Armes.

The island's beauty can be appreciated along several eucalyptus- and pine-shaded paths. For beachgoers, **Plage d'Argent,** to the west, and **Plage de la Courtade,** to the east, are each an easy 10- to 15-minute walk from the main village.

Much of **Île de Port-Cros,** the hilliest and wildest of the three main islands, is France's smallest national park, created in 1963. A trail from the post office in the main village accesses an 18.6-mile (30 km) network of walking trails across the island. Offshore is a marine nature reserve: From the beach at La Palud, on the island's north shore, snorkelers follow an underwater trail *(sentier sous-marin)* to see sponges and octopuses.

Ninety percent of **Île du Levant,** the easternmost island, is a military camp, but its claim to fame is that its remaining space has been a nudist colony since the 1930s.

HYÈRES

The most venerable and southerly of the Côte d'Azur's resorts is dignified and old-fashioned Hyères. In the 19th century, it was a favorite wintering place for such notables as the Empress Eugénie, Queen Victoria, and Edith Wharton. Despite development of its coastal suburbs, Hyères has retained its slightly faded charm. A profusion of palm trees and Moorish architecture imparts an exotic quality on the broad 19th-century boulevards. Through a medieval gatehouse is a quaint old town, with streets offering lovely gardens and sea views. The 12th-century **Tour St.-Blaise** and **Église de St.-Paul** hint at the city's former status. ∎

Hyères
- 🅜 109 E2
- **Visitor information**
- ✉ 3 ave. Ambroise Thomas
- ☎ 04 94 01 84 50
- www.ot-hyeres.fr

Ferries to the islands
Transports Maritimes et Terrestres du Littoral Varois (tel 04 94 58 21 81, www.tlv-tvm.com) has ferryboats that sail year-round from Gare Maritime de la Tour Fondue near Hyères to the Porquerolles. Round-trip ticket: $$$$. For the other two islands, TLV ferries depart from Port d'Hyères.

St.-Tropez

THE 15TH-CENTURY FISHING VILLAGE OF ST.-TROPEZ CERtainly was idyllic when the first artists, headed by postimpressionist Paul Signac, arrived at the turn of the 19th century, admiring its clear, beautiful light. Then Brigitte Bardot starred in the 1956 film *Et Dieu Créa la Femme (And God Created Woman)*, and St.-Tropez broke from obscurity, becoming an international symbol of the French high life. The favored getaway for Pablo Picasso and Giorgio Armani, the place where Mick married Bianca in 1971, St.-Tropez has become a household word, synonymous with glitz and glamour. Even so, its medieval lanes, hidden plazas, and apricot-colored houses, all overlooking the azure Bay of St.-Tropez, remain as picturesque as ever.

Market days
Tues. & Sat.

St.-Tropez
🔼 109 F2
Visitor information
✉ Quai Jean-Jaurès, ave. Général de Gaulle
☎ 08 92 68 48 28
www.ot-saint-tropez.com

Jutting out of the midst of the great Massif des Maures, St.-Tropez occupies one of the most remote spots along the Côte d'Azur. It was destroyed by the Saracens in the Middle Ages, then revived in the 15th century by a group of Genoese families, when it became a tiny self-governing republic thanks to an offer made by a Genoese nobleman to repopulate the place. In 1637, the locals defeated a Spanish fleet that was threatening the coastline. Worried by this

display of military prowess, Louis XIV immediately removed all privileges. Nevertheless, the victory is still celebrated every June 15.

St.-Tropez slipped into obscurity until 1892, when Paul Signac arrived and built a villa that became a haven for artists—most notably Raoul Dufy, Henri Matisse, and others associated with fauvism. They reveled in the area's gorgeous scenery, creating masterpiece after masterpiece. You can see some of their efforts at the **Musée de l'Annonciade** *(place Georges-Grammont, tel 04 94 97 04 01, closed Tues. & Nov., $)*. Look for the superb views of St.-Tropez by Signac ("Saint-Tropez, au Soleil Couchant" or "Saint-Tropez at Sunset," 1896; and "Saint-Tropez, le Quai," 1899) and Albert Marquet ("Saint Tropez, le Port," 1905). The

museum is housed in the 16th-century deconsecrated chapel of the Annunciation.

Some say that St.-Tropez's limelight has passed. While *le jet-set* of the 1960s is indeed long gone, St.-Tropez's moneyed mystique is alive and well. For proof, stop by the **Vieux Port** (Old Port), crammed with shiny yachts—many chartered for more than $100,000 a week. As their captains and crews casually take in the sunset with a toast of Cristal, the "other side" sits steps away at the touristy cafés, sipping espresso and dreaming of being rich.

From the port, narrow streets crowded with fancy boutiques and swank bistros wind uphill to the 16th-century citadel. It offers magnificent harbor views and a skimpy historical exhibit in the **Musée Naval.**

Despite its sparkling reputation, some corners of St.-Tropez remain unassuming and downright ordinary. In the heart of town, old-timers have played *pétanque* at the plane-tree-lined **place des Lices** for more than a century. This square is the site of the weekly markets, feasts of fruit, vegetables, honey, wine … and, since nothing is too ordinary here, perhaps a movie star or two. Bardot, who still lives in St.-Tropez, is said to be a regular. Cafés surrounding the square include the notable **Le Café,** on the former site of the legendary Café des Arts; stars are said to still hide out in the restaurant at the rear.

St.-Tropez has no real beach of its own. The closest are **Bouillabaisse,** to the west; **Les Graniers** in Baie des Cannebiers, just past the citadel; and **Les Salins** on the cape, a 3-mile (5 km) drive away. The most famous is **Plage de Pampelonne,** south of St.-Tropez, edged with cafés and restaurants, including the renowned Club 55. At the very northern end is **Plage de Tahiti,** traditionally the haunt of celebrities. ∎

Musée Naval
- ✉ Mont de la Citadelle
- ☎ 04 94 97 59 43
- 💲 $

Le Café
- ✉ Place des Lices
- ☎ 04 94 97 44 69
- 🕐 Hours vary with season

St.-Tropez's hinterlands

Gassin

🗺 109 F2

Visitor information

✉ Mairie (Town Hall)

☎ 04 94 56 62 00

Ramatuelle

🗺 109 F2

Visitor information

✉ Office de Tourisme, place de l'Ormeau

☎ 04 98 12 64 00

www.ramatuelle-tourisme.com

VINE-STRIPED HILLSIDES, FAR-OFF—AND CLOSE-UP—VIEWS of sparkling Golfe de St.-Tropez, a cluster of medieval hill towns: These are some of the more peaceful pursuits waiting just beyond St.-Tropez's buzz, in the remote Massif des Maures.

Southwest of St.-Tropez, you come to the first of the hill towns, sleepy **Gassin** atop a rocky spur. Right away, you're treated to an amazing view, as far as the Golfe de St.-Tropez, with a composition of pink and red flowers, woodlands, undulating vineyards, and sparkling waters straight out of an Impressionist painting. The first mention of Gassin goes back to 1234, when the *castrum,* or castle, surrounded by ramparts, occupied today's rue de la Tasco. Follow **Leï Barre Promenade**—the medieval terrace marking the former rampart boundary—past a bevy of restaurants, each with

prime vistas, including one aptly named Bello Visto. At the promenade's end, the panorama takes in the Baie de Cavalaire and the Îles d'Hyères (see p. 127). Then wander the maze of atmospheric *ruelles,* with their bougainvillea-draped porticos and medieval gates. One street, tiny **l'Androuno,** is said to be the world's narrowest; only one person can pass at a time.

To the southeast, **Ramatuelle** is another medieval hill town. The central place d'Ormeau—Square of the Elm Tree (though the elm died and was replaced with an olive tree in 1983)—with its souvenir pottery and soap shops, is a touch touristy,

Enclosed by ramparts, toylike Ramatuelle dates back to the Middle Ages.

but its ruelles with their ancient houses are charming as can be. The **Église Notre-Dame,** just off the square, dates from the 17th century, its bell tower a former lookout post. Inside, look for the bust of St.-André—Ramatuelle's patron saint—carved from a fig-tree stump.

Just outside town, on the RD89, the **Moulins de Paillas** are stone windmills used until the turn of the 20th century. The spot, 1,066 feet (325 m) above sea level, offers dizzying views over Baie de Cavalaire and the town of La Croix-Valmer on one side, Ramatuelle on the other.

Down at sea level, breezy, carefree **Cavalaire-sur-Mer** is a popular family resort, with a boules court in the middle of town and a pretty marina filled with yachts and working fishing boats. Every September, tuna fishermen set out from the marina, returning to sell their catch. On rue du Port, the **Casino du Golfe** is the St.-Tropez

peninsula's only casino. Several beaches are worth a look, including the **Plage de Bonporteau,** at Cavalaire's west end. In August 1944, Allied forces landed on Cavalaire's shores to secure a southern beachhead in their effort to liberate Provence. Many memorials commemorate the lives lost during the valiant struggle.

Cavalaire is a good place for water-oriented activities, including microlight flying, sailing, windsurfing, and, with its offshore wrecks and subsea flora and fauna, scuba diving. Regular ferry services leave for the Îles d'Hyères.

Heading back inland and farther north, you can see **Grimaud** for miles around, the remains of its feudal castle crowning a cluster of stone houses. The joy here is to wander the perfectly restored lanes, admiring the porticos, stone stairways, bougainvillea-festooned facades, and blooming flowerpots. To visit, there are the castle ruins, abandoned after the French Revolution, as well as two mills, the restored **Moulin à Vent de Saint-Roch,** a flour mill built in the 17th century, and the remains of the 17th-century **Moulin à Huile de l'Hôpital,** the town's largest oil mill. Learn about the region at the **Musée des Arts et Traditions Populaires** (a folk museum). The picturesque **Chapelle des Pénitents Blancs** (1482) houses the shrines of St.-Théodore and St.-Lambert.

CÔTES DE PROVENCE

The vines covering St.-Tropez's hinterlands are part of the Côtes de Provence appellation—producing mostly rosés—which extends from Cannes to Marseille and as far north as the Haut-Var. You'll see *domaines* (vineyards) advertised everywhere, most offering *dégustations* (tastings). Pick up information at the St.-Tropez tourism office. ■

Cavalaire-sur-Mer
🗺 109 F2
Visitor information
✉ Office de Tourisme, Maison de la Mer
☎ 04 94 01 92 10

Grimaud
🗺 109 F2
Visitor information
✉ 1 blvd. des Aliziers
☎ 04 94 55 43 83
www.grimaud-provence.com

Musée des Arts et Traditions Populaires
✉ 53 montée Hospice, Grimaud
☎ 04 94 43 39 29 (Office de Tourisme)
🕐 Closed Sun.

Le Thoronet's cloister epitomizes the abbey's clean, elegant lines.

Côtes de Provence estate crawl

An idyllic realm of medieval villages, pine and cork oak forests, vineyard-covered valleys, and plenty of opportunities to taste the local wine await on this bucolic drive in the Vallée Intérieure of the central Var—one of the Côte de Provence's five discreet regions that have been given the *appellation d'origine contrôlée.*

Begin in **Les Arcs** ①, with its medieval core and Villeneuve castle (offering dining and rooms). Four-and-a-half miles (7.2 km) east of town, on the D91 toward La Motte, the **Château Ste.-Roseline** ② *(tel 04 94 99 50 30, www.sainte-roseline.com, chapel closed Mon. & a.m.)* is an offbeat castle in a vineyard setting, where you can taste a *cru classé* wine produced since the 14th century. The adjacent chapel houses a 1975 mosaic by Marc Chagall, as well as the corpse of Ste.-Roseline herself (1263–1329) within a glass casket. Roseline cared for peasants during the Saracen invasions and, upon her death, her corpse is said to have not decomposed.

Just south of Les Arcs on the N7, you can taste (and buy) 16 different Côtes de Provence wines at the **Maison des Vins** ③ *(RN 7, tel 04 94 99 50 20).* Locals highly recommend the restaurant, La Vigne à Table. From here, continue on the N7 through Vidauban, then head in the direction of Le Thoronet via the D84. Right away you'll see vineyards, then wind through woodsy hills interspersed with vines and hamlets. About 7.5 (12 km) on, turn right on the D17, continuing on the D79, which will

bring you through Le Thoronet to the abbey of **Notre-Dame-du-Thoronet** ④ *(tel 04 94 60 43 90, $$),* one of three Cistercian houses in Provence (Silvacane and Sénanque are the others). Largely built between 1160 and 1175 of vivid rose stone, it is one of Provence's purest examples of Romanesque architecture. The church was constructed first, so the monks could pray as soon as possible. A self-guided tour visits the church, monks' dormitories, and cloisters.

From the abbey, follow the tiny D279 then D13 to the picturesque village of **Carcès,** perhaps stopping to taste at one of the domaines along the way. You can also taste in town. Charming **Cotignac** ⑤ lies 5 miles (8 km) away, via the D13, its medieval houses cozying against a hillside. Above, tufa cliffs hold caves once hollowed out for wine cellars and even residences. You can hike to them. From here, the D50 leads to **Entrecasteaux,** another picturesque medieval town.

Toward **Salernes** ⑥ via the D31, the scenery alternates between vineyards and piney hills. Near town, signs for *terres cuites* (baked earth) appear, as this village has been famous for its enamel tiles since the 18th century.

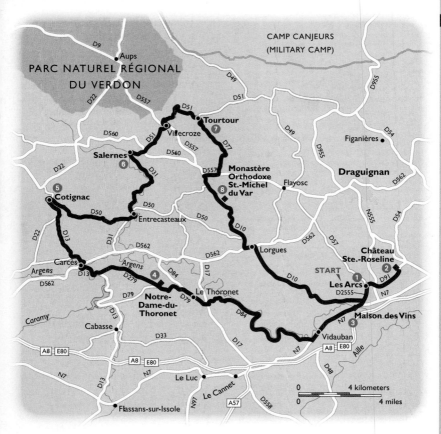

Pretty **Villecroze** is only 3 miles (5 km) away via the D51. Its *vieux village* harbors pastel-shuttered houses dripping with flowers. The town is set against tufa cliffs full of caves—*grottes troglodytes*—where a local lord lived in the 1500s. Tours are offered; they are reached through the town park *(next to the tennis courts).*

Take the D557 to the D51, a twisty, high-to-the-sky road that explains the nickname of **Tourtour ⑦**, your destination—"village in the sky." Views atop this perch are stupendous, while the village, with its houses of pale, locally quarried stone, is charming as can be. The central square is lined with restaurants and cafés. There is a restored 17th-century *moulin à huile*, which presses olives after the harvest in mid-December and serves as an art gallery the rest of the year; the medieval **Tour Grimaldi** watch tower; and two châteaux, one that now houses the *mairie* (town hall), the other an art gallery.

From here, drop back down to Earth via the

> ▲ See area map p. 109
> ► Les Arcs
> ⟳ 60 miles (95 km)
> ⏱ A full day
> ► Les Arcs
>
> **NOT TO BE MISSED**
> • Notre-Dame-du-Thoronet
> • Tourtour

D77, through scrabbly ecru cliffs and pine trees. Take a right on the D557 toward Lorgues, then a left on the D10. Soon you pass the turnoff for the **Monastère Orthodoxe St.-Michel du Var ⑧** *(1909 rte. Lorgues, tel 04 94 73 75 75)*, a historic monastery that can be visited. The large town of **Lorgues** offers more chances for wine-tasting. Return to Les Arcs via the D10 and D57. ∎

More places to visit in Aix, Marseille, & the Var

AUBAGNE
Filmmaker and writer Marcel Pagnol was born in this pretty Provençal town in 1895. While its outskirts have suffered a bit in the name of progress, its tree-shaded *vieille ville* remains much as Pagnol might have known it. The tourist office offers several Pagnol-themed tours, including a day-long, 5.6-mile (9 km) hike covering sites related to his life. ◪ 108 C2 **Maison du Tourisme d'Aubagne** ✉ Ave. Antide Boyer ☎ 04 42 03 49 98

BRIGNOLES
Get past the industrial outskirts to discover the charming historic core of this little town, once famous for sugar plums sent to the royal courts of Europe. Later, it became rich through bauxite mining. **Place Carami** is the old town's focal point, where locals lounge at *terrasse* cafés beneath plane trees. The **Musée du Pays Brignolais** *(place des Comtes de Provence, tel 04 94 69 45 18, closed Mon.–Tues., $)* has santons, paintings by the local Parrocel family, and a re-creation of a Provençal kitchen. ◪ 108 D2 **Maison du Tourisme** ✉ Hôtel Claviers, 10 rue du Palais ☎ 04 94 69 27 51

LA CIOTAT
The world's first movie was premiered here in September 1895, the work of the local Lumière brothers. They showed their *L'Entrée d'un Train en Gare de La Ciotat (The Arrival of a Train at La Ciotat Station)* at their father's theater, the **Théâtre Eden,** which still stands on boulevard Anatole France. Today, film history comes to life at the **Éspace Simon Lumière** *(20 rue du Marechal Foch, tel 04 42 71 61 70),* with photos, posters, and a film archive. Artists including Georges Braque (1882–1963) loved painting the **Vieux Port,** which still possesses some charm. ◪ 108 C2 **Office de Tourisme** ✉ Blvd. Anatole France ☎ 04 42 08 61 32, www.laciotat.com

LA GARDE-FREINET
Celebrated for its chestnuts and chestnut cream, this medieval town lies buried deep in the Massif des Maures. A signposted circuit takes you past the village's old fountains and washtubs *(ask at tourist office).* Another walk leads to **Fort Freinet,** a 15th-century castle carved out of stone, with fabulous views. ◪ 109 F2 **Maison du Tourisme de La Garde-Freinet** ✉ 1 place Neuve ☎ 04 94 43 67 41

OPPIDUM D'ENTREMONT
Perched on an aerie 1,200 feet (367 m) above the edge of a plateau, with a 656-foot-wide (200 m) view of the valley below, Entremont was the capital of the advanced Celto-Ligurian tribe. They ruled between the third and second centuries B.C., when the Romans destroyed the city at the request of the Marseillais. Excavations have exposed a residential zone and traces of shops and warehouses. Of particular note are the number of decapitated statues that have also been uncovered, spearheading a debate: Were the heads of vanquished enemies removed by war chiefs as evidence of their bravery? Or did the tribe practice the ritualized preservation of the heads of the deceased for the creation of reliquaries? The current thought combines both theories. Many of the statues and objects found at Entremont are on display at the **Musée Granet** in Aix-en-Provence (see p. 112). ◪ 108 C3 ✉ 1.8 miles (3 km) north of Aix-en-Provence via ave. Solari (D14) ☎ 04 42 21 97 33, www.entremont.culture.gouv.fr 🕒 Closed Tues.

SALON-DE-PROVENCE
In this busy, modern city, the sight to see is the **Maison de Nostradamus** *(13 rue Nostradamus, tel 04 90 56 64 31, $),* the little house near the château where the famous physician and seer lived from 1547 until his death in 1566. Nostradamus's most famous work is *Les Centuries,* a compilation of predictions written in the future tense in rhyming quatrains. This achievement, along with other aspects of his life, is depicted through a series of tableaus. He is buried in the 14th-century **Église St.-Laurent,** north of the town center. ◪ 108 B3 **Office de Tourisme de Salon** ✉ 56 cours Gimon ☎ 04 90 56 27 60, www.visitsalondeprovence.com ∎

The fabled French Riviera lives on in movie-star-spangled Cannes, famous for its high life and scenery, while surrounding towns pay tribute to perfume-making and contemporary art (starring Picasso).

Côte d'Azur: Cannes & around

Arman's "To My Pretty," a tribute to Picasso, stands on the Musée Picasso's terrace in Antibes.

Musée Picasso in Antibes features some of the Catalan artist's best works—and exquisite views.

Côte d'Azur: Cannes & around

PALM TREES, BODY-SQUEEZED BEACHES, LANGUOROUS SEA BREEZES, AND A sparkling blue sea: This is the heart of the French Riviera, stretching from Cannes to Cagnes-sur-Mer and reaching inland to Grasse, Vence, and other hill towns. This realm also reveals major contributions to modern art (spearheaded by Pablo Picasso), perfume, and military architecture.

Cannes is all about strolling along La Croisette, its famed esplanade, taking in grandiose hotels, bather-packed beaches, and the star walk near the Palais des Festivals et des Congrès, site of the awards ceremony for the International Film Festival every May. Another world exists atop Le Suquet hill, the old quarter with a medieval castle overlooking the glistening bay. Offshore, on Île Ste.-Marguerite, the mysterious Man in the Iron Mask was locked up by King Louis XIV in the late 17th century. The eucalyptus-scented island, along with nearby Île St.-Honorat, is one of the Îles de Lérins, a tranquil escape from the coast's buzz.

After World War II, Picasso moved to the Côte d'Azur, where his works took on the joyful, colorful mood of the surrounding scenery. He helped revitalize the pottery industry in Vallauris, whose main street is now packed with pottery shops (of differing quality).

Picasso at one point lived in the perfectly preserved hill town of Mougins, now most famous for its Moulin de Mougins

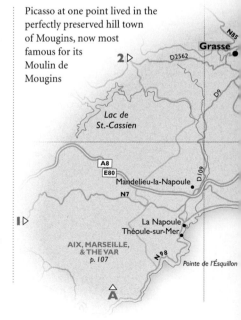

restaurant. Nearby Grasse has been the world's perfume capital since the 16th century, when Catherine de Médicis introduced the concept of scented leather gloves. Today, three perfumeries offer tours, and several museums in the town center provide further insight into the perfume business.

Vence is a pleasant enough hill town, but most people pilgrimage here for one thing—the little white chapel designed by Henri Matisse in the 1950s. From the colorful stained-glass windows to the monochromatic Stations of the Cross to the priests' vestments, Matisse created it all, in what he considered to be his greatest lifetime achievement.

More modern art awaits in another hill town, the nearby St.-Paul-de-Vence. The Maeghts built their art museum in the 1970s, a (then) state-of-the-art temple to house their extensive collection of 20th-century art. Giant sculptures by Miró, Calder, and de Staël dot the terraced grounds.

Georges Braque, Marc Chagall, and Henri Matisse were some of the "unknown" artists who gathered at the town's Colombe d'Or, where they exchanged paintings for food and lodging. Owner Paul Roux built up one of the

most important private collections of 20th-century art in the process. One can only imagine what those struggling artists would think if they knew the price diners pay to view their works today (the only way to see them).

Picasso experienced some of his most prolific months in the moneyed town of Antibes, where he worked out of the ancient Grimaldi castle. The château now holds the Musée Picasso, one of the world's greatest collections of his art. Poised on the Mediterranean, Antibes has several more museums tucked away in its old quarter, including a small but interesting archaeological museum and a fort designed by the great military architect Vauban. The Summer Season was invented on nearby Cap d'Antibes, where F. Scott Fitzgerald, Ernest Hemingway, and their friends frolicked in the surf.

Two more hill towns worth a stop are tiny Biot, a major glassblowing center, and Cagnes-sur-Mer, featuring another Grimaldi castle, which now houses several eclectic art collections, and the last home of Auguste Renoir, a house museum that appears just as if the Impressionist artist might return any moment. ■

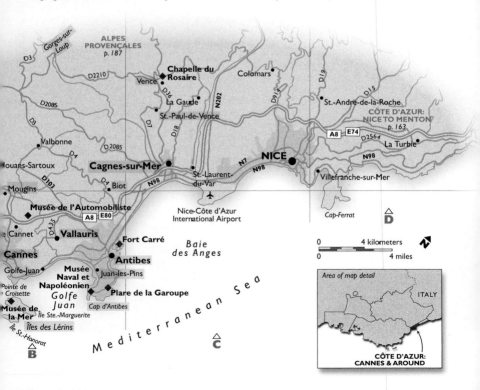

Cannes

Market days
Tues.–Sun.

Cannes
🅐 137 B1
Visitor information
✉ Palais des Festivals
☎ 04 92 99 84 22
www.cannes.fr

Cannes's old port, with the historic Le Suquet quarter beyond, gives a different take on this town famed for its movie stars and film festival.

ALONG THE PALM-SHADED LA CROISETTE, CANNES'S famed seaside esplanade, camera-toting tourists intermingle with young bronzed couples sporting the latest trends, Chanel-chic ladies walking poodles, artists bent over their canvases, probably a movie star or two—you never know. The translucent blue sea shimmers on one side, lapping exclusive, parasol-dotted beaches, while on the other side tower exclusive hotels. There may not be many museums or monuments to visit, but who needs them, in this most glittery, sophisticated resort, where seeing and being seen is what it's all about? For ten days each May, this atmosphere culminates in the world-renowned International Film Festival.

When Lord Brougham, lord chancellor of England, stopped in Cannes in 1834 to avoid a cholera outbreak, the tiny, tenth-century fishing hamlet's future changed forever. He built a Palladium-style villa in Le Suquet quarter, his mates followed, building their own glamorous villas, and ever since Cannes has been associated with luxurious tourism. Palatial hotels were built in the 20th century, including the Carlton, the Martinez, and the Majestic—though only the Carlton remains today.

Cannes got its true stamp of glitz and glamour in 1939, when it

was selected to host the Festival International de Cinéma (see p. 44). Louis Lumière, inventor of cinema, was prepared to preside over the first festival, but World War II intervened. It was not until 1946 that Cannes had its day, when films such as Jean Cocteau's *La Belle et La Bête* and Alfred Hitchcock's *Notorious* had top billing at the old Palais des Festivals (since replaced by the Noga Hilton). Cocteau described the event as "a living comet that has touched down for a few days on La Croisette." Today, the red carpet unfurls at the **Palais des Festivals et des Congrès,** a blocky structure built in 1982 on the headland between the Baie des Cannes and the Vieux Port. More than 50 festivals, congresses, and trade fairs take place here the rest of the year, and the building also contains a casino and nightclub. Outside, the handprints of stars are immortalized in the pavement—Gérard Depardieu, Johnny Hallyday, and Catherine Deneuve are some of the French favorites.

SIGHTS

La Croisette, one of France's loveliest boulevards, runs east from the Palais des Festivals to the Pointe de la Croisette. Glamorous villas and clubs once lined its length, long since replaced by apartment blocks, grand hotels, and designer boutiques. Of the belle époque era, only the wedding-cake **Inter-Continental Carlton Hotel** survives, a pompous neobaroque palace designed by Charles Dalmas. Shortly after the Carlton opened in 1912, it attracted Europe's *haut monde,* including royalty, to be followed later by screen stars. Here,

Carlton Hôtel

✉ 58 La Croisette

☎ 04 93 06 40 06

The Carlton Hotel's two corner cupolas are said to have been inspired by the bosom of La Belle Otèro, one of Cannes's grandes dames. She "consoled" turn-of-the-20th-century American millionaires and Russian dukes who passed their winters gambling away estates in distant lands.

for instance, Elizabeth Taylor checked in, successively, as Mrs. Hilton, Mrs. Todd, and Mrs. Fisher. The ultimate in luxury, even its standard rooms boast marble-encrusted bathrooms, while the deluxe rooms guarantee exquisite views over the bay.

Really, suntanning is what Cannes is all about. So it's been, ever since Coco Chanel (1883–1971) got too much sun here by accident in 1923 and returned to Paris, where the press and fashion world assumed the ultrafashionable woman had started a new trend. Gleaming, golden bodies in skimpy bathing suits continue the craze. Most of the best beaches are private, taken over by hotels across the street. If you don't have a key to one of those luxury rooms, you'll find two small public bathing areas at either end of La Croisette; more public beaches await along boule-

vard du Midi, farther west of La Croisette.

After a day at the beach, the thing to do is promenade. A favorite spot is **rue d'Antibes,** a few streets north of La Croisette, where chic boutiques tempt with their expensive wares. One street farther north, **rue Meynadier** is a bit more down-to-earth, with discount clothes, outlets, souvenir shops, and gourmet food stores in 18th-century facades. The roof-covered **Marché Forville,** at the street's western end, is the town's primary fruit, flower, and vegetable market; it's open every day but Monday.

Quaint **rue St.-Antoine** winds up into the city's oldest quarter—**Le Suquet,** with its fabulous views over the city, the sea, and the yacht-filled Vieux Port. It's topped by the 17th-century **Église Notre-Dame d'Espérance,** the adjoining Cistercian **Chapelle de Ste.-Anne,** and a castle erected by Lérins monks in the 11th and 12th centuries. Ste.-Anne houses a collection of musical instruments, while the castle's square tower contains the **Musée de la Castre.** The latter focuses on local history and displays antiquities collected by eccentric world traveler Baron Lycklama.

On the town's eastern side, in the **Quartier de la Californie,** you'll discover the baroque **Chapelle Bellini** *(allée de la Villa-Florentina)* and the blue-domed **Église Orthodoxe St.-Michel-Archange** *(30 blvd. Alexandre III),* evidence of the town's early popularity among the Russian aristocracy.

A 15-minute boat ride from the Vieux Port brings you to the **Îles des Lérins** (see p. 162), best known for the infamous prisioner, the Man in the Iron Mask, held at Fort Royal. ∎

Man in the Iron Mask

The mysterious Man in the Iron Mask arrived on Île Ste.-Marguerite in April 1687. Who was he? No one knows for sure. Voltaire, who spoke to the mystery man's former servants, believed he was the elder brother of Louis XIV—the inspiration for Alexandre Dumas's novel *Le Vicomte de Bragelonne,* written in 1848–1850. Others have surmised he was the illegitimate son of Anne of Austria (wife of Louis XIII), or of she and Cardinal Mazarin; the bastard son of the Duke of Beaufort (Louis XIV's brother); the bastard son of Charles II of England; or, perhaps, even Count Mattioli, imprisoned for selling to Spain the details of the negotiations between Louis XIV and Charles III of Mantua.

Whatever the case, the masked man was given preferential treatment, as if he were indeed a blue blood. Among the many legends is the one about the woman who came to visit and had a son by him. The child was sent to Corsica to be raised by a woman who knew nothing of his past, only that the child should be given the best possible attention, since he was of good breeding *(de buoné-parté).* His foster mother thereby named the boy Buonaparte ... the future Napoléon? The Man in the Iron Mask left the island for the Bastille in 1698, where he died in 1703. He was buried in St.-Paul cemetery under the name of Marchiali, carrying the secret of his identity to the grave. ∎

Fort Royal, Île Ste.-Marguerite

Musée de la Castre

✉ Château de la Castre, place de la Castre

☎ 04 93 38 55 26

🕐 Closed Mon.

💲 $

Grasse

Grasse

🗺 136 B2

Visitor information

✉ 22 place du Cours Honoré-Cresp

☎ 04 93 36 66 66

Museums website
www.museesdegrasse.com

Musée International de la Parfumerie

✉ 8 place du Cours

☎ 04 93 36 80 20

🕐 Closed for renovations until May 2008

💲 $

Parfumerie Galimard

✉ 73 rte. de Cannes

☎ 04 93 09 20 00

Parfums Molinard

✉ 60 blvd. Victor Hugo

☎ 04 93 36 01 62

Musée d'Art et d'Histoire

✉ 2 rue Mirabeau

☎ 04 97 05 58 00

🕐 Closed Tues. Oct.–May, & Nov.

💲 $

Villa-Musée Fragonard

✉ 23 blvd. Fragonard

☎ 04 97 05 58 00

🕐 Closed Tues. Oct.–May, & all Nov.

💲 $

THE FRAGRANCE OF FLOWERS PERMEATES THE COBBLED lanes of Grasse's *vieille ville*, where perfume-making was born in the 1500s—and raised to high art. A visit to this charming village just north of Cannes, with its ancient houses, insightful museums, and several perfumeries, is not only pleasant but an education.

Founded by Romans, Grasse was a bustling miniature republic in the Middle Ages, with tanning its most important industry. Then, in the 16th century, Catherine de Médicis, who disliked the smell of glove leather on her hands, saw the potential of the area's mild weather and fine soil to grow flowers—jasmine, roses, tuberose—for scented gloves. The glovemakers split from the tanneries, and when perfume became à la mode in the 18th century, they were poised for success. The industrial revolution of the 1800s redefined the perfume industry, as Grasse used new techniques of distillation, *enfleurage* (a process of extracting scents), and organic synthesis to produce fine fragrances that took the world by storm. These days, much of the industry focuses on creating fragrances for household products, but fine fragrances for major perfumes remain part of Grasse's prestige and allure.

PERFUME SIGHTS

Wade through the traffic and crowded succession of roundabouts to the large vieille ville, at the top of town, where most of the sights are found. You'll want to park your car, since the town's steep staircases and tiny, hilly roads are best explored on foot.

Begin your tour at the nearby **Musée International de la Parfumerie.** The International Museum of Perfume traces the history of perfume and how it is made, from the harvesting and treatment of raw materials to the launching of the finished product. A greenhouse on the third floor showcases irises, jasmine, and other plants chosen carefully for their aromatic qualities.

Grasse has five major fragrance houses, three of which are open to the public: Fragonard, Galimard, and Molinard. The only one in the old town proper is **Fragonard** *(20 blvd. Fragonard, tel 04 93 36 44 65)*, housed in the original perfume factory dating from 1782; it has a perfume museum, showcasing 3,000 years worth of bottles, perfume coffers, and beauty cases from around the world—including soap and lipstick molds from the early 20th century and a rare collection of pomanders from the 16th and 17th centuries. Downstairs, join a guided tour through the small factory where perfume is made to this day.

Fragonard has another, more modern factory just south of town *(les 4 chemins, rte. de cannes, tel 04 93 77 94 30)*. The two other perfumeries, **Galimard** and **Molinard,** offering free tours of their factories as well, are also south of town.

OTHER SIGHTS

Back in the old town, several other museums are worth a peek. The Fragonard-sponsored **Musée Provençal du Costume et du Bijou** *(2 rue Jean Ossola, tel 04 93 36 44 65, closed Sun. Nov.–Feb.)* displays Provençal costumes and jewelry dating from the 18th and 19th centuries. Each costume, encased in a glass dome, presents some aspect of Provençal culture—beginning with a 1750 Louis XV-era beige-and-pink flowered dress "à la française," also

called a "Watteau," for the romantic artist who depicted such dresses in his paintings; and including a wedding and artisan dress.

Down the street from Fragonard, the **Musée d'Art et d'Histoire de Provence** is housed in one of Provence's most elegant buildings, dating from the late 1700s. Inside you'll find a rich collection of furniture, paintings, and objets d'art charting high-class life in the 1800s, including Moustiers faïence, ceramics from Vallauris, and Provençal Nativity scenes. A French-style garden, designed by Viscount de Nouailles in 1967 according to 18th-century plans, has roses and lemon trees.

On the other side of the Jardin Public, the **Villa-Musée Fragonard** is a small but special place. Grasse-born painter Jean-Honoré Fragonard, celebrated for his romantic paintings and por-traits, lived in this charming 17th-century villa in 1790 and 1791 (the Fragonard perfumery adopted his name upon its founding). A mix of original drawings and paintings and replicas hang on the walls. Nearby, the **Musée de la Marine** explores Grasse's military ties through the story of Admiral de Grasse, hero of the American Revolutionary War.

Burrowed deep in the old town on place du Petit Puy Godeau, is the Romanesque **Cathédrale Notre-Dame-du-Puy,** dating from the 12th and 13th centuries and rebuilt in the 17th. Inside, to the altar's right, hang three early Rubens (1601), including "Le Couronne-ment d'Épines" ("The Crown of the Thorns") and "Le Crucifié" ("Christ Crucified"). In the Chapelle du St.-Sacrement look for Jean-Honoré Fragonard's 1754 "Lavement des Pieds" ("Christ Washing the Feet of the Apostles"). ∎

A copy of **Jean-Honoré Fragonard's** "Love's Progress in a Young Girl's Heart," commissioned by the comtesse du Barry, Louis XV's most beautiful mistress, hangs in the Villa-Musée Fragonard.

Musée de la Marine
✉ 2 blvd. du Jeu de Ballon
☎ 04 93 40 11 11
🕐 Closed Sat.–Sun.

The art of the perfumer

As beautiful as a symphony, a fine fragrance contains a complex combination of raw materials that harmonize to create the perfect composition. As a composer combines the notes of different instruments, the perfumer adds individual scents—fittingly called notes—to create the desired statement: luxury or passion or mystery or a day at the beach. It's a science that takes place in a lab, but one that requires the art of imagination and creativity and passion. Above all, however, the perfumer must have a good nose.

Everyone has the same number of olfactory receptors in their nose and upper palate—about five million. What separates the perfumer from everyone else is that he or she, through years of apprenticeship and an inherent talent to smell, can dissect a fragrance into various parts, taking smell to an incredible depth. A good "nose," as they are called in the industry, can identify more than 700 smells (most of us are lucky to remember 50). They must be able to recognize smells in minute concentrations, some as little as two parts per million, and they must be able to retain them for weeks, months, even years. And that's just the start of it. These rare experts must then figure out how to blend the smells successfully.

There are more than 4,000 possible smells available to the perfumer—lemon and grapefruit are light and clean; balsam is woodsy yet delicate; lavender and basil are pungent and refreshing; vanilla is rich and exotic. They don't all have to be lovely scents. Cassis (black currant) smells like cat urine, but combined with certain other scents provides an underlying anchor. The ugly white ambergris root is what creates the silvery base of Chanel No. 19. There are also synthetic notes; the synthetic chemical aldehyde, for instance, which smells like starched laundry, is what gives Chanel No. 5 its sparkle.

To make it more complicated, fragrances go through many different phases once they come in contact with the skin. These are generally classified as top, middle, and base notes and must be perfectly blended to round out a perfume.

Creating the fragrance's first impression, the "top note" is very light and evaporates quickly, lasting perhaps just a few minutes. Top notes are usually citrus and fruity, for instance cucumber or mint. As the top note fades, the "middle" or "heart note" forms the perfume's character and body, the one that is detectable after the fragrance has been on the skin a few minutes. It consists of heavier ingredients—geranium, lavender, pear, rose—that last a couple of hours and account for 60 to 70 percent of the blend. The "base" or "bottom note" emerges slowly, after several hours of wearing. It is richly scented—sandalwood, musk, patchouli—creating the lasting notes of the fragrance. It serves as the foundation upon which the perfume is based and evaporates slowly, lasting up to seven or eight hours.

THE BUSINESS

In the olden days, the only way into the perfume business was to be born into it. These days, future perfumers can learn the art at various institutes and schools, where in endless drills they learn the raw materials, how to smell, and the proper fragrance vocabulary, as well as the chemistry of fragrances and how to put scents together.

After three years, students become technicians. The key to becoming a true perfumer, however, is to truly and passionately understand how to put a fragrance together—and this is where the artistic side comes in. Some people inherently have it. Some people can learn it through five, ten, fifteen years of hard work. And some people never get it.

There are 400 perfumers in the world, more than half of whom reside in the United States. Only 20 percent of perfumers focus on fine fragrances, where all the glitz and glamour is, while the others come up with the fragrances for household products such as detergents, cat litter, garbage bags—little niceties that, given the smelly alternative, are really a big deal. ■

Above: Fragrant jasmine—one of the costliest fragrances—grows in abundance in the hills around Grasse.

Above: Copper stills were once used to distill the perfume essence. Right: A beautiful flacon is the final touch in creating an exquisite scent; the notion of designing a bottle for a specific fragrance took root in the 19th century.

Vence

Market days
Tues.–Sun.
Flower market at
place Grand Jardin

Vence
◪ 137 C2

**Visitor
information**
✉ Place du Grand-
Jardin
☎ 04 93 58 06 38

**Fondation Émile
Hugues**
✉ Château de
Villeneuve, place de
Frêne
☎ 04 93 58 15 78
🕐 Closed Mon.
$ $$

**Chapelle du
Rosaire**
◪ 137 C2
✉ 466 ave. Henri
Matisse
☎ 04 93 58 03 26
🕐 Closed Fri. & a.m.
$ $

A 12TH-CENTURY TROUBADOUR CALLED VENCE "LE DOUX répaire" ("sweet nest"), while Nostradamus in the 1500s wrote, "Garden of Vence, marvel of Provence." The town's tightly walled medieval heart remains a pretty, fountain-adorned village, but the main reason people come here sits about half a mile north of town: Henri Matisse's endearing, light-filled Chapelle du Rosaire.

Strategically located 6 miles (10 km) from the sea, Vence was early on an important episcopal city. Its most famous bishops were fifth-century St.-Véran, who organized the town's defenses against Visigoth invaders, and 12th-century St.-Lambert, who defended the town's rights against its new baron, Romée de Villeneuve, igniting a rivalry between nobility and clergy that would last until the bishopric was dissolved after the Revolution. Besieged by Huguenots during the Wars of Religion, the town did not fall, a fact commemorated each Easter with a festival.

The lovely setting did not miss the attention of artists—Matisse, Raoul Dufy, Jean Dubuffet, and D. H. Lawrence are some of the creative minds who showed up in the early 1900s. Russian artist Marc Chagall lived in Vence between 1950 and 1966 (he's buried in nearby St.-Paul-de-Vence, where he also lived). It's still a lively art town, with several galleries and frequent summertime outdoor exhibits.

MEDIEVAL VENCE
Through **Porte du Peyra,** the main 13th-century gate, you see the **Fontaine du Peyra,** built in 1822 to replace a 1578 version. Its clear mineral water comes from the River Foux just above the village; an old marble plaque lists the different amounts of minerals present. On the square's western edge stands the Château de Villeneuve and its 12th-century watchtower. Inside, the **Fondation Émile Hugues** features a permanent art collection and an annual series of exhibitions.

From here, turn right on shop-filled rue du Marché, then left on rue Alsace-Lorraine to place Clemenceau. The square is dominated by the *mairie* (town hall) and the Romanesque cathedral, built in the 11th century on the site of a Roman temple to Mars and restored in the baroque period. Be sure to peek at Chagall's mosaic of Moses in the bulrushes in its baptistery.

CHAPELLE DU ROSAIRE

A 20-minute walk from the town center, across the River Foux and up avenue Henri Matisse, awaits this famous little chapel. Upon moving to Vence from Nice in 1941 to escape Allied bombings, Henri Matisse, then in his late 70s, fell ill and was nursed back to health by the town's Dominican sisters. In gratitude, he designed this chapel for them; it is still used by the Dominican nuns of the Rosary.

The chapel looks traditional on the outside—a whitewashed villa with blue and white tiles on its low-slung roof, topped by a 43-foot-tall (13 m) wrought iron cross and bell tower. Two simple black-and-white ceramics by Matisse hint that this is no ordinary chapel, including the "Mary, Jesus, and St. Dominic" over the front door. In fact, Matisse claimed this chapel, built at the end of his life, between 1948 and 1951, was his masterpiece, a "conclusive achievement of a whole life of labor and the flowering of a huge sincere and difficult striving."

You walk down the steps into the chapel's interior, a dazzling white space bathed in the subaqueous light of three stained-glass windows. The two southern windows feature yellow and blue leaves on a green background, while the chancel window has blue cactuses and golden flowers.

Simple black-lined drawings on white ceramics—representing the colors of the Dominican habit—are the only other adornments. In the nave is a Nativity scene, and overlooking the altar a large St.-Dominic. The Stations of the Cross are line drawings jumbled together in one tableau, with each station hand-numbered accordingly.

Matisse designed every detail of the building, down to the candlesticks, cross, priests' vestments, and the altar, constructed from a piece of a Roman stone bridge that once spanned the River Gard. In the adjoining hall, some of his colorful priests' vestments are on display, as well as working sketches. ■

Matisse's Chapelle du Rosaire, a triumph of light, space, and deliberate use of color

St.-Paul-de-Vence

St.-Paul-de-Vence
🅜 137 C2
Visitor information
✉ Maison de la Tour,
2 rue Grande
☎ 04 93 32 86 95
www.saint-
pauldevence.com

WALLED WITHIN ANCIENT RAMPARTS, THIS IMMACULATE medieval town north of Cagnes-sur-Mer, with its high-end boutiques and art galleries, caters to well-to-do tourists. It also offers one of the Provence's most sublime 20th-century art museums—the Fondation Maeght.

Sitting atop its hilltop aerie, St.-Paul-de-Vence was a flourishing medieval town, doing a fine business in wine, figs, olives, and orange trees. It took on its first note of importance in the 1500s, when François I enlarged the existing town with ramparts and fortifications to guard its strategic position overlooking France and the Savoy (Italy). Many of the ramparts exist to this day.

The town declined until after World War I, when leading artists from the school of Paris began commuting by streetcar from near-

by Cagnes. Picasso, Braque, Matisse, Signac, Renoir, Dufy, Soutine, and Russian artist Marc Chagall (who's buried in the village cemetery) are among those who arrived with drawing notebooks, paint boxes, sometimes canvases. Their destination: Café Robinson, the town's only inn at the time. It was run by Paul Roux, who accepted paintings in exchange for meals and lodging—eventually amassing a priceless art collection. Today, the inn is known as the fabled **Colombe d'Or** restaurant (see Travelwise p. 222), and some of those famous paintings are displayed on its walls—for the viewing of patrons only (alas, the price does not come cheap).

MEDIEVAL VILLAGE

Once occupied by the workshops of weavers, shoemakers, and saddlers, the old town's beautiful 16th- and 17th-century stone buildings—many still bearing the coats-of-arms placed by the original builders—are now filled with a madhouse of boutiques, souvenir shops, antique stores, and, above all, art galleries. Along rue Grande alone, the main street through town, you'll find 36 of the town's 64 art galleries. The tourist office, located just beyond the Porte Nord de Vence (Vence's North Gate), has a list of galleries, as well as a map highlighting the village's main historic points. Seven landmarks have been listed as historical monuments.

Of the historical sites, the most interesting is the Gothic **Église Collegiale,** located at the village's

The Église Collegiale, in the heart of St.-Paul-de-Vence, contains many ecclesiastical treasures.

highest point on place de la Mairie. Dating from the 12th century, the ocher-walled structure went through many alterations until the 18th century; only the choir remains from the 12th-century building. The church is filled with art: Don't miss the painting of Ste.-Catherine-d'Alexendrie, attributed to Tintoretto, hanging to the left as you enter. The last altar on the right is St.-Clément's chapel, a masterpiece of baroque architecture from the 18th century, with a fantastic bas-relief of St.-Clément's martyrdom. Adjacent, the 17th-century **White Penitent's Chapel** houses several masterpieces, including the "Transfiguration," after Raphael, and two 17th-century frescoes representing St.-Pierre and St.-Paul. Nearby is the 12th-century *donjon* (castle keep).

Across from the church, the **Musée d'Histoire Locale** is a tad hokey in its presentation of historical wax-figure scenes, but it does give a good sense of the town's past, ranging from François I's visit in 1538 to assess the need for fortification, to Vauban's inspection in 1701 of the newly built walls, to the mayor's success in 1870 in saving the ramparts from demolition. The photography room has special exhibits taken from the municipal photo library, often showing celebrities in the local setting.

St.-Paul is a wealth of architectural beauty. Keep an eye out for the 1850 **Grande Fontaine** *(place de la Fontaine),* a fountain overlooked by beautiful old dwellings; the **Pontis,** a medieval street bridge over the rue Grande; and the **Placette,** literally, "small square," whose fountain has been running since 1611.

FONDATION MAEGHT

Tucked away in pinewoods north-

St.-Paul-de-Vence's cobbled streets and fountains survive from medieval times.

Musée d'Histoire Locale

✉ Town center, opposite church

☎ 04 93 32 41 13

🕐 Closed Nov., & Sun. & Tues.

💲 $

Fondation Marguerite et Aimé Maeght

✉ Just outside village via La Colle, then up Montée des Trious

☎ 04 93 32 81 63

www.fondation-maeght.com

⑤ $$$

Designed by Catalan architect José Luis Sert, the state-of-the-art Fondation Maeght showcases one of the world's greatest collections of 20th-century art.

west of town, the Fondation Maeght showcases an extraordinary collection of modern and contemporary art in a harmonious natural setting. Marguerite and Aimé Maeght were art dealers and publishers who collected, for starters, Picassos, Matisses, Légers, Chagalls, Calders, and Giacomettis. Only the most modern of buildings could house this sublime art collection, so the Maeghts commissioned Catalan architect José Luis Sert to design their museum. The collaborative result is a low-slung, split-level structure with winglike expansions on the roof for circulation, set amid terraced gardens. Glass walls bring the indoors and outdoors together. Their museum, built "as a gift to the people," opened in 1964.

Inside, the works are regularly rotated, so you never know exactly what you're going to see—perhaps Bonnards, Kandinskys, Légers,

Matisses, and/or Barbara Hepworths. Whatever the case, you won't be disappointed. Temporary exhibitions are just as extraordinary.

Outside, gigantic sculptures are integrated into the building design and surrounding terraces and gardens. Some of the favorites are "Les Poissons" (1964), a mosaic pool by Georges Braque; a courtyard featuring Alberto Giacometti's spindly statues, including "Man Walking"; and a fountain by Pol Bury. The biggest draw is undoubtedly Joan Miró's labyrinth, in which a maze of outdoor rooms feature whimsical ceramic sculptures and fountains.

Also on the grounds is the **Chapelle Saint-Bernard,** built by the Maeghts upon their son's death at age 11. Among its treasures is a stained-glass window by Georges Braque, "Oiseau Blanc et Mauve" ("White and Purple Bird," 1962), over the altar. ■

Antibes

THIS OLD MEDITERRANEAN FISHING TOWN COUNTS among its blessings Europe's largest yacht harbor (a thousand slips), sandy beaches, and a picturesque old town filled with boutiques, restaurants, and a bustling marché Provençal. But the main reason to visit is the Musée Picasso, an old castle overlooking the sea where after World War II a 65-year-old Pablo Picasso created masterpiece after joyful masterpiece, many of which are now showcased within its walls. Nearby, exclusive Cap d'Antibes is where the Summer Season was invented.

An active trading port since its earliest times, Antibes came into its own in the fifth century B.C. with the arrival of Greek traders, who called their fortified town Antipolis—meaning "city opposite," for its position across from Nice. The Romans took over in the first century B.C., renaming it Antiboul. For centuries Antibes remained the only metropolis between Marseille and Italy.

After being besieged in the 16th century by Charles V of Spain, François I and his successors—realizing the city's strategic importance on the border of France and the Savoy (Italy)—began strengthening its fortifications. Overlooking the bay, St.-Laurent Tower became Fort Carré. The stronghold was finished in 1710, with the completion of the ramparts entirely encircling the town. It was here that Napoléon Bonaparte was imprisoned for a week in 1794 after the fall of Robespierre. En route to his return to glory, Napoléon stepped ashore at Golfe-Juan in 1815.

Today, Antibes is a lively, active port town, with cultural sights to visit and buzzing restaurants and cafés at which to linger. The residents include many English, Irish, and Aussies who help crew yachts (which explains the large number of English-speaking pubs).

VIEIL ANTIBES
Tucked behind the ancient seawall close to the sea, little cobblestone lanes crisscross Antibes's old town, where honey-hued houses contain shops full of Provençal wares and restaurants with inviting sidewalk seating. **Porte de France,** on rue de la République, is one of the last remaining vestiges of the city wall.

Keep walking down rue de la République (in the direction of the sea) and you will come to plane-shaded place Nationale and charming **Musée Peynet et du Dessin Humoristique.** Popular cartoonist Raymond Peynet, best known for his "Lovers" series—all the craze in postwar France—lived in Antibes. The museum displays more than 300 of his pictures, cartoons, and sculptures.

Following tiny rue Sade, you will come to the **marché Provençal,** a profusion of stalls beneath a 19th-

Beaches
Antibes has 48 beaches, from small rocky coves to long sandy stretches. The best beaches are found between Antibes's port and Cap d'Antibes: Plage de la Salis and Plage du Ponteil, just south of place Albert 1er. On Cap d'Antibes, the Plage de la Garoupe is where Fitzgerald, Picasso, and Hemingway swam together and conversed under parasols sipping sherry. The golden crescent is today sliced into various beach clubs. ■

Market days
Daily

Antibes
137 B1

Visitor information
11 place du Général de Gaulle
04 92 90 53 00
www.antibesjuanlespins.com

Musée Peynet et du Dessin Humoristique
Place Nationale
04 92 90 54 30
Closed Mon.
$

Marché Provençal
Cours Masséna
Open every a.m. except Mon. June–Aug.

Musée de la Tour
Tour Gilli, Cours Masséna (covered market)
04 93 34 13 58
Open Wed., Thurs., Sat., & Sun. p.m.
$

Église de l'Immaculée Conception
Rue St.-Esprit

Musée d'Histoire et d'Archéologie
Bastion St-André, ave. Amiral de Grasse
04 93 34 00 39
Closed Mon
$

Vauban's Fort Carré has stood sentry over Antibes's harbor since the 17th century.

century canopy stacked high with flowers, goat cheeses, olives, honey, and olive oil. Nearby, at the southern end of cours Masséna, is **Musée de la Tour,** part of the old town gates and now a local history museum.

Around the corner via rue du Bateau awaits the Musée Picasso and, down the far steps, the **Église de l'Immaculée Conception,** Antibes's former cathedral. Its colorful baroque facade belies the rather plain interior, though its treasures include a wooden crucifix from 1447 and a 15th-century altarpiece discovered in the walls in 1938, having been concealed during the Revolution.

Follow the ramparts southward to the **Musée d'Histoire et d'Archéologie,** which offers a tiny yet interesting exhibition on the town's Roman heritage. Housed in the St.-André Bastion, built by Vauban at the end of the 17th century, the structure's brick-vaulted galleries still exude a military feel. The collections, however, take you back 2,000 years to the Romans: their sarcophogi, *amphorae,* and coins (including several from the time of Constantine the Great).

Star-shaped **Fort Carré** (Square Fort), dominating the

Fort Carré

 137 B1

✉ Rte. du Bord de Mer (N98)

☎ 06 14 89 17 45

🕐 Guided tours every half-hour between 10 a.m. & 4 p.m. Tues.–Sun.

💲 $

Note: It takes some work to visit the fort. Park at the Fort Carré parking area on ave. du 11 Novembre, cross the street, and look for the green arrows that lead to the site. Be prepared for a hike. You can also walk from the port along the sea (it takes about 30 minutes), or take a shuttle.

Musée Picasso

✉ Château Grimaldi, place Mariejol

☎ 04 92 90 54 20

🕐 Closed Mon.

💲 $$

approach to Antibes from Nice, appears foreboding atop its hilltop roost. Indeed, after Provence became French in 1481, and Nice remained Italian, this was the last stronghold between France and the states of the duke of Savoy (Italy). Under the auspices of Louis XIV, Vauban (see sidebar p. 156) improved on the 16th-century fortress, including larger firing holes for 18 cannon. There is not much to actually see, but guided tours illume its fascinating history.

MUSEÉ PICASSO

After World War II, Pablo Picasso was offered space in the Grimaldi Castle, built in the 12th century (and revamped in the 16th). Thus begun a period of crazed activity—between mid-September and mid-November 1946—in which the Catalan artist created some of his most famous works. Newly in love with beautiful, young Françoise Gilot and seduced by the south's brilliant light, he experimented with not only painting, but pottery and sculpture, too. When Picasso left, he gave the museum all the work he had done—24 paintings, 80 ceramics, 44 drawings, 32 lithographs, 11 oils on paper, 2 sculptures, and 5 tapestries—

**Hôtel du Cap
Eden-Roc**
Blvd. Kennedy, Cap
d'Antibes
04 93 61 39 01
www.edenroc-hotel.fr

**Musée Naval et
Napoléonien**
137 B1
Ave. Kennedy
04 93 61 45 32
Closed Sun.–Mon.,
& Oct.
$

composing one of the world's greatest Picasso collections.

You'll find Picasso's works on the second floor. Themes from Greek mythology, as well as the beauty and lighthearted nature of the Mediterranean coast, recur from one work to the next. Fauns, centaurs, sea urchins, and fish are common motifs. One room contains pencil sketches that show Picasso's working process; the honing of a theme in many different ways (notice the erasure marks). In another room, Michel Gima's black-and-white photos provide an intimate look at the artist at the château.

The works culminate in "La Joie de Vivre," a 4-by-8-foot (1.2 m x 2.4 m) tableau centered around a dancing woman-flower (said to be Françoise) who is bathed in light. Around her, a centaur plays a flute

and fauns dance—seemingly capturing Picasso's own joy of life. On the ground floor, temporary exhibits showcase 20th-century trends. Don't miss the terrace, where a permanent collection of sculptures by local artist Germaine Richier are poised against the breathtaking backdrop of the Mediterranean; other artists represented here include Joan Miró ("Sea Goddess") and Anne and Patrick Poirier.

CAP D'ANTIBES

Grandiose villas set amid imported tropical flora confirm the cape's fabled reputation as a playground for the rich and famous. Indeed, you'll have to be rich and/or famous (or know someone who is) to get a peek beyond the peninsula's iron gates and high hedges. At the very least, you can wander verdant

Fort St.-Elme in Collioure demonstrates Vauban's masterful five-point-star design.

Master builder

By the early 1500s, with the use of gunpowder in firearms that could knock down walls, the era of impregnable castles was over. A new kind of fortification was needed. Along came the citadel, or fortress, designed to perfection by Sébastien le Prestre de Vauban. Born in 1633 near Vallon, Vauban was

Louis XIV's chief military engineer by the age of 22. Not only was he a brilliant geometrist, he was also a soldier who fought in every battle during Louis XIV's reign. In short, he knew what it took to besiege a fortification and figured out how to prevent such sieges. Using a five-point star superimposed upon another and circumscribed within a ten-point star, he devised a means of extending the outerworks so far that no enemy could begin to attack at close range. He also incorporated stronger defense characteristics, such as building on a high point of land and using broad, low walls with bastions to enable soldiers to fire in any direction. Vauban's fortresses are sprinkled throughout Provence, including Fort Carré at Antibes and the citadels at Villefranche-sur-Mer, Sisteron, and Entrevaux. Citadels based on his principles were built up until World War I. ■

lanes and admire from afar.

The legacy began just after World War I, when painter Gerald Murphy (1888–1964) and his wife, Sara, paid to have the Hôtel du Cap remain open after April (in those days, people *wintered* along the coast). Gerald invited close friend F. Scott Fitzgerald, and soon a whole line of fashionable New Yorkers followed, including Dorothy Parker and Ernest Hemingway. Soon, the trend of sunbathing, plus the parties and drinking that went along with it, took off, and other high-class hotels began opening in the summer months as well.

In the opening paragraph of *Tender is the Night*, Fitzgerald pictured the grand **Hôtel du Cap** (see Travelwise pp. 220–221) as such: "On the pleasant shore of the French Riviera, about halfway between Marseille and the Italian border, stands a large, proud, rose-colored hotel. Deferential palms cool its flushed façade, and before it stretches a short dazzling beach." The hotel is now pale yellow, with gray-green shutters, but it still reigns as the doyenne of venerable hotels, drawing leading authors, film stars, politicians, and aristocrats. If you don't want to pay the price of a room, consider an apéritif at the **Pavillon Eden-Roc,** the hotel's restaurant, with its sweeping white terrace overlooking the sea.

Just down the road, the small **Musée Naval et Napoléonien** has interesting Napoléon memorabilia, including swords, one of his many hats, and military documents, as well as family belongings, including Empress Josephine's tiny tapestry shoes. It is housed in the Tour du Grillon, the remnants of an ancient battery used by Napoléon in 1794.

Also worth seeking out is **Parc Thuret,** in the center of the peninsula, a botanical garden begun in the mid-19th century to acclimatize tropical plants and trees to southern France; the **Phare de la Garoupe,** a lighthouse with a fabulous view; and the neighboring **Sanctuaire de la Garoupe,** a sailor's chapel containing votive offerings to Our Lady of the Sea—sculptured ships, needlepoints of Jesus, and images of healed body parts. ∎

Sanctuaire de la Garoupe on Cap d'Antibes contains a collection of ex-votos, the oldest of which commemorates a surprise Saracen attack on Antibes.

Parc Thuret
- 62 blvd. du Cap, Cap d'Antibes
- 04 97 21 25 03
- Closed Sat.–Sun.

Phare de la Garoupe
- Rte. Phare

Sanctuaire de la Garoupe
- Rte. Phare

Napoléon in Provence

Every year, on the first weekend in March, the town of Antibes hosts a reenactment of one of history's most famous comebacks: the celebrated landfall of Napoléon Bonaparte from Elba, which marked the beginning of the emperor's dramatic return to power and subsequent final defeat at Waterloo.

Europe's leaders thought they had rid themselves of the diminutive Corsican general for good when they exiled him in 1814. Napoléon had wreaked havoc on the continent the previous 20 years. He had fought Austria, Russia, Italy, Spain, Holland, Prussia, Malta, Turkey, Portugal, Egypt, Switzerland, and the British at every turn, using his

superior military skills to lead France to an unprecedented period of European domination. At the peak of his strength, the empire and its associated allies stretched from the Atlantic Ocean to the Black Sea.

So when the 44-year-old French commander was defeated by a large coalition of forces in 1814 and banished into exile to Elba, a small Mediterranean island midway between the French island of Corsica and the Tuscan Italian coast, the continent beyond the Gallic borders breathed a collective sigh of relief.

Not so fast. The terms of the Treaty of Fontainebleau were surprisingly generous to Napoléon. He was given the grandiose title of

Imperial Emperor of Elba, making him more a head of state, albeit of a tiny realm, than a prisoner. Foreign dignitaries visited and were granted audiences with the island's new ruler. It was a far cry from the treatment you might expect of a hated, feared, and vanquished foe. He was even allowed to bring a retinue of nearly a thousand troops to attend to his needs in a style befitting an Imperial Emperor.

It was with these troops that, only nine months after his arrival, Napoléon sailed from Elba and headed unchecked toward the southern French coast, launching his audacious bid to return to power. While he knew he had previously won the hearts and minds of his army while waging his wars of conquest, Napoléon could not know how he would be received in his effort to overthrow King Louis XVIII, who had reestablished the pre-Revolutionary

Bourbon dynastic line in France after Napoléon's demise.

On March 1, 1815, Napoléon and his troops reached the coast of Provence at Golfe-Juan, just outside Antibes, close to where he had ignominiously left France for exile the year before. He was at first greeted with ambivalence, as Provence had long been a stronghold of Bourbon support. While no royalist forces initially helped their former commander, neither did they confront him. Napoléon began a 240-mile (386 km) march north to Grenoble, through the towns of Grasse, Mougins, St.-Vallier-de-Thiey, Castellane, Digne-les-Bains, and others. Along the road, popular sentiment started to turn, as loyalty to Napoléon, especially among peasants and the military, began to outweigh support for the king. On March 7, in a celebrated and pivotal incident outside Grenoble, a regiment of royalist troops sent by Louis confronted their former general at gunpoint. Napoléon stepped forward, opened his overcoat to offer himself as a target, and boldly challenged any soldier who wished to kill their emperor to do so then. En masse the troops rallied to Napoléon's side, adding to his growing tide of support. Napoléon swept north through Grenoble and on toward the capital. Within two weeks, the king had fled, and Napoléon marched triumphantly into Paris to begin his famous Hundred Days, his short return to power that would end in total defeat at the Battle of Waterloo.

Today, many travelers enjoy driving the Route Napoléon, a tourist route that retraces the mountain course that Napoléon and his men followed. Where they found danger, cold, and the imminent risk of arrest or death, today's traveler will instead discover charming towns, some of the world's best wineries, perfumeries, delightful cafés, and comfortable inns. Maps and information can be picked up at the tourist office at Golfe-Juan's Vieux Port.

Much of Napoléon's story in Provence is told at the Musée Naval et Napoléonien, located on Cap d'Antibes, just south of Antibes (see p. 157). — *by Larry Porges* ∎

A 19th-century Artaria print depicts Napoléon's landing at Golfe-Juan in 1815, the first step in his bid to return to power.

Biot

Shop after shop in Biot purveys the town's famous glassware.

BUBBLE-DOTTED GLASSWARE, CALLED *VERRE À BULLES,* IS the craft of choice in this picturesque medieval walled village—evident in the abundance of *verreries* in the surrounding area.

Market day
Tues.

Biot
🅜 137 B2
Visitor information
✉ 46 rue St.-Sébastien
☎ 04 93 65 78 00

It wasn't always so. Before the 1950s, pottery was Biot's main industry. Just before he died, painter Fernand Léger (1881–1955) bought a plot of land south of town, intending to set up a studio and produce ceramic sculptures. His widow, Nadia, organized the **Musée National Fernand Léger** *(chemin du Val du Pôme, tel 04 92 91 50 30, closed* Tues., $) in the space, covering most of the artist's career—from his early Impressionist efforts to his large, bold "machine art" canvases of the 1920s and '30s. In total, there are 348 original pieces, including mosaics, sculptures, oil paintings, and sketches.

Glassmaking arrived in town in 1956, with the establishment of the **Verrerie de Biot** *(chemin des Combes, tel 04 93 65 03 00),* below the old town. Eloi Monod, a potter and engineer who wanted to revive the craft of glassblowing in Provence, opened the factory with one blower and one glassmaker. Today, the complex—half factory, where you can watch men in shorts blow hot globs of glass into delicate shapes, half showroom, where you can buy the end product—has 70 workers. For a fee *($),* you can take a guided tour that explores the history of glassmaking. Several other glassblowers have opened in the area as well.

Tourists flock to the medieval quarter of hilltop Biot, its main **rue St.-Sébastien** lined with glass shops. Of historical interest: The **Musée d'Histoire et de Céramique Biotoises** *(9 rue St.-Sébastien, tel 04 93 65 54 54, closed Mon.–Tues. & Nov., $)* has local costumes and artifacts, including domestic ceramics for which the town was originally known. On the far side of St.-Sébastien, quiet **place des Arcades** is surrounded by Italian loggias, brought by Italians who settled here after the Black Death. Overlooking the square, the village church boasts altarpieces by Louis Bréa and Giovanni Canavesio. ∎

Cagnes-sur-Mer

Cagnes-sur-Mer

⚠ 137 C1

Visitor information

✉ 6 Blvd. Maréchal
Juin

☎ 04 93 20 61 64
www.cagnes-
tourisme.com

TUCKED AMID THE COAST ROAD SPRAWL BETWEEN
Antibes and Nice, Cagnes offers a few gems worth stopping for: the
medieval Haut-de-Cagnes and its castle-museum, and the olive grove
estate where the Impressionist artist Renoir spent his later years.

There are three Cagnes: Cros-de-Cagnes, a seaside development; Cagnes-sur-Mer, an inland commercial area; and Haut-de-Cagnes, the medieval bourg. To visit the pedestrianized old village (the most interesting part), follow signs for Haut-de-Cagnes. You will have to leave your car at the bottom of the hill and walk up the steep, cobbled streets. With its fine Renaissance houses and the small **Église St.-Pierre,** there are plenty of reasons to stop and catch your breath.

At the top of the hill, the Grimaldis of Monaco built the Château Grimaldi—now the **Château Musée** (*place Grimaldi, tel 04 92 02 47 30, closed Tues. & 3 weeks Nov., $*)—as a fortress-prison when they became lords of the area in 1309. In the early 1600s, Jean-Henri Grimaldi transformed the edifice into a palace. He commissioned Genoese artists to paint the interior; their efforts include the "Fall of Phaethon" in the main hall. The château today houses eclectic displays, including one devoted to olive culture and another to modern Mediterranean art. Another room has an unusual collection of portraits of 1930s chanteuse Susy Solidor—more than 40 works by the likes of Jean Cocteau and Raoul Dufy.

Pierre-Auguste Renoir moved to Cagnes in 1903 for relief from his arthritis. He bought an olive grove to the east of town, known as Les Collettes, where he built a house and studio and worked until his death in 1919. Here he painted some of his most famous works, including "Washerwomen at Cagnes" and "The Farm at Les Collettes." The **Musée Renoir** (*19 chemin des Colettes, tel 04 93 20 61 07, closed Tues. & mid-Oct.–early Nov., $*) remains virtually as Renoir left it, including some of his paintings on the walls and everyday items lying about—among them his painter's coat and wheelchair. ∎

The Château Musée—the Grimaldi family's home until the French Revolution—features a two-story courtyard.

More places to visit in Cannes & around

GORGES-SUR-LOUP

In the lofty hinterlands of Grasse and St.-Paul-de-Vence, the rugged, waterfall-strewn Gorges-sur-Loup is a hiker's paradise. The D2210 delves into the heart of this cliff-shadowed region, passing a handful of villages along the way. In **Le-Bar-sur-Loup,** ancient houses surround the former château of the lords of Bar. The Gothic **church of St.-Jacques** is lovely, but most people come to see the famous painting "Danse Macabre," the "Dance of Death," based on a 15th-century town legend about citizens who held a party during Lent and dropped dead. Nearby **Pont-du-Loup** is the home of **Confiserie Florian** (tel 04 93 59 32 91), the renowned sweets kitchen, with free samples offered at tour's end. The golden-stoned village of **Tourrettes-sur-Loup,** farther east, is famous for its violets, celebrated with the Fête des Violettes every March. 🅰 137 B2

ÎLES DES LÉRINS

In the fifth century, the monk St.- Honorat and seven of his disciples founded an abbey on the island that bears his name today, just offshore of Cannes. The abbey of Lérins became famous throughout the Western world, and pilgrims have visited its seven chapels since medieval times (the present abbey dates from the 19th century). A group of Cistercian monks lives there now. Honorat's sister established a convent on a neighboring island, today's **Île Ste.-Marguerite,** which is most famous for its 17th-century prisoner, the Man in the Iron Mask (see sidebar p. 141). The fort where he was held now contains the **Musée de la Mer** (tel 04 93 43 18 17, closed Mon. & 3 weeks Jan., $), which details the fort's history and shipwrecks. You can also visit the masked man's cell. 🅰 137 B1 ✉ 15-min. boat ride from Cannes's Vieux Port; buy tickets from concessionaire at the end of quai Laubeuf.

JUAN-LES-PINS

To the west of Cap d'Antibes, Juan-les-Pins first came to life in the 1920s, when Americans brought the fun-loving way of life … and jazz. When the Jazz Festival of Juan-les-Pins was launched in 1960, all the big names were here: Louis Armstrong, Ella Fitzgerald, Duke Ellington, Sarah Vaughan, Ray Charles. The festival is still held every July. The rest of the time, Juan-les-Pins retains the hedonistic aura of its early days, coming alive at night, every night, all night long, with restaurants and nightclubs galore. 🅰 137 B1 **Office de Tourisme** ✉ 51 blvd. Guillaumont ☎ 04 97 23 11 10 ∎

Tourettes-sur-Loup, city of violets, charms with medieval ambiance in its narrow streets.

Slow-moving, sultry, with an Italian accent, this sun-kissed niche is anchored by Nice, Monaco, and Menton. Chic beach resorts, a prince's palace, and height-defying hill towns are just some of its charms.

Côte d'Azur: Nice to Menton

Changing of the guard at Monaco's palace

Surf's up in Nice, where beaches are pebbly and warm waters beckon

Côte d'Azur: Nice to Menton

IN FAR SOUTHEASTERN PROVENCE, THE SOUTHERN REACHES OF THE ALPS crowd down to the sea, creating a spectacular backdrop for Nice, Monaco, and Menton. Warm blue waters make for lazy days by the seashore, while a collection of world-class museums showcase Henri Matisse, Marc Chagall, Raoul Dufy, and other postimpressionists who were seduced by the region's beauty. You will be, too.

France's fifth largest city, Nice is a pastel showcase of Italianate architecture. The Promenade des Anglais—a beachfront esplanade dating from 19th-century British who enjoyed their daily constitutional with sea breezes—is now dominated by runners, bikers, in-line skaters, and walkers. Mazelike streets crisscross Vieux Nice, ideal for an afternoon stroll, while several art museums feature a strong collection of naïf, postimpressionist, and modern art. The Cathédrale Orthodoxe Russe St.-Nicolas is a surprise; the ornate, onion-domed church represents the large Russian population that flocked here before the Russian Revolution.

Eastward, three roads cutting across formidable limestone cliffs—called the three corniches—present different-level perspectives over the mountains and sea. The lower coast road accesses several beach resorts, including Cap-Ferrat, where the Musée-Villa Ephrussi de Rothschild

provides a glimpse into belle époque opulence. The medieval hilltop town of Èze, on the middle road, is

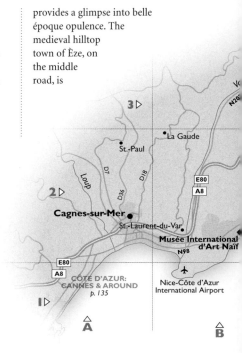

perfectly preserved (and packed with tourists); the climb to the ruins of a hilltop château, now a cactus garden, promises magnificent sea views. The upper road, of course, provides the most glorious panoramas.

On the corniches' other side awaits Monaco, the royal residence of the Grimaldi family since the 13th century. You can visit the magnificent palace when Prince Albert is away, and, on a more melancholic note, stop by the flower-strewn tomb of Princess Grace. Monte-Carlo is the principality's glittery capital, with its world-famous casino dealing in millions of euros a day.

Languorous Menton is said to enjoy the sunniest weather of all Riviera resorts—316 days a year. It's famous for its gardens, lemons, and the artistic legacy of Jean Cocteau. Italy's proximity (just a mile away) is evident in the local accent, Italianate architecture, and especially in the tomato- and garlic-based cuisine.

In surrounding hills, vertiginous roads zigzag to ancient hill towns—Peille, Ste.-Agnès, Coaraze, Peillon, to name a few—virtually untouched by modern day and each one offering dizzying vistas. ■

Renaissance man

Eminently associated with the Côte d'Azur, surrealist film-maker, playwright, writer, actor, set designer, and artist Jean Cocteau (1889–1963) shone for his versatility and brilliance. He wrote volumes of poems (*Aladdin's Lamp*), criticisms (*Le Rappel à l'Ordre*), psychological novels (*Thomas l'Imposter, Les Enfants Terribles*), plays (*La Voix Humaine*), and films (*Le Sang d'un Poète, La Belle et la Bête, Orphée, Le Testament d'Orphée*). He created pebble mosaics, tapestries, pastel drawings, and, in his 70s, he painted frescos in the town hall of Menton and in the chapel of St.-Pierre at Villefranche-sur-Mer. Cocteau insisted that he was primarily a poet and that all his work was poetry—indeed, it is. ■

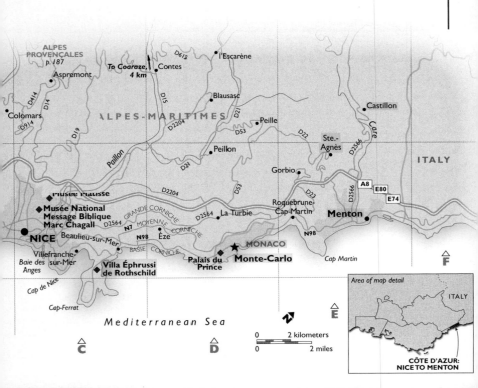

Nice's grand old hotels edge the Baie des Anges.

Nice

BENEATH A BRILLIANT MEDITERRANEAN SUN, NICE BASKS in a long Italian heritage: fashionable and cosmopolitan yet relaxed. The translucent blue-green Baie des Anges washes its southern edge—the only downfall being pebbly beaches. But Nice is also France's fifth largest city, offering a lineup of world-class museums and other cultural sites. And that's the debate—go to the beach, or museums? Hopefully, you'll have time to do both.

Market days
Tues.–Sun.
Flower market at
Cours Saleya

Nice
 165 C1
Visitor information
 5 promenade des Anglais
 08 92 70 74 07
www.nicetourisme.com

Nice became a part of France only in 1860, under the Treaty of Turin, heretofore falling under the reign of the counts of Savoy. The culture is sufficiently suffused with Italian influence—its architecture, cuisine (*pissaladière* and *pistou*, for instance), even language (a regional dialect called Nissart). But Nice's

history also owes something to the British, who discovered the city as a warm winter wonderland in the late 1700s. In 1822 they subsidized a seafront esplanade, the beloved Promenade des Anglais. Queen Victoria stayed in Nice later that century (in the Cimiez Quarter), initiating a long line of aristocrats

the area north and west of place Masséna, including the pedestrian streets of rue de France and rue Masséna. To the east, huddled against the Colline du Château, is Vieux Nice (Old Nice), delineated on its other sides by boulevard Jean-Jaurès and quai des États-Unis. The Promenade des Anglais heads west along the beachfront to the airport, 3.7 miles (6 km) away. North of the center is the wealthy neighborhood of Cimiez.

VILLE MODERNE & PROMENADE DES ANGLAIS

The *ville moderne* (modern town), dating from the 18th and 19th centuries, begins at the River Paillon in the eastern part of the city—though you won't see the river, since its dry bed is buried for most of its length and covered with gardens and boulevards. The modern town's focal points are place Masséna and **Jardins Albert 1er.**

Shaded by palms, the Promenade des Anglais arcs along the seafront, with belle époque villas and casinos on one side, the cobalt sea on the other. Once the place for afternoon constitutionals, the promenade is now taken over by runners, Rollerbladers, and walkers, as well as bench sitters, who stare complacently out to sea.

Among the promenade's most famous landmarks is the **Hôtel Negresco,** built between 1906 and 1912 for the Romanian Henri Negresco in beautiful belle époque style. Check out the elegant Salon Louis XIV and the Salon Royal. The other famous building is the art deco **Palais de la Méditerranée,** once Nice's most famous casino. Built by American millionaire Frank Jay Gould in 1929, it was renovated in 2004 to become a luxury hotel complex.

(continued on p. 170)

who came and built elaborate villas. Among the masses who followed were writers and artists enraptured by the gorgeous setting: Dumas, Nietzsche, Apollinaire, Flaubert, Hugo, Georges Sand, Stendhal, Matisse, and the list goes on.

In recent times, Nice has been plagued with a deserved reputation for crime and corruption—largely due to the exploits of Jacques Médécin, the city's mayor from 1966 to 1990. Considered a virtual dictator by some, he escaped to Uruguay to avoid charges of corruption and fraud but later served a prison term in France. Problems are still present in the 21st century, but Nice's undeniable charms will overcome and seduce you.

The modern city center occupies

Hôtel Negresco
✉ 37 promenade des Anglais
☎ 04 93 16 64 00
www.hotel-negresco-nice.com

Palais de la Méditerranée
✉ 13–17 promenade des Anglais
☎ 04 92 14 77 00
www.lepalaisdela mediterranee.com

Musée International d'Art Naïf A. Jakovsky
✉ Château Ste.-Hélène, ave. de Fabron
☎ 04 93 71 78 33
🕐 Closed Tues.
💲 $

Musée des Beaux-Arts
✉ 33 ave. des Baumettes
☎ 04 92 15 28 28
🕐 Closed Mon.
💲 $

Cathédrale Orthodoxe Russe St.-Nicholas (Église Russe)
✉ Blvd. du Tzarevitch
☎ 04 93 96 88 02
💲 $

Museum discounts

The Musées de Nice offer a 7-day pass for 6 euros, which includes all municipal museums.

Musée Masséna

✉ 65 rue de France
☎ 04 93 91 19 10

Musée d'Art Moderne et d'Art Contemporain (MAMAC)

✉ Promenade des Arts
☎ 04 97 13 42 01
www.mamac-nice.org
🕐 Closed Mon.
💲 $

Matisse's "Fleurs et Fruits" (1953)

(continued from p. 167)

Nearly all the beaches stretch along the sweep of bay between Rauba Capeu and the airport; 15 or so are private (you must be either a hotel guest or pay—about 15 euros for the lounger, 4 additional for a parasol), separated by public beaches in between (these get crowded—show up early. The **Plage Publique de Beau Rivage** is one of the better ones). You can walk along the bay's length (including the private beaches if you stay close to the sea.

THE MUSEUMS

In the west of town, the **Musée International d'Art Naïf A. Jakovsky** presents an international collection of folk art in the lovely pink villa once belonging to parfumier Réné Coty. The collection traces the evolution of primitive painting from the 18th century to the present. French artists include André Bauchant (1873–1958) and Pierre Bonnier (considered the French Grandma Moses).

Hidden away in an elegant neighborhood just east, the **Musée des Beaux-Arts** is housed in another sumptuous belle époque villa, built in 1878 for a Ukrainian princess. The collection, spanning a range of styles from the 15th to 20th centuries, began with the works given to Nice in 1860 by Napoléon III. The most celebrated classical paintings are by members of the van Loo family, including Carle van Loo's enormous "Thésée, Vainqueur du Taureau de Marathon," from the 18th century. The Impressionists, postimpressionists, Nabis, and fauves are well represented, the most important of which are Felix Ziem, Raoul Dufy (a whole roomful, including the locally set "Le Mai à Nice" and "Le Casino de la Jetée–Promenade de Nice"), and Jules Chéret (1836–1932), the creator of modern poster art.

North of here, on the other side of the A7, you are transported to imperial Russia at the **Cathédrale Orthodoxe Russe St.-Nicholas.** Tsar Nicolas II built this ornate edifice between 1903 and 1912 in memory of a young tsarevitch who died in town in 1865. Evoking early 17th-century style, the

grandiose church is topped by six sparkling onion domes, its interior filled with carvings, icons, frescoes, and a wonderful iconostasis. It served many exiled Russians who fled to Nice after the Revolution.

Poised about midway along the Promenade des Anglais, the recently renovated **Musée Masséna** is housed in the 1898 Italian-style Palais Masséna. The museum features a locally accented collection of furniture, paintings, religious art, and ceramics. Its highlights include works by Nice's primitive painters and Napoléon's coronation robe and a copy of his death mask.

In the modern town, you come to the ultramodern **Musée d'Art Moderne et d'Art Contemporain** (MAMAC), showcasing European and American art from the 1960s on. The building comprises four marble-coated towers linked by steel walkways, all enclosed in glass. All the big names are here, including Andy Warhol and Roy Lichtenstein. An entire section is devoted to Nice-born Yves

Belle époque beauties

Wedding-cake mansions. Pastel-frosted villas. Garlanded palaces: The belle époque style flourished in Nice at the turn of the 20th century, when colossal classical buildings were smothered with profusions of carved garlands, flowers, and shields. Here are some of Nice's most beautiful examples:

Conservatoire de la Musique (24 blvd. de Cimiez)
Hôtel Excelsior Régina (71 ave. Régina)
Hôtel Negresco (37 promenade des Anglais)
L'Alhambra (46 blvd. de Cimiez)
Musée des Beaux-Arts (33 ave. des Baumettes)
Villa Raphaeli-Surany (35 blvd. de Cimiez) ∎

The Hôtel Negresco is one of Nice's few remaining turn-of-the-20th-century grandes dames.

Musée Paleontologie Humaine de Terra Amata
✉ 25 blvd. Carnot
☎ 04 93 55 59 93
⊕ Closed Mon. & 1st 2 weeks in Sept.
$ $

Musée National Message Biblique Marc Chagall
▲ 165 C2
✉ Ave. du Dr. Menard
☎ 04 93 53 87 20
www.musee-chagall.fr
⊕ Closed Tues.
$ $$

Musée Archéologique

✉ 160 ave. des Arènes de Cimiez

☎ 04 93 81 59 57

🕐 Museum & ruins: Closed Tues.

💲 $

Musée Matisse

🅰 165 C2

✉ 164 ave. des Arènes de Cimiez

✉ 04 93 81 08 08

www.musee-matisse-nice.org

🕐 Closed Tues.

💲 $

Boat tours

One-hour coastal boat tours depart from Nice's quai Lunel to round exquisite satellite bays of Cap de Nice, Villefranche-sur-Mer, and Cap Ferrat before cruising Nice's Baie des Anges (Trans Côte d'Azur, tel 04 92 00 42 30. www.trans-cote-azur.com)

Opposite: The first painting in Marc Chagall's Biblical Message Cycle, "Création de l'Homme," shows an angel of God carrying a sleeping Adam toward Earth. Painted in 1956–1958, it hangs in Nice's Musée National Message Biblique.

Klein (1928–1992), whose two major works—"Garden of Eden" and "Wall of Fire"—can be seen on the rooftop terraces.

A short walk east of the port, the **Musée Paleontologie Humaine de Terra Amata,** built over a site where mammoth hunters camped 400,000 years ago, gives a look at Europe's earliest inhabitants.

Jumping north of Vieux Nice, you'll come to one of Nice's major draws, the **Musée National Message Biblique Marc Chagall.** The small, modern museum centers on Chagall's Biblical Message Cycle, a collection of 17 enormous paintings of biblical inspiration and composing the largest public collection of the Russian artist's works. In the main gallery, 12 large paintings painted between 1954 and 1967 illustrate scenes from the first two books of the Old Testament, Genesis and Exodus. They are simply magical with their whimsical, colorful depictions of flowers, goats, and floating couples. A smaller room houses five paintings in the "Song of Songs" series, based on another Old Testament book. Graceful and lyrical in their composition, they are all done in shades of red that are somehow peaceful, not jarring.

Chagall's large mosaic depicting the prophet Elijah in his chariot of fire is displayed over a fountain, and preparatory sketches are also on display. Poke your head into the auditorium, where the artist's stained-glass windows depict the creation of the world.

If you follow boulevard de Cimiez north up into the Cimiez Quarter—the once fashionable hill-top neighborhood for British holidaymakers—you'll come to the **Musée Archéologique,** the ruins of the ancient city of Cemenelum, the Roman capital of the Alpes-Maritime, dating from A.D. 69. A haphazard display of vases, sarcophagi, and glassware dug up at the site are found in the museum, while a short path outside winds through the ruins—which include an amphitheater and public baths.

But the reason to make the trek this far north is the fabulous **Musée Matisse,** housed in a 17th-century, poppy red villa. Drawn by the scenery, as well as for health reasons and to be near his friends (Picasso, Renoir, and Bonnard lived nearby), Matisse began living in Nice year-round in 1921 and died here in 1954. The museum's collection of paintings, gouache cutouts, drawings, bronze sculptures, oil paintings, engravings, and illustrated books spans the artist's long career. The visit begins with his dark and somber still lifes, progressing through his Impressionist and fauvist attempts. Well-known pieces include "Fenêtre à Tahiti" (1935–1936) and "Nymphe dans la Forêt" (1935–1943), as well as the works painted in Nice, including "Tempête à Nice" (1919) and "Odalisque au Coffret Rouge" (1926). The visit then launches into into his exuberant, colorful paper cutouts *(gouaches découpées),* a genre he began in 1950 at age 80. Among the famous examples are the Blue Nude series, including "Blue Nude IV" (1952), and the multihued "Danseuse Créole" (1950). In the modern atrium downstairs is the pièce de résistance: the playful "Fleurs et Fruits" (1953), Matisse's largest masterpiece in France (13.5 feet by 28.5 feet/4.1 m x 8.7 m) and his last work before his death.

Adding a personal touch, the museum also displays everyday objects that inspired Matisse—Chinese vases, plates, pitchers, and bold-printed fabrics that take on exuberant life in his paintings. ∎

Creating paradise

Breeze-riffled palms and burgeoning lemon trees, curtains of bougainvillea and flocks of hibiscus, bloom-studded succulents and cactuses, all set against a dazzling blue sea—this magical land could only be the Côte d'Azur, muse of artists and writers, antidote for cold northern winters. But it wasn't always so.

In the early 1800s, the dry countryside around Cannes harbored onions, chickpeas, and olives—not very attractive to the wealthy English, who, adoring the area's temperate climate, spent their winters here. Used to luxuriant gardens, they rushed to surround their opulent villas with exotic plants, from palms to cactuses to avocados. As the Côte d'Azur became fashionable, a profusion of flora spread across its parched landscape, bit by bit transforming into the lavish paradise it is today. Glamorous and eclectic, the gardens they created are everywhere—from little residential plots to city plantings to private collections, some of which can be visited by appointment. Indeed, there are few places in the world that possess such beautiful gardens as the Côte d'Azur. Here are some of the best.

JARDIN EXOTIQUE, ÈZE

The Jardin Exotique's beautiful cactus garden crowns the picturesque old hilltop village of Èze, set among vestiges of the ancient castle. Sea views extend out over red-tiled roofs. ✉ rue du Château ☎ 04 93 41 10 30 💲 $$

HYÈRES'S GARDENS

Overlooking the red-tile-roofed old town, the **Jardin Provençal** unites two fabulous gardens. Packed with rare plants, brightly flowered **Parc Ste.-Claire** surrounds the 19th-century castle where American novelist Edith Wharton resided (and died) between 1927 and 1937. Cobbled paths wander up the hill to **Parc St.-Bernard,** specializing in Mediterranean plants (including 20 varieties of rosemary, 15 of phlomis, and 25 different cistus). At the top of the park, above montée de Noailles, is the **Villa Noailles,** a cubist mansion enclosed within part of the old citadel. It was designed in 1923 by Robert Mallet-Stevens for the Vicomte Charles de Noailles, a patron of modern art. It's most famous for its concrete-and-glass cubist triangle garden by Gabriel Guevrekian. The villa plays host to temporary contemporary art shows (Wed.–Fri. p.m. April–Oct.). Be sure to walk to the west of the park and farther up the hill to the ivy-twisted castle remains, offering stunning views out to the Îles d'Hyères. **Office de Tourisme d'Hyères** ✉ 3 ave. Ambroise Thomas ☎ 04 94 01 84 50, www.ot-hyeres.fr

MENTON'S GARDENS

Menton's splendid microclimate nurtures an abundance of subtropical Edens. The **Jardin Botanique Exotique du Val Rahmeh** (ave. de St.-Jacques, Garavan, tel 04 93 35 86 72, closed Tues. Oct.–March, $$) was founded in the late 19th century by Lord Radcliffe, governor of Malta. A pebbly path takes you through a variety of tropical and subtropical plantings collected from as far away as the Himalayas and New Caledonia. Guided visits are offered. Nearby, the Valencia-style **Jardin Fontana Rosa** (ave. Blasco Ibañez, $$) is the 1920s creation of Spanish novelist Vicente Blasco Ibañez. It is full of roses, citrus trees, and water, as well as ceramic figures evoking great literary figures such as Cervantes and Victor Hugo. The **Jardin de Maria Serena** (Promenade Reine Astrid, Garavan, tel 04 92 10 97 10, guided visits Tues. 10 a.m., $$) is famed for its palm trees. The garden surrounds the Second Empire–style Villa Maria Serena, designed by Charles Garnier in 1866. North of town, the **Jardins des Colombières** (372 rte. de Super Garavan, tel 04 92 10 97 10, closed Sept.–June, $$), designed between 1918 and 1927, is painter and garden-designer Ferdinand Bac's last and best known garden. It showcases a series of little gardens, each inspired by a personality of Greek mythology.

VILLA THURET, CAP D'ANTIBES

The famous botanical gardens of Villa Thuret is where, in 1865, G. Thuret established a botanical testing site with the aim of introducing more varied flora to the Riviera. Today,

some 3,000 plant species representing the Riviera's extreme variety of microclimates and soil types flourish in this strolling wonderland, with 200 new species introduced every year. ✉ 62 blvd. du Cap, Cap d'Antibes ☎ 04 97 21 25 03 🕓 Closed Sat.–Sun. See also Monaco's Jardin Exotique (see p. 181) and Villa Ephrussi de Rothschild (see p. 186). ■

Cactuses, such as these at Monaco's Jardin Exotique, are among the hardy plant choices at the disposal of Riviera gardeners.

The Three Corniches

Villefranche-sur-Mer

165 C2

Visitor information

✉ Place François-Binon

☎ 04 93 01 73 68

A GIANT WALL OF LIMESTONE CLIFFS TOWERS ABOVE THE blue sea between Nice and Menton, making access between the two towns historically difficult. Over the centuries, three different roads—each higher than the next—have been cut into the rock to transport people back and forth. The Basse Corniche, also known as the Corniche Inférieure, follows the coastline's contours, accessing a string of seaside resorts; the Moyenne Corniche, which has featured in many Hollywood films, twists through tunnels and along dramatic cliff edges; and, higher still, the Grande Corniche offers the grandest views of all. Each road offers a selection of sights to see—be aware that you can't necessarily reach one from the other.

La Turbie's Trophée des Alpes

BASSE CORNICHE (N98)

Built in the 1860s to bring gamblers to the new Monte-Carlo casino, the Basse Corniche opened up once isolated fishing villages that have since blossomed into seaside resorts (explaining the common lines of traffic along the way). Leaving Nice on the N98, you almost immediately come to **Villefranche-sur-Mer,** an immaculately maintained village stacked up the hillside. It's always been a hardworking fishing town, though these days you'll see everything from yachts to battleships in its deepwater harbor. In town, seek out the **Chapelle de St.-Pierre** on the waterfront, a tiny chapel whose thick walls and barrel vaults were decorated in 1957 by Jean Cocteau (see sidebar p. 165). The poet, novelist, playwright, filmmaker, and painter spent part of his childhood in Villefranche, and he dedicated this work to the fishermen. Clean, free-flowing black lines, accented with pastel washes, depict, to the left, "Homage to the Women of Villefranche" and, on the right, "Homage to the Gypsies" (of Les Stes.-Maries-de-la-Mer). The remaining images, in the nave and apse, represent scenes from St. Peter's life. In 1560 the dukes of Savoy built the **Citadelle St.-Elme** on the hill overlooking the harbor. Today the fort houses the **Musée Volti**, which displays sculpture and modern art.

Just beyond Villefranche is **Cap-Ferrat,** a flowery peninsula studded with belle époque estates. Most mansions are hidden behind shrubbery and fences, but there's one that you can visit (for a price)—the sumptuous **Villa Ephrussi de Rothschild** (see p. 186).

In the neighboring quiet resort town of **Beaulieu-sur-Mer,** the **Villa Kerylos** (*impasse Gustave Eiffel, tel 04 93 76 44 09, $$*) offers an unexpected peek into the lifestyle of ancient well-to-do Greeks. German archaeologist Théodore Reinach built this circa-second-century B.C. estate in 1902–1908 according to specific historical references. An audioguide takes you through every room, providing historical details.

Beyond Beaulieu, you are treated to spectacular vistas before easing into **Monaco** (see pp. 178–182).

MOYENNE CORNICHE (N7)

This spectacular drive is reward enough, with its balcony views over cliff and sea. Midpoint you come to the medieval hilltop village of **Èze.** Its nickname, Eagle's Nest, accurately describes its dizzying roost

1,550 feet (472 m) directly above the sea. The views are stupendous—a fact not lost on ancient Phoenicians, Romans, Ligurians, and Saracens, all of whom prized the perch as a lookout. With such altitude, it's hard to believe that Èze was historically a fishing village, whose poor fishermen had quite a trek after a day's work. While today's town caters mostly to tourists with its bevy of galleries and souvenir shops, the small church of Èze, rebuilt with a classical facade and two-story tower between 1764 and 1771, is worth a stop. Steep, shop-filled lanes climb up to the **Jardin Exotique,** a cactus and succulent garden planted among the old castle ruins.

GRANDE CORNICHE (D2564)

The stunning Grande Corniche, capping the cliff tops 1,600 feet (487 m) above the sea, originally was the Romans' Via Aurelia, used to conquer the west. In the town of **La Turbie,** you can't miss the **Trophée des Alpes** (Trophy of the Alps; *18 ave. Albert 1er, tel 04 93 41 20 84, closed Mon., $$*), the domineering monument denoting Augustus' victory in 13 B.C. over 44 Ligurian tribes. Built in 6 and 5 B.C., it was restored between 1929 and 1933. ∎

Picturesque Villefranche-sur-Mer

Chapelle de St.-Pierre-des-Pêcheurs

- ✉ Place Pollonais, Villefranche-sur-Mer
- ☎ 04 93 76 90 70
- 🕐 Closed Mon. & mid-Nov.–mid-Dec.
- 💲 $

Musée Volti

- ✉ Citadelle, ave. Sadi Carnot, Villefranche-sur-Mer
- ☎ 04 93 76 33 33
- 🕐 Closed Tues.

Èze

- 🗺 165 D2
- **Visitor information**
- ✉ Office de Tourisme, place Général de Gaulle
- ☎ 04 93 41 26 00

Jardin Exotique

- ✉ Rue du Château, Èze
- ☎ 04 93 41 10 30
- 💲 $$

Monaco & Monte-Carlo

EBULLIENT WITH LEGENDARY GLAMOUR AND GLITZ,
Monaco delivers with a fairy-tale castle perched high atop Le
Rocher—the Rock. But Monaco is also a 21st-century, forward-thinking place, thanks to the late Prince Rainier III who, during his reign
from 1949 to 2005, fashioned his principality into a dynamic, glittering, high-rise-filled enclave. Its belle époque Monte-Carlo Casino is
the fabled venue where fortunes are won and lost.

Monaco
 165 D2

Visitor information
✉ 2a blvd. des
Moulins, Monte-Carlo
☎ 92 16 61 16
www.monaco-
tourisme.com

On Jan. 8, 1297, Francesco Grimaldi,
dressed as a monk, overpowered the
guards of the Genoan fortress built
on the Rock of Monaco. He was
the first Grimaldi to reign over
Monaco, the beginning of the
world's oldest ruling monarchy.
Charles VIII, king of France, first
recognized Monégasque independence in 1489. During the French

Revolution, the royal family was
arrested and imprisoned, but later
released. The Grimaldi family
returned to the throne under the
1814 Treaty of Paris.

Monaco's absolute monarchy
was replaced in 1911 by a constitution, which was reformed by Prince
Rainier in 1962. Francesco's descendent, Prince Rainier expanded the

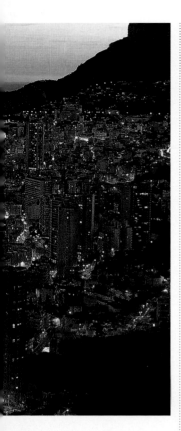

size of the municipality by 20 percent. Upon his death in 2005, his son, Albert II, ascended to the throne as the new sovereign and seems to have effectively settled into his new role.

Banking and industry are important in Monaco, but tourism has been the most obvious source of foreign revenue since the 1800s, when a railway from Nice first brought people to the newly built casino, opera house, and expensive villas that have turned the state into a playland for the rich.

Philadelphian film star Grace Kelly came to Monaco in 1954 to film *To Catch a Thief* and ended up capturing Prince Rainier's heart. Their storybook romance ended tragically in 1982 with her death in a car accident.

Monaco is tiny—less than a mile (2 km) square. Only 5,000 of its 30,000 residents are Monégasque citizens, with the rest being French, Italians, and others who have come for fun, sun, and tax breaks.

Built around the steep sides of the yacht-filled Port de Monaco, Monaco is divided into three main *quartiers:* Monaco-Ville, the ancient quarter atop the 197-foot-high (60 m) cliff along the port's south side, where most of the sights are found; Monte-Carlo, with its casino and annual Grand Prix, on the port's north side; and Fontvieille, the residential and commercial area southwest of Monaco-Ville.

VISITING MONACO

Monaco-Ville possesses a mix of royal glamour and medieval charm. You enter via the steep **Rampe Major,** approaching the palace square past the statue of Francesco Grimaldi, furtive and mysterious in his cloak. Beyond looms the **Palais du Prince,** Prince Albert's royal residence (Princesses Caroline and Stéphanie live down the street). Built on the site of a 13th-century Genoese fortress, the palace has been refined over the centuries, metamorphosing from a skeletal fortress into an elegant residence with a Renaissance facade. Out front a carabineer—palace guard—stands frozen in his immaculate red-and-white uniform; changing of the guard takes place daily at 11:55 a.m.

Your ticket permits entrance into 15 rooms of **Les Grands Appartements** (State Apartments), with an audioguide narrating detailed historical information on the principality and the royal family and highlighting various objets d'art and Grimaldi portraits. First stop is the **Courtyard of Honor,** in Italian Renaissance style. The horseshoe staircase, its balustrades decorated with three million stones

Calling Monaco
When calling Monaco, the international prefix 00 377 must be dialed, followed by the 8-digit number.

Palais du Prince
◩ 165 D2
✉ Place du Palais
☎ 93 25 18 31
www.palais.mc
🕐 Open only when the prince is not home, usually June–mid-Oct.
💲 $$ (combined ticket with Napoléon museum: $$)

Musée Collections des Souvenirs Napoléoniens et des Archives Historiques du Palais
✉ Place du Palais
☎ 93 25 18 31
www.palais.mc
🕐 Closed Nov.–May
💲 $ (combined ticket with palace: $$)

Cathédrale de Monaco
✉ 4 rue Colonel, Bellando de Castro
☎ 93 25 01 04

**Musée
Océanographique**

Ave. St.-Martin

93 15 36 00

www.oceano.mc

$$$

**Musée des
Timbres et des
Monnaies**

Terrasses de
Fontvieille

93 15 41 50

$

**Collections des
Voitures
Anciennes**

Terrasses de
Fontvieille

92 05 28 56

www.palais.mc

$$

of Carrara marble in geometric patterns, is where the head of state addresses Monégasques during important state matters. You are taken through the **Gallery of Mirrors,** used as an antechamber for guests awaiting reception by the royal family. The gold-and-white hallway, adorned with crystal-drop chandeliers and marble floor mosaics, is filled with Ming vases, Japanese cups, busts of Prince Charles III, and other treasures.

The palace's highlight is the **Throne Room,** the setting for official Monégasque court events since the 1500s. This is also the room where, in 1956, the civil marriage between Prince Rainier III and Grace Patricia Kelly was celebrated by the prime minister. Looking quintessentially regal with its red-damask walls alternating with gilt wood panels, its centerpiece is the lacquered gilt throne in Empire style, crowned by a canopy

of Vienna velvet, on which the prince rests his crown. In one corner you can't ignore the 1982 portrait of the glowing royal family dressed in casual clothes and broad smiles, painted just months before Princess Grace's fatal car crash.

The palace's east wing houses the **Musée Collections des Souvenirs Napoléoniens et des Archives Historiques du Palais.** This is Prince Louis II's (Albert's great grandfather) private collection of objects relating to Napoléon: guns, flags, clothing snippets (including a swatch from a cloak he wore the day he was crowned emperor by Pope Pius VII at Notre-Dame in Paris), medals, and heraldic devices. An audio-guide provides details on some of the more interesting pieces, including the tricolor sash worn by General Bonaparte in 1796.

From the palace, signs lead to the **cathedral,** rebuilt in 1878 using white stone from La Turbie.

Centuries of Grimaldis are buried here, including Princess Grace (her flower-strewn tomb is the last one as you circle the altar counterclockwise)—marked plainly with the words "Gratia Patricia, MCMLXXXII." Of particular interest are the circa 1500 retable to the right of the transept, painted by Louis Bréa, and the episcopal throne in white Carrara marble.

The world-renowned **Musée Océanographique,** its grandiose facade rising from a towering cliff, was founded in 1910 by Prince Albert I, and underwater-explorer Jacques Cousteau ran it for years. The rarest fish of the seven seas swim in 90 tanks, and there are a display of living coral and a shark lagoon.

FONTVIEILLE

In Fontvieille, the neighborhood to the southwest of Le Rocher, three museums are found on one level of the Centre Commercial (a shopping center): the **Musée des Timbres et des Monnaies** (Museum of Stamps and Coins), covering four centuries of Monégasque minting; **Collections des Voitures Anciennes** (Collection of Antique Cars), Prince Rainier's antique car collection, including the 1956 Rolls-Royce Silver Cloud that carried the prince and princess on their wedding day; and the **Musée Naval** (Naval Museum), Prince Rainier's scale models of famous boats and ships.

Some 7,000 varieties of cactuses and succulents are found at the **Jardin Exotique,** built into the side of a rock farther up the hill. Your ticket also gets you into a cave complex, full of stalagmites and stalactites, and the **Musée d'Anthropologie Préhistorique** (Museum of Prehistoric Anthropology). The latter looks at the history of the human race, including the inhabitants that settled in the Monaco area some million years ago.

Musée Naval
✉ Terrasses de Fontvieille
☎ 92 05 28 48
$ $

Jardin Exotique
✉ Blvd. du Jardin Exotique
☎ 93 15 29 80
$ $$ (includes anthropological museum)

Nijinsky, Stravinsky, Picasso, and Cocteau are among the generations of patrons who have sat among princes and dukes in the Hôtel de Paris's ornate café.

Casino de Monte-Carlo

✉ Place du Casino

☎ 92 16 20 00

www.casino-monte-carlo.com

🕐 Salons Européens: noon–late daily, slot machines 2 p.m.–late daily; Salons Privés: 4 p.m.–late daily Club Anglais: 10 p.m.–late daily

💲 Entrance to Salons Européens: $$$ Entrance to Salons Privés & Club Anglais: $$$$$

The Casino de Monte-Carlo, known as the "cathedral of hell" in its 19th-century heyday

MONTE-CARLO

Its reputation for flamboyant glamour and opulence preceding it, Europe's most fabled casino needs no introduction. It's named for Prince Charles III, who opened the casino in 1865 to raise much-needed revenue for the principality. His plan worked—"Mount Charles" was so successful that five years after the opening, taxation was abolished (and still is).

The first gaming tables were housed in various venues until 1878, when architect Charles Garnier, of Paris Opéra fame, designed the present belle époque beauty, with its green copper cupolas, rococo turrets, and gold chandeliers. The sumptuous opera house was part of his plan as well.

The casino's facade appears imposing, but anyone can wander its ornate entrance hall. To the right as you enter are public slot machines. Ahead is the candelabra-lit two-story atrium entrance hall, paved in marble and ringed with a forest of ionic columns.

One door leads into the **Salle Garnier,** the opera house, with its luxurious red-and-gold decor accented with bas-reliefs, frescoes, and sculptures. Top-notch international performances of opera, ballet, and concerts have been staged here for more than a century.

The gaming halls are just as opulent, comprising a succession of rococo rooms with mirrors, frescoes, bas-reliefs, and gilded mahogany. Even if you're not a high roller, it's worth paying the fee just to take a look at these fabled rooms (*a dress code is enforced; tie and jacket can be rented at bag check. Passport required*). Roulette, trente et quarante, and slots are played in the **Salons Européens** (European Rooms), while European and English roulette, trente et quarante, chemin de fer, blackjack, and craps are the games of choice in the **Salons Privés** (Private Rooms).

The casino sits on an urban hilltop surrounded by fancy hotels (including the **Hôtel de Paris;** *tel 92 16 30 00),* special-occasion restaurants, and the world's most expensive boutiques (Hermès, Cartier, Chrstian Dior). ■

Nice's hinterlands

Ste.-Agnès, the coast's loftiest village at 2,132 feet (650 m; see p. 186)

THE CRAGGY PEAKS RISING STEEPLY BEHIND NICE SHELTER a collection of lofty *villages perchés*, their foundations laid during Roman invasions in the second century B.C. The access roads may be tiny, twisty, and steep—at times even tortuous—but the dizzying views alone are worth the white knuckles.

Clinging to a rock above the River Paillon de Contes, fortified **Contes,** 9.3 miles (15 km) northeast of Nice, was a medieval market for olives and ceramics. Olives have been crushed at the **Moulin à Huile de la Laouza** *(ave. Raiberti, tel 04 93 79 28 73)* since the 13th century. The 16th-century **Église Ste. Marie Madeleine** boasts a retable by François Bréa.

North via the D15, remote **Coaraze** is one of the area's most untouched villages, its narrow streets winding up to a 14th-century church. Toward Monaco, off the D21, **Peillon** clutches its rocky promontory overlooking a valley of pine and olive trees. The view from the church, at the top of the main street, takes in the whole area. The **Chapelle-des-Pénitents-Blancs,** near the village entrance, has a group of frescoes of the Passion by Giovanni Canavesio, dating from 1489. The fact that boutiques have been banned may explain the lack of tourist hordes.

The road to sky-high **Peille** is breathtaking—for its narrow cliff-side engineering and tiny two-way tunnels as well as for its views. A quiet, undiscovered village is your reward. Some of the buildings date from the 14th through 16th centuries; place de la Colle has the finest ones. At the **Musée du Terroir,** a tiny local museum, descriptions are written in Pelhasc, a dialect specific to Peille. ■

Musée du Terroir
✉ Place de l'Armée, Peille
☎ 04 93 91 71 85
🕐 Open Sun p.m. only

Menton

Menton

🅰 165 E2

**Visitor
information**

✉ Office de Tourisme,
Palais de l'Europe,
8 ave. Boyer

☎ 04 92 41 76 76

www.villedementon
.com

**Musée Jean
Cocteau**

✉ 165 E2

✉ Le Bastion, quai
Napoléon III

☎ 04 93 57 72 30

🕐 Closed Tues.

💲 $

Hôtel de Ville

✉ 17 rue de la
République

☎ 04 92 10 50 00

🕐 Salle des Mariages:
closed Sat.–Sun.

💲 $

**Musée de
Préhistoire
Régional**

✉ Rue Loredan-Larchey

☎ 04 93 35 84 64

🕐 Closed Tues.

**Basilica St.-
Michel-Archange**

✉ Parvis St.-Michel

**Musée des
Beaux-Arts**

✉ Ave. de la Madone

☎ 04 93 35 49 71

🕐 Closed Tues.

IN THIS ENCHANTING TOWN NEAR THE ITALIAN BORDER, you'll find one of the Côte d'Azur's most stunning tableaus: Beneath a bright blue sky, apricot-hued houses march up the hillside toward Alpine peaks, the turquoise sea lapping at their base. It's beautiful, but practical, too. The geography ensures that Menton is the Riviera's warmest resort, with winter temperatures rarely dropping below 50°F (10°C) and tropical foliage blooming year-round. No wonder people compare it to the Garden of Eden. A museum created by artist extraordinaire Jean Cocteau, baroque churches, and miles of beaches are just some of its lures.

The Romans called the area Sinus Pacis (Gulf of Peace) and set up the garrison of Lumone on Cap-Martin, but no colony. With little outside interaction, the isolated Gulf of Peace remained virtually undeveloped until the 19th century. Lord Brougham, an eccentric Englishman, discovered the place around 1830 while seeking a warm winter haven. Since then, Menton has grown into a well-moneyed, genteel resort (elderly British flock here in winter) with an Italian flair—the border is only a mile away. You'll hear plenty of Italian interspersed with French, and many restaurant menus feature northern Italian fare.

The **Promenade du Soleil** winds along the seashore from the boat-filled harbor in the town center, past beaches, restaurants, and apartment houses built in the 1930s for well-to-do Parisians. It leads to **Cap-Martin** a mile away, where palm trees shade beautiful old villas.

The tiny-turreted bastion standing sentinel over the harbor dates from the 17th century. Today it's more famous for the museum inside, the **Musée Jean Cocteau,** set up by the onetime Menton resident himself (1889–1963; see sidebar p. 165). It's a good guess that, given the meandering-line style of the pastels and pencil sketches found here, Cocteau probably would not have attained

much notice as an artist had he not been so talented in other realms. Nevertheless, the works here are his key pieces: pebble mosaics, his first tapestry, as well as several pastels from his "Inamorati" ("Lovers") series. Cocteau is buried outside, his tombstone reading "Je reste avec vous" ("I stay with you").

Across the street stands the **Halles Municipales** (Town Market), its stalls overflowing with fresh lobsters, crayfish, almond-and-marzipan tarts, big red tomatoes, and lemons, lemons, lemons. Menton is famous for its lemons—celebrated in February with the Fête des Citrons. Seek out that *délice Mentonnais*—a lemon butter crust covered with lemon crème brûlée and red fruits.

From the market, stroll through the place aux Herbes to **rue St.-Michel,** bustling with shops, restaurants, and cafés. On the next street over, rue de la République, you'll find the **Hôtel de Ville.** Cocteau transformed the walls of its **Salle de Mariages** in the 1950s with marriage-related scenes: In front, a Niçoise lemon picker marries a local fisherman, while on the right-hand wall, a wedding scene features people in Maghreb costumes, perhaps referring to Saracen roots of many Mentonnais. The opposite wall contains one of Cocteau's favorite subjects, Orpheus in the

scene where the mythic poet discovers that his beloved is dying.

The earliest known visitor to Menton—the *Nouvel Homme de Menton*—arrived 30,000 years ago. See his skull, and learn about the region's prehistory, at the nearby **Musée de Préhistoire Régional.**

VIEUX MENTON

The Italianate houses of the *vieille ville* step up the hillside along twisty medieval streets. To explore it, follow rue St.-Michel east to place du Cap, where rue des Logettes accesses narrow rue des Écoles Pie, which switchbacks up the hill. Finally you come to place de la Concéption, home to the 1762 **Chapelle des Pénitents Blancs** *(open Mon. 3–5 p.m.),* with its magnificent baroque facade.

The prize awaits in the parvis St.-Michel just below, the **Basilica St.-Michel-Archange,** said to be southern France's largest baroque church. Built between 1619 and 1653, its gilded marble interior features a high altar surmounted by a statue of an armor-clad St. Michael, the town's guardian saint, made of polychrome wood (1820). The chapel to the altar's right, dedicated to Ste.-Devote, belonged to the Grimaldi family. In the saint's picture above the altar, you can make out in the background a view of Monaco Rock.

On the town's west end, the tired-looking **Musée des Beaux-Arts** houses a collection of European paintings spanning the Middle Ages to modern times. A couple of highlights: Louis Bréa's "Virgin and Child" and onetime Menton resident Graham Sutherland's surrealist "La Fontaine." More interesting is the building itself: The pink-white Palais Carnolès, inspired by the Grand Trianon at Versailles, was built in the 1700s as the summer retreat for the Grimaldi princes. The ornate first-floor ceilings bespeak something of the bygone splendor. Outside, terraced gardens and citrus-tree-shaded promenades shelter the sculpture collection, with works ranging from Thomas Gleb's "Moines d'Eternit," eerie white cloaked figures with no faces, to Jean Terzief's more traditional "Baigneuse." ∎

Jean Cocteau covered the walls of Menton's Salle de Mariages, in the 17th-century Hôtel de Ville, with esoteric wedding scenes in the 1950s.

More places to visit from Nice to Menton

CASTILLON

An earthquake in 1887 destroyed Castillon, 7.4 miles (12 km) north of Menton via the precarious D2566 en route to Sospel, then it was bombed in 1944. The Provençal-style village you see today, dating from 1951, is considered a model of modern rural planning. It is a self-proclaimed artisan village, with several shops purveying stained-glass windows, artwork, clothing, even a microbrewery. The **Syndicat d'Initiative** *(rue de la République, tel 04 93 04 32 03)* has expositions of local art. ⚠ 165 E3

STE.-AGNÈS

Clinging to a pinnacle 2,559 feet (780 m) above sea level, this is Europe's highest seaside village; the views from the southern parking lot are breathtaking. Once a Saracen stronghold, the town is a medieval haven of cobbled lanes, vaulted archways, and underground caverns. Peek into the **Éspace Culture et Traditions** (Center of Culture and Tradition) at the Office de Tourisme for displays of local artifacts. **Fort Maginot de Ste.-Agnès** *(tel 04 93 35 84 58, open daily p.m. July–Sept., Sat.–Sun. p.m. rest of year, $)* was built in 1932 as part of the French military's futile defense effort against Italy. Higher up at the château ruins, participate in an ongoing archaeological dig that has turned up Bronze Age artifacts. ⚠ 165 E2 **Office de Tourisme** ✉ 51 rue des Sarrasins, Ste.-Agnès ☎ 04 93 35 84 58

MUSÉE VILLA ÉPHRUSSI DE ROTHSCHILD

Though Béatrice Ephrussi, a Rothschild baroness, already owned a Monaco mansion, she couldn't give up the opportunity of owning another on Cap-Ferrat, on land that King Leopold II had planned to carve out for himself. Her vision became this pink-confection, Venice-style villa overlooking the sea, its elegant rooms centered around a covered patio with pink marble colonnades and mosaic floor. The villa is full of paintings, furniture, and objets d'art, many dating from 18th-century France, the baroness's favorite style and period. Some of the rare pieces include a Savonnerie carpet; furniture once belonging to Marie-Antoinette; and a collection of Vincennes, Sèvres, and Dresden porcelain. Don't miss the baroness's suite, with its painted ceiling from the 18th-century Venetian school and, in the adjoining bathroom, her traveling cases that she took throughout her world journeys.

Even considering these treasures, the villa's most splendid aspect is its themed gardens—seven of them. The French garden is the main one, with a lily-pad-dotted pool, dancing fountains, and a Temple of Love replicating the Trianon at Versailles. There are also a Provençal garden, filled with olive trees and lavender; a lapidary garden, with sculptures too large to be displayed in the villa; and Spanish, Japanese, Florentine, and exotic gardens.

The main ticket admits you to the ground floor and gardens. For a couple more euros, you get a guided tour of the first floor, which includes the tapestry room and the *singeries* room, decorated with monkeys. ⚠ 165 C1 ✉ 1 ave. Ephrussi-de-Rothschild, Cap-Ferrat ☎ 04 93 01 33 09, www.villa-ephrussi.com $ $$ ■

Just desserts

A province so rich in natural flavors bodes well for sweets and desserts. Lavender and thyme appear in crème brûlée, as well as in jams and honey, while nougat made from black honey is considered essential for the Noël meal. But the fun comes in tasting different regional specialties. *Navettes* from Marseille are cookies flavored with anise and orange blossom, and *gâteaux secs aux amands* from Nîmes are almond biscuits. The Aix specialty is *calisson*, a melon-and-almond sweet glazed in sugar. Apt is known for its *fruits confits* (crystallized glazed fruit), while the Vaucluse features Cavaillon melon accompanied by muscat from Beaumes-de-Venise. St.-Tropez offers *tarte Tropézienne*, a cream-filled sandwich cake, while the nearby Massif des Maures focuses on chestnuts: *glace aux marrons glacé* is chestnut ice cream and *crème des marrons* is chestnut cream. Nice offers *socca*, a chickpea crêpe; *berlingots* are mint-and-lemon hard caramels from Carpentras; and that's just a start ... ■

Hills grow to knife-edged, snowcapped peaks in this Alpine realm of Provence, featuring such natural splendors as the Parc National du Mercantour and the Gorges du Verdon.

Alpes Provençales

Wheat-speckled lavender blooms

Alpes Provençales

THE SOUTHERN ALPS END ABRUPTLY JUST INLAND FROM THE MEDITER-
ranean Sea, providing an unexpected foray into remote mountainscapes—the domain of
chamois, ibex, and bearded falcons. Towns are few and far between, in this region where
hiking, skiing, white-water rafting, and canyoning reign. But here, too, you'll find fields
of lavender, faïence, and other more familiar aspects of Provence.

Perhaps the greatest surprise is the Parc
National du Mercantour, a wilderness escape
where jaggy peaks rise abruptly to the sky.
Roads are tortuous and steep, with many *lacets*
(hairpin turns)—providing magnificent,
white-knuckle views. This is a world of rare
and endangered flowers, endless hiking trails,
and high-altitude camps. Isola 2000 is the

famous ski resort where the Niçois head in
winter, while the Vallée des Merveilles harbors
some of the world's oldest etchings, dating
from the Bronze Age.

The mountains taper farther west, setting
the scene for the Gorges du Verdon, Europe's
largest canyon. This is an outdoor enthusiast's
dream, with white-water rafting, bungee

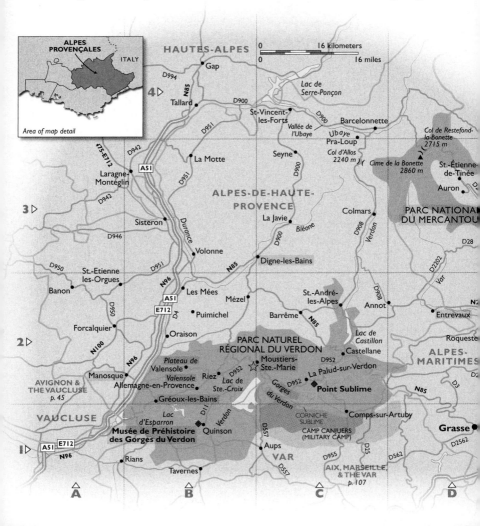

Sheep graze on the Col d'Allos, deep in the southern Alps.

jumping, and rock climbing.

A popular base at the canyon's eastern edge, the village of Castellane is Provençal in feel, with its central *boules* court, terrace cafés, and warm-hued buildings. Moustiers-Ste.-Marie, on the canyon's western side, has been world famous for its faïence for centuries. Shop after shop features the exquisite porcelainware, some better quality than others.

Westward, the plateau de Valensole is a bucolic world of medieval villages and forested hills … and fields and fields of lavender. During their peak bloom in late June and July, the air fills with a purple-blue aura and, as the harvest begins, their distinct pungent scent. ■

Lavender festivals

Games, competitions, music, floats, and food, all having to do with lavender, celebrate the height of lavender season. These are some of the season's best festivals:

Digne-les-Bains beginning of Aug.
Esparron-sur-Verdon mid-Aug.
Ferrassière end of June
Riez second half of July
Sault mid-Aug.
Valensole end of July
Valréas beginning of Aug.
Volvent beginning of Aug. ■

(Map)

ITALY

Isola 2000
Col de Tende tunnel
Vallée des Merveilles
Madone de Fenestre
Mont Bégo
St.-Sauveur-sur-Tinée
St.-Martin-de-Vésubie
Tende
La Brigue
St.-Dalmas-de-Tende
Gorges de Bergue
Fontan
Gorges de Saorge
Saorge
Vallée de la Roya
Breil-sur-Roya
ITALY
Sospel
Contes
Menton
MONACO
Monte-Carlo
Vence
NICE
CÔTE D'AZUR: NICE TO MENTON *p. 163*
Cagnes-sur-Mer
Mediterranean Sea
Antibes
CÔTE D'AZUR: CANNES & AROUND *p. 135*
Cannes

**Parc National
du Mercantour**
🅜 188 D3
**Visitor
information**
✉ Administrative head-
quarters, 23 rue
d'Italie, Nice
☎ 04 93 16 78 88
www.parc-
mercantour.com

**MAIN PARK
VISITOR
CENTERS
Breil-sur-Roya**
✉ 17 place
Bianchéri
☎ 04 93 04 99 76
Sospel
✉ 19 ave. Jean
Médecin
☎ 04 93 04 15 80
Tende
✉ 103 ave. du 16
Septembre 1947
☎ 04 93 04 73 71
**St.-Martin-de-
Vésubie**
✉ Place Félix
Faure, St.-Martin-de-
Vésubie
☎ 04 93 03 60 00
**Bureau des
Guides du
Mercantour**
✉ Place du Marché,
St.-Martin-de-Vésubie
☎ 04 93 03 31 32

**Opposite:
Nicknamed
the Switzerland
of Nice, St.-
Martin-de-
Vésubie has been
a mountaineering
center since the
19th century.**

Parc National du Mercantour

HIGH UP IN THE ROCKY PEAKS BEHIND MENTON AND NICE, only 25 miles (40 km) from the sea, Mercantour National Park is one of Provence's best kept secrets. In this spectacular Alpine realm, spreading across seven valleys and covering more than 171,250 acres (69,300 ha), you'll find an amazing diversity of scenery: wild canyons, olive groves, lily-scattered prairies, glacial lakes at the base of craggy peaks, and emerald green rivers racing through narrow gray-rock gorges. More than 2,000 species of flora thrive here, some of which live nowhere else. And the abundant wildlife includes the shy ibex, chamois, even wolves. Among archaeological treasures is the spectacular Vallée des Merveilles, with its thousands of Bronze Age petroglyphs. And the park's list of attributes goes on and on.

Created in 1979, the park is one of France's seven national parks. It borders on Italy's Parco Naturale Alpi Marittime, so that the two parks create a vast protected area in the heart of the Maritime Alps.

Located at the crossroads of Mediterranean and Alpine biomes, Mercantour harbors a profusion of varied wildlife species. Ermines, marmots, boars, and foxes are some of the most common critters. The wolf has migrated back from Italy after 50 years of absence. Six ongulés (hoofed animals) live here—the most celebrated being the nimble, sure-footed chamois, a small antelope that can leap as high as 6.5 feet (2 m) and as far as 20 feet (6 m); wild mountain sheep (mouflon), introduced in 1950 from Corsica for hunting purposes and, despite its name, poorly adapted to mountain life; and ibex, a wild mountain goat with large recurved horns.

In the skies above, look for golden eagles, falcons, and vultures—including the gypaète barbu (bearded vulture), with a wingspan of up to 10 feet (3 m).

The diversity of flora is just as incredible. This is the only place in France you can travel from the Mediterranean biosphere all the way up to the Alpine, experiencing all the flora in between: from lavender and olive trees below 2,300 feet (700 m); to fir trees, Norway spruce, and Norway pine between 2,300 and 5,000 feet (700 and 1,500 m); giving way to larch trees above that; and, above 8,000 feet (2,500 m), scrabbly patches of rhododendron, Alpine grass, and lichens.

Of 4,200 known plant species in France, 2,000 are found here, 200 of which are rare, and 30 endemic (found nowhere else in the world). For example, the *Saxifraga florulenta moretti*, which flowers once every ten years, grows only here, specifically at elevations between 8,000 and 10,000 feet (2,500 and 3,000 m). The Bérard thistle is one of the blooms that have survived from the Tertiary period, adapting to the cold climate. In the meantime, species such as the Asian lily have been brought from far away by wind or birds.

There is an abundance of outdoor activities: hiking, mountain biking, spelunking, canyoning, white-water rafting, kayaking, paragliding, and, in winter, skiing—and that's just a start. You can join

Isola 2000 Chalet d'Acceuil
☎ 04 93 23 15 15
www.isola2000.com

guided tours of archaeological sites, birds-of-prey evenings, and much more. Seek out the different Maisons du Parc (visitor centers) throughout the park for information.

From the south, you will most likely enter the park via Menton (through Sospel) or via Nice (through the Vallée de la Vésubie or the Vallée de la Tinée).

VALLÉE DE LA ROYA

One of Mercantour's most striking valleys, the Roya Valley, on the park's eastern edge, became French in 1947. Until then, King Victor Emmanuel II

The Couvent des Franciscans' church choir, Saorge

of Italy used it for his hunting grounds. A string of medieval towns dot the River Roya from south to north, with **St.-Dalmas-de-Tende** being the gateway to the fabled Vallée des Merveilles.

In the valley's south, linked to the coast via Sospel, is charming **Breil-sur-Roya,** feeling very much like a 17th- or 18th-century mountain town with its ancient buildings. Seek out 18th-century **Sancta-Maria-in-Albis,** a dazzlingly baroque church with frescoed ceilings and gilded decorations; the magnificent altarpiece dates from the 12th century. With the turbid River Roya running through town, it's no surprise that Breil is a hub of kayaking and white-water rafting.

From Breil the N204 heads north along the Roya through the **Gorges de Saorge,** leading to the spectacular village of **Saorge,** its boxy little houses holding dearly to the sheer cliff. The only way to get here is from behind, via the village of Fontan. Don't miss the **Couvent des Franciscains** *(tel 04 93 04 55 55, closed Tues. April–Oct., $)*, south of the village, with its baroque church and cloister adorned in 18th-century frescoes showing the life of St. Francis.

Northward, the spectacularly Alpine **Gorges de Bergue** bring you to **St.-Dalmas-de-Tende,** the main gateway to the Vallée des Merveilles (see below). Farther on you pass through picturesque La Brigue to **Tende,** with its medieval bourg; the ruins above the village are those of a castle once belonging to the Counts of Tende. Don't miss the **Musée des Merveilles** *(ave. du 16 Septembre 1947, Tende, tel 04 93 04 32 50, closed Tues., 2 weeks March, & 2 weeks Nov., $)*, which provides a thorough account of the geological and archaeological history of the Vallée des Merveilles through displays, dioramas, and a film. Copies of the valley's ancient etchings help identify the petroglyphs.

VALLÉE DES MERVEILLES

Sometime between 2800 and 1300 B.C, during the Bronze Age, shepherds migrated seasonally to the

remote Vallée des Merveilles, where they scratched tens of thousands of rock carvings into stone walls at the foot of Mont Bégo. Among the drawings are pointed shapes identified as knives, arrows, and other weapons, and witchlike figures called *orants*. The site's original purpose is unknown, though possibly it was used for worship.

VALLÉE DE LA VÉSUBIE

The Valley of the Vésubie, accessed via the D2565 north of Nice, weaves in and out of park boundaries. Less wild than its counterparts, the green valley still has its share of heart-stopping views. Its main outdoor base is the medieval village of **St.-Martin-de-Vésubie,** where you can hike in summer and ski in winter. Don't miss the view out onto the valley from place de la Frairie, behind the church.

VALLÉE DE LA TINÉE

In winter, Niçois head to the slopes of **Isola 2000** via the narrow D2205, through the heart of the Tinée Valley. **Isola village,** 11 miles (18 km) from the slopes, is charmingly

medieval, with cobbled streets and the chapel of Ste.-Anne. Northwest of Isola village, **St.-Étienne-de-Tinée** offers ample summertime walking adventures around the 9,383-foot (2,860 m) **Cime de la Bonette.**

VALLÉE DE L'UBAYE

Seven mountain passes link the Valley of the Ubaye to the outside world, including **Col de Restefond-la-Bonnette,** one of Europe's highest passes, at 8,900 feet (2,715 m). **Barcelonnette** is this remote valley's only town, founded by the count of Barcelona in 1231. Some 5,000 Barcelonnette residents followed the lead of the Arnaud brothers, who emigrated in 1821 to Mexico and established a textile empire. In time, some returned home, building Mexican-style villas and farmhouses. This curious history is retold at the **Musée de la Vallée** (*10 ave. de la Libération, tel 04 92 81 27 15, closed Sun.–Mon. & a.m. Sept.–June, $*).

The Ubaye Valley is best known for its white-water rafting. ■

Vallée de la Tinée

Vallée des Merveilles
You can walk in yourself, but the rugged region is extremely high in altitude—it's not for amateurs. From St.-Dalmas-de-Tende, take the D91 to Lac des Mesches, then proceed on foot or by 4WD vehicle approved by the national park. You can also access it from Madone de Fenestre, in the Vésubie Valley to the west. Mountain shelters are available for overnight stays. The less adventurous can take a guided walk, arranged through Merveilles Gravures et Découvertes (10 montée des Fleurs, Tende, tel 06 86 03 90 13); half-day and full-day tours leave regularly June–Sept. There are also 4WD tours. ■

Gorges du Verdon

Parc Naturel Régional du Verdon

 188 B2–C2

✉ BP 14, Domaine de Valx, Moustiers-Ste.-Marie

☎ 04 92 74 68 00

Moustiers-Ste.-Marie

 188 B2

Visitor information

✉ Place de l'église

☎ 04 92 74 67 84

www.ville-moustiers-sainte-marie.fr

AT FIRST GLANCE, THE RIVER VERDON'S UNEARTHLY light jade color takes your breath away. Its name—meaning "gift of green"—couldn't be more apt. Vertiginous limestone cliffs loom high above, some more than 2,300 feet tall (700 m)—the ensemble creating Europe's wild Grand Canyon. This natural paradise, located within an hour of the Côte d'Azur, is among France's unsung secrets, perhaps because the only way in—and out—is along one of France's scariest roads. Sporting types will love the outdoor opportunities.

The canyon's most impressive section zigzags 13 miles (21 km) between **Moustiers-Ste.-Marie** and **Castellane.** Both towns are good bases, with Castellane being a camper's haven, and pretty Moustiers (see p. 198) catering more to the inn crowd. Both towns offer a choice of outfitters.

The canyon provided a refuge for humans as far back as the second century B.C., when Ligurians hid out here from Romans. In the fifth century, monks lived in the canyon's

Some gorge activities

Aquatic hiking *(randonée aquatique)* This adventure trek can include sliding down waterfalls and paddling through rapids.

Bungee jumping *(saut en élastique)* The most popular spot is the Pont de l'Artuby, 600 feet (182 m) above the water, considered one of Europe's best drops.

Canyoning Guides take you hiking, climbing, and rappelling down ravines.

Climbing 933 climbing routes have been classified on the Verdon cliffs. The most famous, **Falaise de l'Escales** (Stopover Cliff), is 1,000 vertical feet high (300 m).

Hiking You can walk most of the canyon's length on the difficult GR4. There are two must-do hikes for serious hikers: the 9-mile (14 km) **Martel Trail,** which roughly follows Martel's 1905 route into the gorge; and the 3.4-mile (5.5 km) **Imbut Trail,** which ends at the Imbut, where the River Verdon disappears into rocks.

White-water rafting, kayaking, canoeing The trip through the 18.6-mile-long (30 km) canyon drops several hundred yards down between rock walls—passing through impressively named rapids, such as Niagara and Cyclops. This trip—passing through Class III and IV rapids—is for experienced boaters only, or those on a guided trip.

Other activities Horseback riding, trout fishing, hang gliding, parasailing, hot-air ballooning.

Information Ask at regional outfitters, or visit ProvenceWeb (www.provenceweb.fr). ∎

caves as hermits. More recently, the only humans who knew the deepest gorges were 19th-century woodcutters, who rappelled down cliffs looking for boxwood stumps for *boules.* French explorer Edouard Martel (1859–1938) was the first to penetrate the canyon's length, during a three-day expedition in 1905. His group braved torrents, navigated chaotic rocks—and not one member could swim! A plaque commemorates their accomplishment at **Point Sublime,** on the Rive Droite. Only with the construction of the Corniche Sublime in 1948 could the gorge be reached by car. The entity was made a parc naturel régional in 1977. ∎

Castellane
Ⓜ 188 C2
Visitor information
✉ Office de Tourisme, rue Nationale
☎ 04 92 83 61 14
www.castellane.org

La Palud-sur-Verdon
Ⓜ 188 C2
Visitor information
✉ Syndicat d'Initiative, Le Château
☎ 04 92 77 32 02

Aiguines
Ⓜ 188 C2
Visitor information
✉ Office de Tourisme, ave. Tilleuls
☎ 04 94 70 21 64

Opposite: Europe's largest canyon does not disappoint, with plunging limestone walls, vertiginous views (especially along the Route des Crêtes, seen here)— and a plethora of outdoor adventures.

Driving the Gorges du Verdon

This circuit around the canyon begins in Moustiers-Ste.-Marie and proceeds along the Rive Droite, highlighting the spectacular Route des Crêtes. You can detour to (or overnight in) Castellane before returning along the Rive Gauche, fittingly called the Corniche Sublime. Lookout points *(belvédères)* along the way provide the perfect opportunities to stop and admire the endless views.

RIVE DROITE (NORTH)

From the pretty town of **Moustiers-Ste.-Marie** ❶ (see p. 198), follow the D952 toward the Rive Droite. On this tiny, twisty road high above the gorge, generally lacking guard rails, you climb past views of far-off Lac de Ste.-Croix, then descend on the edge of a cliff, with the raft-filled **River Verdon** far below.

The road makes a hairpin turn at

Rafting the Verdon

Belvédère de Mayreste ❷, where, if you scramble 500 feet (150 m) up the rocks, you get your first overall view of the canyon.

Farther along, the road climbs past the **Relais des Gorges,** a snack bar. Beyond, the landscape flattens into a plateau, wide enough for fields of lavender, and then you descend to **La Palud-sur-Verdon** ❸, one of the canyon's major activities hubs.

Just out of town is where you pick up the D23—the **Route des Crêtes** ❹. The dizzyingly high, 14-mile (23 km) road follows

the plateau's edge, where sometimes only empty space exists between you and the valley floor, 2,300 feet (700 m) below. Keep an eye out for raptors soaring on thermals beneath you. Wild goats may also be spotted.

A little more than midway along the Route des Crêtes, the **Refuge des Malines** offers snacks and drinks overlooking one of the canyon's most sublime views (no bathroom, though). The trailhead for the popular **Martel Trail** is found here. Back in the car, you are treated to a couple more gorge views before turning back toward town.

Back at La Palud, turn right on the D952 (ignoring the Route des Crêtes sign this time) and proceed through woods, past valley views and wildflower fields, snaking down to **Point Sublime** ❺. Park at the designated lot and walk up the hill, following the blue blazes, to the grand view of **Samson Corridor**—the entrance to the Grand Canyon.

Beyond the tunnel, the road slips into the narrow **Clue de Carejuan** and from there you have a choice—continue on the D952 to Castellane or cross over the Pont de Soleils to begin the drive along the Rive Gauche.

RIVE GAUCHE (SOUTH)

The D955 takes you through tiny Soleils, beyond which you see Trigance's crenelated castle topping a hill. Turn right on the D90, which winds to medieval **Trigance** ❻— pleasant enough with a couple of restaurants. The castle is home to a gourmet restaurant.

Beyond, the road climbs through fields and woods, with far-off mountain views. At the D71, turn right toward Aiguines. The road descends, and you come to the **Balcons de la Mescla** ❼. A short path leads to an overview of where the Artuby and Verdon Rivers meet. Just down the road, more views await, as well as a snack bar-restaurant, **Le Relais des Balcons.**

The road then winds down to **Pont de l'Artuby** (Artuby Bridge), 600 feet (180 m)

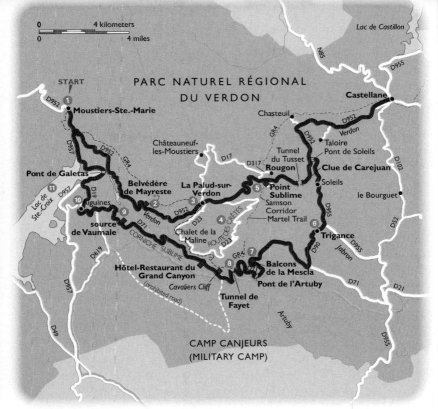

above the river. The bridge is Europe's highest, a popular spot for bungee jumpers. Beyond, you are on the gorge's edge, with pullovers from which to safely admire the views. Climbing a bit, you come to the **Tunnel de Fayet** ⑧; pull over at its exit for a magnificent view of the Verdon 1,000 feet (300 m) below.

Moving away from the gorge, the road follows **Cavaliers Cliff,** bringing you to the **Hôtel-Restaurant du Grand Canyon,** a concrete concoction with vistas from its terrace. Behind the hotel, the Rive Gauche footpath begins its journey to the bottom of the gorge.

The road closely traces the canyon, with pullouts offering chances to stop. Fill your water bottles with cool, sweet water at the **source de Vaumale** ⑨ (Vaumale spring), then proceed to the road's highest point—more than 2,625 feet (800 m) above the Verdon. Far away lie the turquoise waters of Lac de Ste.-Croix, one of the artificial lakes created by dams.

From here, the road twists down to **Aiguines** ⑩, a pleasant town with a centuries-old legacy of "turning boxwood"

- 🅰 See area map p. 188
- ▶ Moustiers-Ste.-Marie
- 🔄 50 miles (80 km)
- 🕐 A full day
- ▶ Moustiers-Ste.-Marie

NOT TO BE MISSED
- Route des Crêtes
- Point Sublime
- Tunnel de Fayet

to make boules (lawn-bowling balls). The town's 17th-century castle *(private),* flanked by four pepperpot turrets covered with glazed tiles, was built by Balthazar de Gauthier.

Beyond town you enter the watery wonderland of the **Lac de Ste.-Croix** ⑪, where all kinds of water sports equipment can be rented. Take a dip before taking the quick jaunt back to Moustiers via the D957—with one last stop: The **Pont de Galetas,** where you can stand on the bridge and watch the lake spilling into the river. ∎

Market day
Fri.

**Moustiers-Ste.
Marie**
🗺 188 B2
**Visitor
information**
✉ Office de Tourisme,
place de l'église
☎ 04 92 74 67 84
www.ville-moustiers-
sainte-marie.fr

Moustiers-Ste.-Marie

MOUSTIERS IS KNOWN FOR FINELY PAINTED TIN-GLAZED ceramics, or faïence. Every historical museum in Provence boasts some sample from Moustiers's heyday, between 1689 and the late 19th century, when talented artisans produced exquisite pitchers, plates, and saucers, some destined for the king of France himself. In the age-old tradition, more than 20 *poteries* flourish here once again, selling their wares in tiny boutiques on often crowded lanes. Nonetheless, Moustiers remains one of Provence's most picturesque villages, with its red-roofed buildings clutching a steep hillside beneath two towering cliffs, a gold star strung between.

**Painting in the
Moustiers way**

Land. He vowed that if he returned safely to his hometown, he would suspend a chain bearing a star between the two cliffs overhanging his village. Ever since, the star has been replaced when it falls. In the Middle Ages, pilgrims flocked to the church following an increase of miracles taking place here. A steep, winding path leads from rue Bourgade to the church, with 14 Stations of the Cross along the way.

Back in town, Moustiers is a fine place to stroll, its tiny, pedestrian-only lanes lined with old taupe buildings and tiny, flowery squares. Water runs in abundance through numerous fountains and basins, and a rushing mountain stream drops right through town. With 30-odd shops selling faïence, you will quickly become an expert—some are obviously better quality than others. Most of the shops make their own pottery, in workshops outside town.

A stop at the small **Musée de la Faïence** (*Hôtel de Ville, tel 04 92 74 61 64, closed Tues., Jan., & a.m. Sat.–Sun., $*), near the village entrance, provides a good overview. A video (in French) explains the process of faïence making and display cases show some of the city's finest historical pieces.

Moustiers also serves as an outfitting base for the Gorges du Verdon (see pp. 194–197). ∎

No one knows for sure who hung the star, which dangles directly above the Romanesque **Chapelle Notre-Dame-de-Beauvoir,** the little church tucked hard among the rocks above the village. Legend describes it this way: During the Crusades, the knight Blacas d'Aups was taken prisoner in the Holy

Moustiers's famous faïence

It's said that in 1668 a monk from Faenza shared the secret of porcelain glazing with Pierre Clérissy of Moustiers. The town's earthenware industry was never the same again. As the economy suffered during the Spanish Wars of Secession, King Louis XIV encouraged the nobility to melt down their gold and silver to help finance the war and to use faïence—Moustiers faïence—instead. At this time, the production of ceramics, previously geared toward the lower class, shifted to the creation of fine tableware with stanniferous glazes. Only blue and pale cream were used at first in designs depicting hunting and biblical scenes. The 18th century saw more detailed biblical and allegorical scenes. Emerging from this came a period in which grotesque figures, dwarfs, clowns, and birds were scattered among vegetation. New colors, too, were introduced: red, orange, purple, green, yellow. At this time, more than ten million decorative, utilitarian, and religious items were being produced. But, with the hardships of the Revolution, plus the exhaustion of local clay quarries (not to mention the rising competition of English bone china), the last oven went cold in 1874. Marcel Provence reestablished a kiln in 1927, the start of Moustiers's modern porcelain era. ■

Plateau de Valensole

If you want to see fields and fields of summertime-blooming lavender, the hot, dry plateau de Valensole is the place to go. A cluster of unspoiled historic villages make visiting this region a delight.

Valensole is the plateau's main city, built on a site previously occupied by Romans. Stroll the medieval streets around the **Église St.-Blaise.**

In **Riez,** an old lavender-distilling center to the south, you'll find a typical Provençal town through medieval gates, with vaulted passages and tiny streets. Among its fine buildings is **Hôtel de Mazan,** dating from the Renaissance. On the town's southern outskirts are four granite columns in a field, believed to have been part of a first-century A.D. temple of Apollo. Opposite, you'll spot one of the oldest baptisteries in France, from

the sixth century; a small museum of archaeological finds is inside.

Nearby **Allemagne-en-Provence** has a Renaissance château, begun in the late 12th century and still inhabited *(tel 04 92 77 46 78, closed Nov.–March, $$)*; tours are offered. The town's name dates back to the Wars of Religion, when the baron of Germany besieged the place. ■

Lavender potpourri

Valensole
🗺 188 B2
Visitor information
✉ Office de Tourisme, place Héros de la Résistance
☎ 04 92 74 90 02

Lavender country

Perhaps no other scent so readily defines Provence than the pungent, heady aroma of lavender, and no other scene than the fields and fields of the tiny purple buds growing in a profusion of mounds beneath a blue summer sky. Beloved for its scent, valued for its medicinal and soothing qualities, lavender has been used since Roman times—and the industry is still going strong.

The ancient Romans used lavender flower heads to scent their clothes and public baths. In fact, the origin of the name comes from the Latin *lavare,* meaning "to wash." Lavender's antidotal qualities have also been known as long, with Mithridates, king of Pontus, inventing in the first century B.C. a famous remedy against insect bites called *Thériaque.* During the Middle Ages, when many believed that plague was spread by vapors in the air, lavender was sprinkled on floors and burned on streets and in disease-infested houses. It was also used to treat insomnia and drive away lice, moths, and bedbugs.

Lavender's popularity soared in the 16th-century royal courts, where the mode (at least according to Catherine de Médicis) demanded that gloves, handkerchiefs, and wigs be perfumed. Lavender production took off in Provence, but it was not until the 19th century that *lavanderaies* (lavender plantations) popped up throughout the countryside. Although lavender grows wild throughout Provence, at this point fields were planted for the express purpose of cultivation.

LAVENDER PRODUCTION

Lavender belongs to the mint family, which also includes thyme, savory, oregano, and sage. While 70 species and subspecies of lavender have been identified worldwide, only three grow in Provence: true lavender *(la lavande)* is found high up in dry, rocky soil. Aspic, which grows lower down, is similar to la lavande except it has broader leaves and its branches hold a number of stems. And less refined *le lavandin* is a hybrid of la lavande and aspic. For production purposes, la lavande is the most highly regarded by perfume makers for its sweet essential oil, though aspic and

especially le lavandin are more productive and therefore more common—ending up in laundry and household products.

Lavender is planted in long, undulating rows in autumn or spring, with plants taking three or four years to mature. The first flowers appear in June, bursting forth in full glory by the end of the month in a hazy blue aura of beauty.

The harvest takes place from July to mid-August, when the scent overpowers the air. During the three-week harvesting period, mechanized harvesters pick flowers all day, every day. Upon harvesting, the plants are left out to dry, then bundled and packed and sent to the distillery. Here, the essential oil is

extracted: 120 pounds (55 kg) of flowers makes one pound (0.45 kg) of essential oil.

Provence is the world's top lavender producer. The main growing areas are the Alpes-de-Haute-Provence (plateau de Valensole, Vallée de l'Asse), the Vaucluse (plateau de Vaucluse, plateau de Sault), the Drôme (Les Baronnies), and the Rhône River Valley.

LAVENDER ROUTES

A midsummer drive through Provence's blooming lavender fields is one of those memorable lifetime experiences. One of the prettiest areas is around **Sault,** whose tourism office *(tel 04 90 64 01 21, www.saultenprovence.com)* has mapped out seven guided tours. Stops along the way include the **Jardin des Lavandes** *(rte. du Mont-Ventoux, tel 04 90 64 13 08)*, offering floral and perfume workshops; and the **Sentier des Lavandes,** a short walking trail just south of town. The Association des Routes de la Lavande *(www.routes-lavande.com)* has charted out additional scenic drives through laven-

der fields in the Sault area and elsewhere.

Most distilleries are open to the public, offering a first-hand look at the distillation process. **Distillerie des Agnels** in Apt *(rte. de Buoux, tel 04 90 74 34 60)* offers year-round tours.

Several spas cater to lavender's relaxing side. For instance, the **Établissement Thermal de Dignes-Les-Bains** *(rte. des Thermes, Digne-les-Bains, tel 04 92 32 32 92)* offers lavender baths.

Finally, for an excellent overview of the lavender business, be sure to stop by the **Musée de la Lavande** in Coustellet (see p. 79; *rte. de Gordes, tel 04 90 76 91 23, $$).*

For a list of lavender festivals, see sidebar p. 189. ∎

Above left: Romans used lavender oils for bathing, cooking, cleansing, and scenting the air, popular uses to this day. Right: Distilling lavender in the traditional way. Below: Fields and fields of lavender explode into bloom in June and July.

More places to visit in the Alpes Provençales

DIGNE-LES-BAINS

In this genteel spa town, pleasant cafés luxuriate along the shady boulevard Gassendi. Don't miss the **Cathédrale Notre-Dame-du-Bourg,** dating from the 12th and 13th centuries; faint fresco fragments from the 14th and 15th centuries still adorn its walls. World traveler Alexandra David-Néel began her explorations in 1883 at the age of 15 and rarely let up. Having spent much of her life in East Asia, she settled in Digne, at her "Samten Dzong," or "castle of meditation," just south of town. It's now the **Musée Alexandra David-Néel** *(27 ave. Maréchal Juin, tel 04 92 31 32 38),* filled with exhibits on Tibetan art and culture. ⚠ 188 C3 **Office de Tourisme** ✉ Place du Tampinet ☎ 04 92 36 62 62

ENTREVAUX

Full of charm with its drawbridge entrance, tall and narrow houses, and tiny squares, Entrevaux has a few shops and restaurants without being touristy. At the behest of King Louis XIV, Vauban (see sidebar p. 156) fortified the town in the 17th century as part of the defensive line blocking the Alpine pass to defend France from the Savoy (Italy). A serpentine climb up ramps and through fortified doorways brings you high above town to his pinnacle-top **citadel** *($);* its ghostly ruins are in a slow state of restoration. ⚠ 188 D2 **Office de Tourisme** ✉ Porte Royale ☎ 04 93 05 46 73

GRÉOUX-LES-BAINS

Celebrated since Roman days for the curative power of its waters, this affluent spa town is best known for the rather clinical **Thermes de Gréoux-les-Bains** *(rue Eaux Chaudes, tel 08 26 46 81 81, closed Jan.–Feb.).* More than a million gallons (4 million L) of bubbling sulfurous water a day fill its white marble baths, enjoyed by the rheumatic, arthritic, and other sufferers. Shop-lined **rue Grande** crosses the old town, along which you'll find the **Maison de Pauline** *(47 rue Grande, closed weekends, $),* an 1827 house furnished in 19th-century Provençal style. Overlooking the town is a 12th-century **Templar castle,** which you can visit by guided tour *(inquire at the tourism office).* ⚠ 188 B2 **Office du Tourisme** ✉ 5 ave. des Maronniers ☎ 04 92 78 01 08, www.greoux-les-bains.com

MANOSQUE

Housing developments and industrial parks are your first impressions of this bustling city located between the Luberon and wild Haute-Provence. Its town center, however, remains picturesque. **Rue Grande** is the main shopping street, along which, at No. 14, a plaque marks the house where Provençal writer Jean Giono (1895–1970) was born. At No. 21 is a branch of **Occitane,** the Manosque-based purveyor of Provence-inspired cosmetics. ⚠ 188 B2 **Office de Tourisme** ✉ Place du Dr. Joubert ☎ 04 92 72 16 00

MUSÉE DE PRÉHISTOIRE DES GORGES DU VERDON

People were living in caves near Quinson as early as the Paleolithic period. They left behind bone awls, ceramics, and ocher grindstones, as well as the bones of ibex, horses, and beavers—the foundation for this incredibly researched museum of prehistory. State-of-the-art information terminals and computer-generated images help shed light on how early humans lived, while a prehistoric village has been re-created. The museum offers guided tours of the nearby **Grotte de la Baume Bonne,** a major prehistoric site. ⚠ 188 B1 ✉ Rte. de Montmeyan ☎ 04 92 74 09 59, www.museeprehistoire.com ⊕ Closed Tues. Sept.–June 🅢 $$

SOSPEL

The mountain gateway to the Roya Valley, this sleepy Alpine town straddles the River Bévéra. You can't miss the 11th-century **Pont Vieux** (Old Bridge). Its tiny tower was a tollhouse on the medieval salt road between the coast and Italy; today it holds temporary art exhibitions. On place St.-Michel rises **Église St.-Michel,** the epitome of baroque frothiness. Inside, trompe l'oeil murals cover the walls and ceiling, but the pride of place is the magnificent 16th-century retable by François Bréa, "Immaculate Virgin." ⚠ 189 E2 **Office de Tourisme** ✉ 19 ave. Jean Médecin ☎ 04 93 04 15 80, www.sospel-tourisme.com ■

Travelwise

Traditional transport

TRAVELWISE INFORMATION

PLANNING YOUR TRIP

WHEN TO GO

The best months are May and June, when the temperatures are warm and tourists few. Spring brings blooming almond and cherry trees and fields of red poppies. September and October are also good months to visit, with the vendange (grape harvest) beginning September 15. Winter can be cool; the cueillette des olives, however, takes place mid-November through early January, and ski season in the Alps of Haute-Provence is Christmas through March. Summer is often brutally hot, though the lavender fields bloom late June to late July. August can see sudden storms and frequent rain showers. Keep in mind that the cold, northerly mistral wind blows on average 100 to 150 days a year, often reaching 60 mph (100 kmph) and dropping temperatures as much as 20°F (6°C). It is strongest in winter and spring, when it can last for several days at a time.

INTERNET PLANNING

www.beyond.fr
www.discoversouthfrance.com
www.franceguide.com
www.guideriviera.fr
www.provenceweb.fr
www.tourisme.fr
www.visitprovence.com

WHAT TO TAKE

You should be able to buy anything you need in France. Pharmacies offer a wide range of drugs, medical supplies, and toiletries, along with expert advice, but you should bring any prescription drugs you might need. If you wear them, a second pair of glasses or contact lenses is a good idea (and a legal requirement if you plan to drive). Sunscreen and anti-mosquito products are advisable in summer. A warm sweater is useful early and late summer

evenings. In the mountains bring a light, waterproof garment. If you're headed to the Camargue, bring binoculars and lots of mosquito repellent. Lastly, don't forget the essentials: passport, driver's license, ATM card (and/or traveler's checks), and insurance documentation.

INSURANCE

Make sure you have adequate coverage for medical treatment and expenses including repatriation, and baggage and money loss.

PASSPORTS

U.S. and Canadian citizens need only a passport to enter France for up to 90 days' stay. No visa is required. Nationals of the European Union have no entry requirement; a national ID is sufficient.

HOW TO GET TO PROVENCE

BY PLANE

All the major airlines have direct flights to Paris, including American, Continental, Delta, United, and Air France. Delta, Aer Lingus, and Air France fly direct to Nice from New York, though it's often cheaper to fly to Paris and then catch a cheap internal flight or take the TGV train south.

MAJOR AIRPORTS

Aéroport Marseille–Provence
Tel 04 42 14 14 14
www.marseille.aeroport.fr
Located 15.5 miles (25 km) northwest of Marseille, the airport offers 30 daily flights to Paris, with a travel time of 65 minutes. Direct flights to 60 destinations.
Airport shuttle service: Marseille–Provence bus station, tel 04 42 14 31 27. To and from Marseille: shuttle every half hour; travel time 20 minutes. To and from Aix-en-

Provence: shuttle every hour; travel time 30 minutes.
Aéroport Nice–Côte d'Azur
Tel 08 20 12 33 33
www.nice.aeroport.fr
Located 3.7 miles (6 km) west of Nice.

AIRLINES IN FRANCE

Aer Lingus, tel 08 21 23 02 67, www.aerlingus.com
Air France, tel 08 20 32 08 20, www.airfrance.com
American Airlines, tel 08 10 87 28 72, www.aa.com
Continental Airlines, tel 01 71 23 03 35, www.continental .com
Delta, tel 08 11 64 00 05, www.delta.com
EasyJet, tel 08 26 10 26 11, www.easyjet.com
United, tel 08 10 72 72 72, www.united.com

BY TRAIN

The French national railroad, the SNCF (Société Nationale des Chemins de Fer), links Paris and all major cities. There are numerous daily train connections between Paris and Provence via the TGV, with a travel time of 3 hours between the Gare de Lyon and Marseille (see p. 205). You can buy train tickets in advance from your travel agent or SNCF office, or at a station or travel agency (agence de voyage) in France.

TICKET INFORMATION

If you buy your train ticket in France, you must punch it at the time-stamping machine (composteur) at the platform entrance, before you begin the journey. Once stamped, a ticket is valid for 24 hours. An unstamped ticket is not valid (and can result in an on-the-spot fine).

North Americans have a wide choice of passes, including Eurailpass, Flexipass, and Saver Pass, which can only be purchased in the U. S. (Information and reservations 888-382-7245, www.raileurope .com). Discounts are available for students and senior citizens with a student card or passport.

SNCF INFORMATION
Tel 36 35, www.sncf.fr

TGV (Train à Grande Vitesse): The Paris–Méditerrannée train will whisk you to Marseille in 3 hours, with stops (depending on the train) at Avignon and Aix-en-Provence. There are separate schedules from Paris–Charles de Gaulle airport and Paris–Gare de Lyon. Information: tel 36 35. You can reserve your seats and buy tickets directly from the SNCF website, or purchase them at train stations in larger towns. Reservations are required. For more information: www.tgv.com.

PROVENCE'S TGV STATIONS

Avignon TGV Located at town's southern edge, between ring-road and Durance River, 2 miles (3 km) from town center. A shuttle (navette) runs back and forth every 15 minutes between the station and just inside the town wall at Cours President Kennedy.

Aix-en-Provence TGV The train station is about 6 miles (10 km) west of town, with navettes providing direct links to Aix and Marseille. There are also other buses, taxis, and easy access to the A8 autoroute.

Marseille TGV The train station is at the Gare St.-Charles, in the center of town. Buses and taxis can transport you elsewhere, and a navette will take you to the Marignane airport.

GETTING AROUND PROVENCE

BY TRAIN
The major cities of Provence and the Côte d'Azur are linked by excellent rail services (see inside back cover map). Nice is the major rail hub along the Côte d'Azur, and Cannes and Monaco are linked by frequent service.

BY BUS
To get off the tourist path without a car, your best bet is the frequent bus service that links smaller towns and villages. Buses run most frequently Monday to Saturday; there are very few buses on Sunday.

BY CAR
Provence has a good network of roads, from small and often picturesque D roads to autoroutes, often called péages, because a toll (péage) must be paid. Occasionally you pay a fixed fee upon entering a section of autoroute; more often you are given a ticket as you enter, and you pay as you leave according to the distance traveled. Credit cards are accepted in the pay booths. The autoroutes may only be two lanes in each direction, but are the quickest routes. There are gas stations with 24-hour service approximately every 12 miles (20 km), but there are also, more frequently, well-designed parking and picnic places (called Aires). The main routes nationales between towns and cities (N on maps) are generally in excellent condition. Many are two-lane for at least part of their length.

RENTING A CAR
Renting a car in France is expensive. Arrange a car rental with your local travel agent before leaving home; it can be much cheaper. Otherwise there are desks in airports and major railroad stations in France. There are fly-drive options with most flights, and the SNCF offers a train-car rental package.

To rent a car in France you must have a current driver's license (held for at least 3 years) and be at least 21 years old. Some companies will not rent to people under 26 or over 60. Make sure you have information about what to do in case of an accident or breakdown; telephone numbers in case of emergencies; and the procedure to follow. You must carry the relevant car documents with

you, and some identification. It is recommended that you purchase the collision-damage waiver, which costs extra per day, but, in the case of accidental damage to the car, your responsibility will be a few hundred euros at most. Your credit card company may also cover you. Automatic transmission and air-conditioning are luxuries in Europe and come at a price.

Central offices
The largest rental agencies are located at the Marseille–Provence airport.
ADA, tel 08 25 16 91 69, www.ada.fr
Avis, tel 08 20 05 05 05, www.avis.fr
Europcar, tel 08 25 35 83 58, www.europcar.fr
Hertz (at Marseille gare), tel 04 91 05 51 20, www.hertz.fr
Rent-a-Car, tel 08 91 70 02 00, www.rentacar.fr

DRIVING INFORMATION
Accidents See p. 209.
Age limits and licenses The minimum age limit for driving in France is 18 years (21 if you are renting a car). Visitors from North America and the U.K. do not need an international driver's license but must carry their home driver's license.
Breakdown assistance Autoroutes and routes nationales have emergency telephones every mile (2 km). Police stations (gendarmeries) can give information about breakdown services or garages—call them at 17.
Busy periods French roads will be busy from the beginning of July, when school vacations begin, and at their worst around August 15, a major national holiday. Special routes attempt to relieve summer traffic congestion; watch for the small green BIS (Bison Futé) signs that indicate these alternative routes. A brochure in English on the Bison Futé routes is available from French government tourist offices.
Children Children under 10 must travel in the rear seat.

Distances All distances on signposts in France are shown in kilometers (1 km = 0.62 mile).

Drunk-driving The French drunk-driving limit is 50 mg alcohol per 100 ml of blood. This can mean that as little as one glass of beer can take you up to the limit.

Gas Petrol is expensive. Sold by the liter (there are 3.75 L to an American gallon), you'll need either leaded (avec plomb) or unleaded (sans plomb). Most gas stations accept credit cards.

Headlights All vehicles must carry a spare set of lightbulbs.

On-the-spot fines On-the-spot fines may be levied by police for several offenses, including speeding, not wearing seat belts, and not having the car's documentation with you.

Parking Some French towns and cities have blue zones where parking is free for up to an hour. You need to display a parking disk (disque de stationnement), which you obtain from garages, tabacs, and tourist offices. Otherwise most towns have on-street parking machines (horodateurs) from which you buy a ticket to display in your car. Coins required vary from 20 cents to 2 euros. Multistory car parking garages are common; check closing times: Some close overnight and may shut by 8 p.m.

Priorité à droite Traditionally, priority on French roads was given to vehicles approaching from the right, except where otherwise indicated. Nowadays, on main roads, the major road will normally have priority, with traffic being halted on minor approach roads with one of the following signs:
•Cedez le passage: yield
•Vous n'avez pas la priorité: you do not have right of way
•Passage protégé: no right of way
A yellow diamond sign indicates that you have priority, the diamond sign with a diagonal black line indicates that you do not have priority.

Take care in small towns and rural areas without road markings where you may be expected to yield to traffic

coming from the right—especially farm vehicles. If oncoming drivers flash their headlights, it is to indicate that they have priority, not the other way around. Priority is always given to emergency and public utility vehicles.

Road conditions For information about current road conditions, telephone the Inter Service Route line or tune into the local radio frequency (often indicated on signs beside roads). Autoroutes information, tel 08 92 68 10 77, www.autoroutes.fr.

Road signs
•Access interdit: no entry
•Allumez vos feux: switch on lights
•Interdiction de stationner: no parking
•Passage pour piétons: pedestrian crossing
•Rappel (remember): reminder of a previous restriction
•Ralentissez: slow down
•Sens unique: one-way traffic
•Virages sur....km: curves for...km
•Zone bleue: parking disk required

Seat belts The wearing of seat belts is mandatory in both the front and rear seats.

Speed limits There are different speed limits for normal weather and times of poor visibility (heavy rain or fog). Autoroutes have limits of 75–85 mph (110–130 kmph; slower limit applies in poor visibility). Two-lane roads: 60–75 mph (90–110 kmph) Other open roads: 50–55 mph (80–90 kmph) Towns (from entry name sign to exit name sign): 30 mph (50 kmph)

Traffic circles Vehicles already on a traffic circle have priority, except very occasionally in small towns where priorité à droite still applies.

Traffic lights These are sometimes suspended high over the road and can easily be missed.

PRACTICAL ADVICE

COMMUNICATIONS

POST OFFICES
La Poste is open from 9 a.m. to 6 p.m. on weekdays and from 9 a.m. to noon on Saturdays (in smaller towns offices will close for lunch and, in villages may only be open for 2 or 3 hours on weekday mornings). Mail can be delivered to you at a post office if it is marked "Poste Restante" and with the postal code of the Bureau de Poste at which you collect it. The postal code is essential. You will have to pay a fee for each item of mail.

Mailboxes Yellow boîtes postales (mailboxes) are located outside every post office and on walls in larger towns. They may have separate compartments for local mail, départemental (mail within the département), and autres départements/déstinations (elsewhere in France and foreign).

TELEPHONES
Telephone numbers have ten digits usually written into pairs, for example 04 23 45 67 89. Numbers in Provence begin with 04.

To call a French number (for example, 04 23 45 67 89) from abroad, dial the international code (011 from U.S. and Canada, 00 from U. K.), then the code for France (33), followed by the number, omitting the first 0: 011 33 4 23 45 67 89.

To call Monaco, the international prefix 00 377 (011 377 from U.S. and Canada) must be dialed, followed by the 8-digit number.

Phone booths Cabines téléphoniques stand outside larger post offices, in railroad stations and airports, and near roads and parking garages in towns and villages. They take either phone cards or credit cards and occasionally money. Phone cards (télécartes) can be bought at any

tobacconist (*bureau de tabac*).
Making a call Follow the
instructions that will appear on
the telephone's screen: *décrochez*
(pick up the receiver); *inserrez votre
carte* (insert your card or coin);
patientez (wait); *numérotez* (dial the
number); *raccrochez* (hang up).
International calls To make an
international call from France, dial
00 followed by the country's
international code. These can be
found in the front of the *Pages
Jaunes* section of the *annuaire* or
posted in a telephone booth.
Some useful ones are: Australia
61; Canada 1; Ireland 353; U.K. 44;
U.S. 1.

For operator services dial
12. For international directory
assistance, dial 32 12, followed
by the country code.

To dial toll-free numbers
(*numéros verts*), insert a card or
money to make the connection
(coins will be returned, units will
not be registered against cards).
Reduced rate calls in France and
Europe: 7 p.m.–8 a.m. weekdays,
noon Sat.–8 a.m. Mon. For calls
to the U.S. and Canada: 7 p.m.–1
p.m., Mon.–Fri., and all day Sat. &
Sun. Reduced rates also apply on
public holidays.

CONVERSIONS
1 kilo = 2.2 pounds
1 liter = 0.2642 U.S. gallon
1.6 kilometer = 1 mile

Women's clothing

American	8	10	12	14	16	18
French	38	40	42	44	46	48

Men's clothing

American	36	38	40	42	44	46
French	46	48	50	52	54	56

Women's shoes

American	6-6.5	7-7.5	8-8.5	9-9.5
French	38	39	40-41	42

Men's shoes

American	8	8.5	9.5	10.5	11.5	12
French	41	42	43	44	45	46

ELECTRICITY
In France, electricity is 220 volts,
50 Hz, and most plugs have two
round prongs. If you bring
electrical equipment, you will
need an adapter, and, for U.S.
appliances, a transformer.

E-MAIL & INTERNET
If you bring your own computer,
you will need a universal AC
adapter, plus an adapter
between your telephone
plug and the standard T-shape
French receptacle.

Internet cafés exist in
major cities and smaller towns;
often, they are simply a
computer or two hooked up in
a café (or even at McDonald's).
Ask at the local tourist office
for the nearest location.

ETIQUETTE & LOCAL CUSTOMS
Etiquette is very important in
France: Always be ready to
shake hands when you are introduced, and when you meet
friends and acquaintances.
Kissing on both cheeks is also
very common. When entering
any establishment it is polite
to offer a general *Bonjour,
messieurs/dames*. Remember
to use the titles *Monsieur* and
Madame. Young women are
addressed as *Mademoiselle*, a
woman in her 20s or older is
addressed as *Madame*. Address
a waiter as *Monsieur*, and call a
waitress either *Madame* or
Mademoiselle. *Garçon* (boy) is
not acceptable.

When visiting churches and
cathedrals, dress appropriately
and respect the sensitivities of
those who are there for
devotional purposes. Visitors
are requested not to walk
around religious buildings during
services. Even though in most
cases no fee is charged to visit a
church or cathedral, it is polite
to contribute to one of the
boxes requesting donations.

NATIONAL HOLIDAYS
All banks, post offices, and many
museums, galleries, and stores
close on these national holidays:
January 1 (Jour de l'An)
Easter Sunday and Monday
(Pâcques)
May 1 (Fête du Travail)
May 8 (Victoire 1945)
Ascension Thursday (Jeudi de
l'Ascension)
July 14 (Fête Nationale)
August 15 (Assomption)
November 1 (Toussaint)
November 11 (Armistice 1918)
December 25 (Noël)

MEDIA

ENGLISH-LANGUAGE NEWSPAPERS
Newspapers and magazines are
sold in tabacs and *maisons de la
presse*, many of which stock
American or British newspapers
(often the previous day's edition).
International newspapers are
available in airports, major railroad
stations, and most large hotels.

The main national dailies are
Le Monde, conservative *Le Figaro*,
and left-wing *Libération* and
L'Humanité. American and British
dailies—*The International Herald
Tribune*, *The Times*, and *Daily
Telegraph*—are widely available in
Nice, Marseille, and most coastal
resorts.

Regional newspapers contain
national and international as well
as local news, and are often read
more than the national press.
Nice-Matin is the leading regional
daily newspaper; there is also
the Toulon-based *Var* edition
called *Var-Matin*. *La Provence*,
the result of a merger between
Le Provençal and right-wing *Le
Méridional*, has local editions for
Bouches-du-Rhône, Vaucluse,
and Alpes-de-Haute-Provence.

TV CHANNELS
French television offers five TV
channels: TF1, France 2, France 3,
5 or La Cinquième (in the
evening this one becomes Arte,
a combined Franco-German
transmission), and M6. TF1
occasionally shows undubbed
American films with French
subtitles, Arte more frequently
shows subtitled international
films and art programs. Most
American films shown on French
television are dubbed into
French, as are all the American
soaps and serials that make up
the bulk of French TV. France 3

PRACTICAL ADVICE

Région has good shows about Provence. A subscription channel, Canal+, has a monthly program of films, shown at least once in the original language (marked VO—*version original*), as well as sports. The main television news programs are at 1 p.m. and 8 p.m.

RADIO

National channels are broadcast from Marseille (France Bleu Provence, RFM Provence, Radio France Provence). Local French-language radio stations include Radio Provence (103.6 MHz and 102.9 MHz FM) and Cannes Radio (91.5 MHz FM). Popular music channels include Nostalgie FM (98.3 MHz FM) and Chérie FM (100.1 MHZ FM). Riviera Radio (106.3 and 106.5 kHz) broadcasts 24 hours a day in English. In some areas, BBC Radio 4 can be received on long wave (198 kHz). Traffic FM (107.7 MHz FM) broadcasts traffic reports in English, French, and Italian.

MONEY MATTERS

In 2002, the euro replaced the French franc. The euro is available in 500, 200, 100, 50, 20, 10, and 5 euro notes, and 2 and 1 euro coins, and 50, 20, 10, 5, and 1 centime coins.

Most major banks have ATMs outside for bank (ATM) cards and international credit cards with instructions in a choice of languages. You will need a four-digit PIN number. Arrange this with your bank before you leave home. Currency can be exchanged in banks, and Bureaux de Change in train stations and airports. If you're going to use traveler's checks, buy them in euros before you leave home. To cash traveler's checks at the bank have some form of ID (passport) ready. To use a check you will not need a check card, but you may be asked for photo ID.

Visa is the most common credit card accepted. Mastercard (Access/Eurocard) and Diners Club are also widely accepted, while American Express is less popular. Carte Bancaire (CB) is a French card encompassing both Visa and Mastercard.

OPENING TIMES

Nearly all stores and offices close for lunch from noon to 2 p.m., even until 3 p.m. or 4 p.m. Many stores close for the morning or all day Mon. or Wed.
Banks 9 a.m.–5 p.m. Mon.–Sat., closing for lunch
Bureaux de tabac and **maisons de la presse** 8 a.m.–7 p.m. Mon.–Sat., 8 a.m.–noon Sun.
Gas stations usually close at 9 p.m. except on autoroutes.
Grocery stores 9 a.m.–7 p.m. Mon.–Sat., some closing for lunch except Sat. and sometimes Fri.
Museums Closed for lunch noon–2 p.m, except perhaps during the months of July and/or Aug. Municipal museums usually close on Mon., national museums on Tues.
Post offices 9 a.m.–6 p.m. weekdays, closing for lunch, 9 a.m.–noon Sat.
Stores 9 a.m.–7 p.m. Mon.– Sat., closing for lunch; some food stores also open Sun. a.m.

TIME DIFFERENCES

Provence, as the rest of France, runs to CET (Central European Time) 1 hour ahead of Greenwich Mean Time, 6 hours ahead of Eastern Standard Time. New York is 6 hours behind. Remember that France uses the 24-hour clock.

TIPPING

Most restaurant bills include a 15 percent service charge. If it is, *service compris* is indicated at the bottom of the menu. If in doubt, ask: *Est-ce que le service est compris?* It is usual to leave a small additional tip for the waiter if the service has been good. It is customary to tip taxi drivers 10 to 15 percent. It is usual to give porters, doormen, and tour guides a tip of 1 to 2 euros, usherettes and cloakroom attendants 5 euros, and hairdressers 10 percent. There is no need to leave a tip for hotel maids unless you have required out-of-the-ordinary service.

REST ROOMS

Public rest rooms vary considerably—some are still old-fashioned squat toilets. Towns generally have public rest rooms near the *mairie* (town hall) of major towns. Self-cleaning toilet cabins are sometimes available on the street (not wheelchair accessible) for 20 cents. Large department stores have public rest rooms. You can always use the toilet in a bar or café, signposted *les toilettes* or *les WC* (the acceptable thing to do is purchase a drink in exchange). There may be an attendant; tip with small change.

TOURIST OFFICES

An excellent place to obtain visitor information before leaving home is from the French Government Tourist Office: www.franceguide.com. The Montréal office operates a public information hotline (tel 514/288-1904).
U.S.
New York
Maison de la France
825 Third Ave., 29th floor
New York, NY 10022
Fax 212/838-7855
West Coast
9454 Wilshire Blvd., Suite 210
Beverly Hills, CA 90212
310/271-6665
Fax 310/276-2835
Midwest
205 N. Michigan Ave.
Chicago, IL 60601
312/327-0290
CANADA
Montréal
1800 ave. McGill College, Ste. 1010
Montréal, Quebec H3A 3J6
Tel 514/288-2026
Fax 514/845-4868
U.K.
London
178 Piccadilly
London W1J 9AL
Tel 09068 244 123
Fax 0207 493 6594
FRANCE
Maison de la France
20 ave. de l'Opéra
Paris 75001
Tel 01 42 96 70 00
Provence
Nearly every town and village has a

tourist office *(office de tourisme)* offering information on sights, accommodations, restaurants, entertainment, and activities. Many make local hotel reservations.

Comité Régional de Tourisme
Les Docks, 10 place de la Joliette, Atrium 10.5
Marseille 13002
Tel 04 91 56 47 00

TRAVELERS WITH DISABILITIES
An information sheet for travelers with disabilities is published by the French Government Tourist Office. The guide "Où Ferons-Nous Étape?" (in French) lists accommodations suitable for travelers with disabilities, including wheelchair users. It is available by mail from the Association des Paralysés.

APF (Association des Paralysés de France) 17 blvd. Auguste Blanqui, Paris 75013, tel 01 40 78 69 00, www.apf.asso.fr
APF des Bouches-du-Rhône (Marseille) Tel 04 91 79 99 99
APF des Alpes-de-Hautes-Provence (Manosque) Tel 04 92 71 74 50

EMERGENCIES

EMBASSIES IN FRANCE
Canadian Embassy 35 ave. Montaigne, Paris 75008, tel 01 44 43 29 00
Canadian Consulate 37 ave. Montaigne, Paris 75008, tel 01 44 43 29 16
British Embassy 35 rue du Faubourg St.-Honoré, Paris 75008, tel 01 44 51 31 00
U.S. Embassy 2 ave. Gabriel, Paris 75008, tel 01 43 12 22 22
U.S. Consulate 12 blvd. Paul-Peytral, Marseille 13006, tel 04 91 54 92 00

EMERGENCY PHONE NUMBERS
Ambulance (Service d'Aide Médicale d'Urgence, or SAMU): 17

Police secours (police rescue): 17
Pompiers (fire rescue): 18
SOS Help (in English): 01 46 21 46 46

WHAT TO DO IN A CAR ACCIDENT
There is no need to involve the police if you have an accident in which no one has been hurt. The official procedure is for each driver to fill out a *constat à l'amiable*, each signing the other's copy. Phone the rental company and explain what has happened.

If you are involved in a serious road accident, phone the police (17) or fire rescue (18). These numbers are free but in a phone booth you need to insert a calling card to make a connection (no credit is taken).

A number and address in the telephone booth will say where you are, and you may be asked the name of the nearest town so that the operator can identify which département you are in. Alternatively, you may find the local *police secours* number posted in the phone booth.

LOST PROPERTY
If you lose your passport, report first to the police, then to the nearest embassy or consulate (see above). If you are detained by the police for any reason, you are entitled to call the nearest consulate for a member of the staff to come to your assistance.

Lost credit cards
American Express: tel 01 47 77 72 00
Diners Club: tel 08 10 31 41 59
Mastercard: tel 08 00 90 13 87
Visa: tel 08 00 90 11 79

HEALTH
Check that your health insurance covers visits to France. Pharmacies—recognizable by a green cross sign—are staffed by qualified pharmacists who can recommend treatment, and will tell you if you need to see a doctor and where to find one.

For serious physical injury, go to a hospital emergency room *(urgences)*. A pharmacy will be able to direct you. To renew a prescription, take your medicine in its package to a pharmacy. If they do not have that product, they will try to find its equivalent. If they can only sell it to you with a prescription, they will direct you to the nearest doctor.

International Association for Medical Assistance to Travelers IAMAT is a non-profit organization that anyone can join free of charge. Members receive a directory of English-speaking IAMAT doctors on call 24 hours a day, and are entitled to services at set rates.

IAMAT offices
U.S.: 1623 Military Rd. #279, Niagara Falls, NY 14304 tel 716/754-4883
Canada: 1287 St. Claire Ave., W. Toronto, Ontario M6E 1B8, tel 416/652-0137

MEDICAL EMERGENCIES
For an ambulance, dial 15, Service d'Aide Médicale d'Urgence.

French medical treatment is of a high standard, and facilities are generally excellent.

MAJOR EVENTS

Festivities in the south of France are far too numerous to list in their entirety. What follows is a selection of the largest and most well-known events throughout the region. Ask at the local tourist office to confirm dates and pick up information on some of the more obscure events that are set to take place.

JANUARY
Festival International du Cirque de Monte-Carlo (Éspace Fontvieille, Monaco, Office de Tourisme: tel (377) 92 16 61 16) International circus artists compete.

FEBRUARY
Le Chandeleur (2, Basilique St.-Victor, Marseille, tel 04 96 11 22 60) Candlelit procession behind black virgin of Basilique St.-Victor.
Le Corso Fleuri (3rd Sun., Bormes-les-Mimosas, Office de Tourisme: tel 04 94 64 82 57) Flower-adorned floats parade through town.
Bormes Mimosa Procession (3rd Sun.) The blooming of mimosa celebrates the coming of spring.
Menton Lemon Festival (3 weeks in Feb., www.citrons-menton.com) Lemon-decorated floats, lemon-decorated gardens, and more, all related to lemons.

MARCH
Carnaval de Nice (month before Lent, Nice, tel 04 93 92 80 73, www.nicecarnaval.com) Floats, fireworks, and performers. in the region's most celebrated festival.

APRIL
Féria Pascale (Easter Sat.–Mon., Les Arènes, Arles, tel 04 90 96 03 70. www.feriaarles.com) Three days of course Camarguaise.

MAY
Fête des Gardians (1, Arles, Office de Tourisme: tel 04 90 18 41 20) Camarguais cowboys take over the Roman arena.
Féria de Pentecôte (Pentecost weekend, Les Arènes, Nîmes, tel 04 66 21 82 56) Bullfighting, music, and art.
Fête de la Transhumance (Pentecost Mon., St.-Rémy-de-Provence) Traditional festival in which shepherds herd sheep to greener pastures.
Grand Prix de Monaco (Ascension weekend, tel (377) 93 15 26 00, www.acm.mc) Formula One racing cars speed around Monte-Carlo's narrow streets.
Cannes Film Festival (2nd week, www.festival-cannes.fr) Annual international film festival.
La Bravade (mid-May, St.-Tropez, Office de Tourisme: tel 08 92 68 48 28) Celebration of the arrival of headless Christian martyr Torpes (Tropez) in A.D. 68.
Pélerinage de Mai (23–25, Les Stes.-Maries-de-la-Mer, tel 04 90 97 82 55) Gypsies from all over come to honor Sarah, their patron saint.

JUNE
Fête de la Musique (21, www.fetedelamusique.culture.fr) Celebration of music throughout France on the summer solstice.
Les Baroquiales (end June–early July, tel 04 93 04 24 41) Baroque music in Alpine valley churches.

JULY
Festival d'Avignon (3 weeks in July, Avignon, tel 04 90 27 66 50, reservations: tel 04 90 14 14 14, www.festival-avignon.com) Famous theater festival.
Festival Piano (mid-July–mid-Aug., La Roque d'Anthéron, tel 04 42 50 51 15, www.festival-piano.com) Classical piano under the stars.
Jazz à Juan (2 weeks in July, tel 04 97 23 11 11, www.antibesjuan lespins.com) Legendary jazz festival.
Nice Jazz Festival (2 weeks in July, Jardins de Cimiez, Nice, Office de Tourisme: tel 08 92 70 74 07, www.nicejazzfest.com)
Bastille Day (14, throughout France) French national holiday, with balls and fireworks.
Festival Provençal (Avignon & nearby villages, Office de Tourisme: tel 04 32 74 32 74, www.nouvello.com) Celebration of Provençal language and folklore.
Festival de la Sorgue (L'Isle-sur-la-Sorgue, Office de Tourisme: tel 04 90 38 04 78) Folklore, street theater, and a floating market.
L'Été de Vaison (Théâtre Antique, Vaison-la-Romaine, tel 04 90 28 74 74, www.vaison-festival.com) Dance and theater festival.
Les Estivales de Carpentras (Théâtre de Plein Air, Carpentras, tel 04 90 60 46 00) Music, dance, and theater.
Les Chorégies d'Orange (July–Aug., Théâtre Antique & other venues, tel 04 90 34 24 24, www.choregies.asso.fr) Lyric opera in ancient amphitheater.
Festival International d'Art Lyrique (Aix-en-Provence, tel 04 42 17 34 34, www.festival-aix.com) Basic opera with a modern twist.

AUGUST
La Féria Provençale (mid-Aug., St.-Rémy-de-Provence, Office de Tourisme: tel 04 90 92 05 22) Three days of bull races.
Festival de Musique (Aug., parvis St.-Michel, Menton, tel 04 92 41 76 76, www.villede menton.com) Concerts in ancient church square.

OCTOBER
Marseille Contemporary Music Festival (last 3 weeks)

DECEMBER
La Pastorale (Dec.–Jan., throughout Provence) Theatrical announcement to shepherds of Christ's birth.
Fêtes de la Lumière à St.-Raphaël (2 weeks in Dec., St.-Raphaël, Office de Tourisme: tel 04 94 19 52 52, www.saint-raphael.com) Street theater groups and musicians fill the light-adorned town; fireworks on New Year's Eve.

HOTELS & RESTAURANTS

Finding a place to stay in Provence will be a challenge—not because choice is limited, but rather because there is such an enormous selection of appealing hotels. From reconverted medieval châteaus to stately country inns, and Riviera palaces to clifftop villas, there's no shortage of accommodation available for all budgets and tastes. The same goes for restaurants: the legendary *cuisine du soleil* has innumerable disciples in the fertile south, and dining here never fails to be an unforgettable experience.

HOTELS

The following is a selection of good quality hotels throughout Provence and the Côte d'Azur (listed by price, then in alphabetical order). Wherever possible we have chosen hotels that are both individual and typical, perhaps with notable local or historic associations.

In high season, always try to book in advance, if possible confirming by fax. You may be asked for a deposit or credit card number.

No matter when you visit, reservations will be essential. This is particularly the case during July and August, when contacting hotels and restaurants well in advance is imperative. It's also a good idea to check whether or not a town festival is taking place during your trip. Quintessentially French, these are not to be missed, but be forewarned they can make finding accommodation difficult, and in addition might radically change the face of an otherwise sleepy, rural town. November is the traditional time for the tourist industry to go on vacation themselves—meaning hotels and restaurants close up shop.

GRADING SYSTEM

French hotels are officially graded according to a star system, from four to one stars, indicating the minimum level of facilities. The requirements of the lesser grades are assumed in the higher ones. A few hotels in this selection, either restaurants with rooms or château hotels, are not star rated.

✪✪✪✪ Private bath/shower rooms. Restaurant.

✪✪✪ At least 80 percent of the rooms have bath/shower. Breakfast offered in the room.

✪✪ Forty percent of rooms have bath/shower and a telephone in each room.

✪ Plain but adequate accommodation.

CREDIT & DEBIT CARDS

Many hotels accept all major cards, though some smaller ones accept only cash. Abbreviations used are: AE (American Express), CB (Carte Bancaire), DC (Diners Club), MC (Mastercard), V (Visa).

HOTEL CHAINS & GROUPS

U.S. contact numbers:
Concorde Hotels
Tel 800/888-4747
Hilton
Tel 800/445-8667
Leading Hotels of the World
Tel 800/223-6800
Relais & Châteaux
Tel 212/735-2478
French contact numbers:
Maisons des Gîtes de France
Tel 01 49 70 75 75
Many departments have a Loisirs Acceuil booking service to reserve hotels, gîtes, and campsites; ask the French Tourist Office for a list or contact the nearest local tourist office.

RESTAURANTS

Our selection (listed by price, then in alphabetical order) suggests good regional restaurants offering typical local dishes, as well as including some of the great stars of French cuisine. It is always worth seeking out typical local restaurants and sampling the specialties of the area.

L = lunch   D = dinner

Dining hours

Lunch usually starts around midday and continues until 2 p.m. Dinner is eaten around 8 p.m. but may start about 7 p.m.; in smaller places or in the countryside you may be too late after 9 p.m.

At the height of the season, or if you have a particular place in mind, make a reservation.

Restaurants often have outdoor tables for good weather, and even in towns and cities you may find yourself sitting on the sidewalk or in a courtyard. Facilities for outside dining are mentioned here only where the view, or perhaps the garden, is of particular note.

Most restaurants offer one or more prix-fixe menus, set meals at a fixed price, sometimes including wine. Otherwise (and usually more expensively), you order individual items *à la carte*—from the menu.

The French usually eat a salad after the main course and sometimes with the cheese course, which always comes before dessert. Bread and water are supplied free. (French tap water is safe to drink.)

Wine lists are often dominated by local wines, and all restaurants offer a *vin de pays* by the carafe or demi-carafe. Although smoking is now forbidden by law in all public places in France, it is in fact still widely accepted, and you should specify if you prefer a non-smoking *(non-fumeurs)* section.

Cafés

Cafés remain a French institution, good for morning coffee, leisurely drinks, or modest meals. In small towns and villages they are very much the center of local life. Note that drinking at the bar is cheaper than sitting at a table.

Tipping

A service charge is usually included in the bill. Only add more if the service has been particularly good.

HOTELS & RESTAURANTS

▦ **AVIGNON & THE VAUCLUSE**

APT

🍴 AUBERGE DE LUBÉRON
$$$
8 PLACE DU FAUBOURG DU BALLET
TEL 04 90 74 12 50
Typical Provençal food in a peaceful atmosphere, with a terrace and garden. Duck foie gras with *fruit confits*; Luberon lamb with *aubergine confits*. Reservations necessary.
🕐 Closed Sun. D in winter, Mon. (except D in season), & Dec. 23–Jan. 15 🚘 All major cards

🍴 LE CARRÉ DES SENS
$$$
COURS LAUZE DE PERRET
TEL 04 90 74 74 00
Imaginative and healthy cuisine (lemon chicken with wild barley risotto) mixes with a well-stocked wine cellar and contemporary art exhibits, with a dash of Luberon sophistication. The *bar à vins* in back has cheaper dishes that are every bit as delicious.
🕐 Closed Sun. D, Mon., & Nov.–March 🚘 MC, V

AVIGNON

▦ DE LA MIRANDE
🍴 $$$$$ ✪✪✪✪
4 PLACE DE LA MIRANDE
TEL 04 90 14 20 20
FAX 04 90 86 26 85
www.la-mirande.fr
An 18th-century hotel close to the Palais des Papes, with luxurious rooms and tasteful furnishings. The Michelin one-star restaurant offers Provençal specialties such as flavorsome Luberon lamb.
🛈 19 🅿 🚗 🚘 All major cards

SOMETHING SPECIAL

▦ L'EUROPE
Avignon's top hotel—even Napoléon stayed here. The grand entrance to this 16th-century mansion leads onto the peaceful terrace, and tapestries hang in the elegant salon. The Michelin one-star restaurant, La Vieille Fontaine, lives up to the splendor of the establishment. Try *courgette* flowers stuffed with artichoke or roast sea bream with tomato tart.
$$$/$$$$$ ✪✪✪✪
12 PLACE CRILLON
TEL 04 90 14 76 76
FAX 04 90 14 76 71
www.heurope.com 🛈 44 + 3 suites 🅿 🕐 Restaurant closed Mon., Sun. D, & 2 weeks in Aug. 🚗 🚘 All major cards

▦ CLOÎTRE ST.-LOUIS
$$$ ✪✪✪✪
20 RUE DU PORTAIL BOQUIER
TEL 04 90 27 55 55
FAX 04 90 82 24 01
www.cloitre-saint-louis.com
A perfect blend of classical and modern French asthetic sensibilities. Situated in a 16th-century Jesuit cloister, its contemporary touches include a rooftop pool and sun deck.
🛈 80 🅿 Limited 🚗 🚗
🚄 🚘 All major cards

🍴 LA COMPAGNIE DES COMPTOIRS
$$$
83 RUE JOSEPH VERNET
TEL 04 90 85 99 04
Set in a renovated Benedictine convent, the sophisticated atmosphere accentuates the tangy Mediterranean cuisine: grilled Camargue bull and vegetarian delicacies such as Piedmont risotto with radicchio shoots.
🚘 All major cards
🕐 Closed Sun.–Mon.

🍴 BRUNEL
$$
46 RUE DE LA BALANCE
TEL 04 90 85 24 83
An established Avignon favorite. The vegetarian dishes are especially well prepared; try the wild mushroom ravioli.

🕐 Closed Sun.–Mon.
🚘 MC, V

🍴 LE PETIT BEDON
$$
70 RUE JOSEPH VERNET
TEL 04 90 82 33 98
This sweet homey restaurant offers rustic Provençal dishes such as pumpkin soup and veal with sage, with pear cake and baked apple for dessert.
🕐 Closed Sun.–Mon. L, & 3 weeks in Aug. 🚘 All major cards

🍴 L'ÉPICERIE
$
10 PLACE ST.-PIERRE
TEL 04 90 82 74 22
Opposite the 16th-century Église St.-Pierre, this tiny café offers local dishes such as lamb in apricot sauce and a tempting selection of cheeses.
🕐 Closed Sun. & Nov.–March
🚘 All major cards

Across the river in Villeneuve-lez-Avignon:
▦ LE PRIEURÉ
🍴 $$$ ✪✪✪✪
7 PLACE DU CHAPITRE
TEL 04 90 15 90 15
FAX 04 90 25 45 39
www.leprieure.fr
Period furniture and decor take you back in time, in this sumptuous 14th-century priory.

HOTELS
An indication of the cost of a double room without breakfast is given by **$** signs.
$$$$$	over $300
$$$$	$250–$300
$$$	$150–$250
$$	$80–$150
$	under $80

RESTAURANTS
An indication of the cost of a three-course dinner without drinks is given by **$** signs.
$$$$$	over $100
$$$$	$60–$80
$$$	$40–$60
$$	$25–$40
$	under $25

The restaurant is a superb choice for an elegant dinner.

❶ 36 **P** ⬛ ⬛ ⬛ ⬛ All major cards

🏨 L'ATELIER
$$ ○○
5 RUE DE LA FOIRE
TEL 04 90 25 01 84
www.hoteldelatelier.com
A charming, restful, 16th-century house.

❶ 23 **🕐** Closed Jan.–Feb.
⬛ All major cards

BONNIEUX

🏨 LA BASTIDE DE 🍴 CAPELONGUE
$$$ ○○○○
LE VILLAGE
TEL 04 90 75 89 78
FAX 01 90 75 93 03
www.edouardloubet.com
One of the only hilltop hotels in the Petit Luberon, its light, airy rooms, with typical Provençal furniture, look out on the old village. The upscale restaurant's menu features refined dishes fresh from the farm and garden: guinea fowl in truffle sauce and generously seasoned baked John Dory.

❶ 17 **P** ⬛ **🕐** Closed Nov.–Feb. ⬛ All major cards

🏨 HOSTELLERIE DU PRIEURÉ
$$$ ○○○
RUE JEAN-BAPTISTE AURARD
TEL 04 90 75 80 78
FAX 04 90 75 96 00
www.hotelprieure.com
Tastefully renovated 18th-century priory in traditional Provençal style.

❶ 10 **P** **🕐** Closed Nov.–March ⬛ All major cards

🍴 LE FOURNIL
$$$
5 PLACE CARNOT
TEL 04 90 75 83 62
The fountain-graced terrace is an exquisite place to enjoy a southern, 3-hour lunch.

🕐 Closed Mon. & Sat. L Nov.–Feb. ⬛ V

BUOUX

🍴 AUBERGE DE LA LOUBE
$$
BUOUX
TEL 04 90 74 19 58
Below the hamlet of Buoux on the road to Lourmarin, this out-of-the-way restaurant has a 20-year legacy of simple but delicious cooking. Reservations recommended.

🕐 Closed Mon., Thurs., & Sun. D ⬛ No credit cards

CAVAILLON

🍴 LE PRÉVÔT
$$$
353 AVE. DE VERDUN
TEL 04 90 71 32 43
Well-known for its themed seasonal menus, summer is M. Prévôt's brightest moment, showcasing his seven-course menu centered around cantaloupe—Cavaillon's speciality.

🕐 Closed Sun.–Mon.
⬛ AE, MC, V

CHÂTEAUNEUF-DU-PAPE

🏨 LE CHÂTEAU DES FINES ROCHES
$$$ ○○○○
RTE. DE SORGUES
TEL 04 90 83 70 23
FAX 04 90 83 78 42
www.chateaufinesroches.com
Several kilometers out of town amid cypress trees and vineyards, the castlelike manor house features spacious, rustic-style rooms.

❶ 8 **P** ⬛ ⬛ All major cards

🏨 LA SOMMELLERIE
🍴 **$$$** ○○○
RTE. DE ROQUEMAURE
TEL 04 90 83 50 00
FAX 04 90 83 51 85
www.hotel-la-sommellerie.com
A charming 17th-century *bergerie* situated among the famous vineyards now houses this delightful small hotel. Haute-cuisine restaurant.

❶ 14 **🕐** Restaurant: closed

Sat. L, Sun. D, all Mon., & Nov.–March ⬛ All major cards

🍴 LA MÈRE GERMAINE
$$
3 RUE DU COMMANDANT LEMAITRE
TEL 04 90 83 54 37
www.lameregermaine.com
Typical Provençal cuisine, featuring lamb, duck, and fish, is attuned to both the seasons and select vintages. End your meal with a chocolate-and-hazelnut tart. The outdoor seating offers gorgeous vistas.
⬛ All major cards

🍴 LE PISTOU
$
15 RUE JOSEPH-DUCOS
TEL 04 90 83 71 75
An unassuming lunch stop could quite easily turn into a memorable meal—the suggestion du jour here rarely disappoints.

🕐 Closed Sun. D, & all Mon.
⬛ All major cards

GIGONDAS

🏨 LES FLORÊTS
🍴 **$$/$$$**
RTE. DES DENTELLES
TEL 04 90 65 85 01
www.hotel-lesflorets.com
An attractive, quiet restaurant with Provençal decor and a flowery terrace. The menu features natural, typical products and old-time recipes: monkfish braised with orange butter, lamb on a bed of eggplant. Clean, comfortable rooms available, with surprisingly opulent bathrooms.

🕐 Closed Wed. & Jan. & March ⬛ All major cards

GORDES

🏨 LA BASTIDE DE 🍴 GORDES & SPA
$$$$ ○○○○
RTE. DE COMBE
TEL 04 90 72 12 12
FAX 01 90 72 05 20
www.bastide-de-gordes.com
Restored brick *bastide* in the

HOTELS & RESTAURANTS

village, with spacious rooms decorated with antiques. Its three-story spa includes a sauna, hammam, and meditation room. Provençal and Mediterranean cuisine in the well-appointed restaurant.
🛈 45 🅿 🕒 Closed Jan.–Feb. 🕙 🏊 🏊 🞮 AE, MC, V

🏨 DOMAINE DE L'ENCLOS
$$$ ✪✪✪✪
RTE. DE SÉNANQUE
TEL 04 90 72 71 00
FAX 04 90 72 03 03
Private gardens, a bocci ball court, and a heated pool make this an excellent family choice. Rooms are spacious, each with an individual touch. Five-minute walk to town.
🛈 17 🅿 🕙 🏊 🞮 AE, MC, V

🏨 LA FERME DE LA HUPPE
$$$
RTE. D'APT
LES POURQUIERS
TEL 04 90 72 12 25
FAX 04 90 72 01 83
In the peaceful Luberon countryside, this beautiful 18th-century farm, with an inner courtyard, has been renovated in Provençal style.
🛈 8 🕒 Closed Dec.–April 🕙 🏊 🞮 MC, V

🍴 LE MAS TOURTERON
$$$
LES IMBERTS
CHEMIN ST.-BLAISE
TEL 04 90 72 00 16
This old Provençal *mas* with a walled garden serves light, imaginative seasonal cuisine.
🕒 Closed Mon.–Tues. Sept.–June, & Nov.–March 🞮 All major cards

ISLE-SUR-LA-SORGUE

🏨 MAS DE CURE BOURSE
🍴 **$$ ✪✪✪**
RTE. DE CAUMONT
TEL 04 90 38 16 58
FAX 04 90 38 52 31
www.masdecurebourse.com

Comfort and tranquility abound at this 18th-century post-coach stop surrounded by orchards.
🛈 13 🕒 Restaurant closed Nov. 🏊 🞮 MC, V

🍴 LE CARRÉ AUX HERBES
$$
13 AVE. DES QUATRE OTAGES
TEL 04 90 38 23 97
This chic bistro alongside the antique dealers won't disappoint a hungry appetite. Reservations recommended.
🕒 Closed Tues.–Wed., & Jan. 🞮 MC, V

LOURMARIN

🏨 AUBERGE LA FENIÈRE
🍴 **$$$/$$$$$ ✪✪✪✪**
RTE. DE CADENET
TEL 04 90 68 11 79
FAX 04 90 68 18 60
www.reinesammut.com
A stylish mas restored with care, taste, and elegance. Reine Sammut's kitchen is what really put this luxury spot on the map, though, primarily using ingredients from her own garden.
🛈 9 🕒 Closed Nov.–Jan.; restaurant closed Mon. & Tues. L 🞮 All major cards

🏨 HOSTELLERIE LE PARADOU
$$
COMBE DE LOURMARIN
TEL 04 90 68 04 05
FAX 04 90 08 54 94
Peaceful family hotel tucked into the Gorges de Lourmarin. Rooms have views over fields and village.
🛈 9 🅿 🞮 MC, V

🏨 HÔTEL DE GUILLES
$$ ✪✪✪
RTE. DE VAUGINES
TEL 04 90 68 30 55
FAX 04 90 68 37 41
www.guilles.com
Fifty-acre (20 ha) estate for those intent on enjoying the countryside's blooming flowers and whirring cicadas. Charming rooms in Provençal style.

🛈 29 🕒 Closed Nov.–March 🏊 🅿 🞮 AE, MC, V

ORANGE

🏨 HÔTEL ARÈNE
$$ ✪✪✪
PLACE DE LANGES
TEL 04 90 11 40 40
FAX 04 90 11 40 45
www.hotel-arene.fr
The quiet, simple, Provençal-style rooms here are among Orange's most pleasant accommodations.
🛈 30 🕙 🅿 🕙 🞮 All major cards

🍴 LE PARVIS
$$$
3 COURS POURTOULES
TEL 04 90 34 82 00
Braised sea bass is just one of the choices on a haute cuisine menu reknowned for its use of top-notch ingredients.
🕒 Closed Sun. D, Mon. 🞮 MC, V

🍴 L'ORANGERIE
$$
4 PLACE DE L'ORMEAU
PIOLENC 84420
TEL 04 90 29 59 88
This 18th-century auberge with a stone-walled court-yard provides a traditional atmosphere for inventive cuisine: Langoustine with truffle sauce and osso buco of langoustine are favorites.
🕒 Closed Mon. L 🞮 DC, MC, V

ROUSSILLON

🏨 MAS DE GARRIGON
$$$ ✪✪✪
RTE. DE ST.-SATURNIN
TEL 04 90 05 63 22
FAX 04 90 05 70 01
Small, cozy hotel with bold-colored rooms each dedicated to a writer or artist who lived and worked in Provence. Each room has a private terrace overlooking the Luberon.
🛈 17 🅿 🕙 🏊 🞮 All major cards

SAIGNON

🏨 AUBERGE DU 🍽 PRESBYTÈRE
$$ ✪✪✪
PLACE DE LA FONTAINE
TEL 04 90 74 11 50
FAX 04 90 04 68 51
www.auberge-presbytere.com
A wonderful country inn overlooking the town square of one of the Luberon's lesser known hilltop villages. The restaurant serves delightful meals.
🛏 12 ⏰ Closed Wed. & mid-Nov.–Feb. ⬛ MC, V

SÉGURET

🏨 DOMAINE DE 🍽 CABASSE
$$$ ✪✪✪
ST.-JOSEPH
TEL 04 90 46 91 12
FAX 04 90 46 94 01
www.domaine-de-cabasse.fr
An established Dentelles vineyard that also takes in boarders. Perfect for wine lovers and those who appreciate Provençal home cooking.
🛏 12 🅿 ⏰ Closed Nov.–March ⬛ MC, V

🏨 LA TABLE DU 🍽 COMTAT
$$ ✪✪✪
LE VILLAGE
TEL 04 90 46 91 49
FAX 04 90 46 94 27
www.table-comtat.fr
Located at the apex of the village of Séguret, an intimate hotel whose gourmand owners do their best to share a love of fine dining with their guests.
🛏 8 ⏰ Closed Nov.–Feb.
🅿 ⬛ All major cards

VAISON-LA-ROMAINE

🏨 LE BEFFROI 🍽 $$ ✪✪✪
RUE DE L'ÉVÊCHÉ, HAUTE VILLE
TEL 04 90 36 04 71
FAX 04 90 36 24 78
www.le-beffroi.com
A 16th-century mansion perched high up in the

medieval town: country-style antiques, wooden rafters, and ceramic tiles set the mood. The restaurant makes ample use of local products (such as lavender honey).
🛏 22 🅿 ⬛ All major cards

🍽 LE MOULIN À HUILE
$$$$
QUAI MARÉCHAL FOCH
NEAR PONT-ROMAIN
TEL 04 90 36 20 67
Chef Robert Bardot's artful creations are just what you'd expect from a classy Provençal restaurant—*fougasse* with truffle butter and pan-fried red mullet in a shallot and herb sauce are some of the mouthwatering treats.
⏰ Closed Sun. D, & all Mon. ⬛ AE, MC, V

VÉNASQUE

🏨 AUBERGE LA 🍽 FONTAINE
$$$ ✪✪✪
PLACE DE LA FONTAINE
TEL 04 90 66 02 96
FAX 04 90 66 13 14
www.auberge-lafontaine.com
Inviting apartments in an old town house are ideal for longer stays. Includes kitchen, fireplace, bedroom, and dining room.
🛏 5 🔲 🅿 ⬛ AE, MC, V

◼ SOUTH ALONG THE RHÔNE

AIGUES-MORTES

🏨 LES ARCADES
$$ ✪✪✪
23 BLVD. GAMBETTA
TEL 04 66 53 81 13
FAX 04 66 53 75 46
www.les-arcades.fr
Above the arcades housing Aigues-Mortes's best seafood restaurant are nine individually decorated rooms. The building dates from the 16th century, with modern furnishings.
🛏 9 ⏰ Closed Mon., Tues., & Thurs. L 🔲 ⬛ All major cards

🏨 LES TEMPLIERS
$$$ ✪✪✪
23 RUE DE LA RÉPUBLIQUE
TEL 04 66 53 66 56
FAX 04 66 53 69 61
www.hotellestempliers.fr
A thoughtfully restored old hotel within the ramparts, with stone walls, painted beams, and fireplaces in many of the rooms. The courtyard is a haven of tranquility.
🛏 11 🅿 ⬛ 🔲 ⬛ AE, MC, V

ARLES

🏨 LE MAS DE PEINT 🍽 $$$$ ✪✪✪✪
LE SAMBUC
TEL 04 90 97 20 62
FAX 04 90 97 22 20
Converted stables attached to an old Camargue farmhouse hold exquisite rooms with wooden ceilings, white linen furnishings, and antiques.
🛏 8 + 2 suites 🅿 ⏰ Closed early Jan.–March 🔲 ⬛ All major cards

🏨 GRAND HÔTEL NORD PINUS
$$$/$$$$$ ✪✪✪✪
14 PLACE DU FORUM
TEL 04 90 93 44 44
FAX 04 90 93 34 00
Although brought up-to-date, this luxury hotel remains traditionally Provençal at heart. Very popular with bullfighters at festival time.
🛏 25 🅿 🔲 Some rooms ⬛ All major cards

🏨 L'ARLATAN
$$ ✪✪✪
26 RUE SAUVAGE
TEL 04 90 93 56 66
FAX 04 90 49 68 45
www.hotel-aralatan.fr
This 15th-century town house in the heart of Arles overflows with history and furnishings fit for Provençal nobility. Numerous fine touches include a walled garden and Roman excavations.
🛏 47 ⏰ Closed Jan.–Feb. 🅿 🔲 ⬛ All major cards

⬛ Nonsmoking ⬛ Elevator 🔲 Air-conditioning ⬛ Indoor/⬛ Outdoor swimming pool 🏋 Gym ⬛ Credit cards   **KEY**

🍽 L'AFFENAGE
$$$
4 RUE MOLIÈRE
TEL 04 90 96 07 67
The Provençal hors d'oeuvres are the specialty at this former coach house, but the main courses, including lamb grilled in the fireplace, are just as good.
🕐 Closed Sun. & 3 weeks in Aug. 🚫 No credit cards

🍽 LA GUEULE DE LOUP
$$$
39 RUE DES ARÈNES
TEL 04 90 96 96 69
First-floor wood-beamed restaurant above the kitchen serves Midi classics with an original twist like *charlotte d'agneau* with eggplant and red pepper coulis; and *tarte tatin* of turnips with foie gras. Reserve ahead.
🕐 Closed Jan., Sun., & Mon. L 🚫 MC, V

🍽 LE CILANTRO
$$
31 RUE PORTE DE LAURE
TEL 04 90 18 25 05
New arena-side bistro on the tip of everyone's tastebuds—the tongue-twisting dishes *(risotto carnaroli aquarello)* are delightfully surprising.
🕐 Closed Sat.–Mon. L 🚫 All major cards

🍽 CAFÉ LA NUIT
$
PLACE DU FORUM
TEL 04 90 49 83 30
Favorite local café, decorated to look like van Gogh's painting "Café du Soir."
🚫 MC, V

LES-BAUX-DE-PROVENCE

🏨 LA BENVENGUDO
$$$ ✪✪✪
1 MILE (2 KM) S OF LES BAUX
TEL 04 90 54 32 54
FAX 04 90 54 42 58
www.benvengudo.com
Tucked beneath the Alpilles, a manor-hotel with an elegant garden. The lounge and dining room are in Provençal style;

some rooms have private terraces. Tennis.
ℹ 20 + 3 suites 🅿
🕐 Closed Nov.–Dec. 🚫 🏊
🚫 AE, MC, V

🏨 LE MAS D'AIGRET
$$$ ✪✪✪
D27A
TEL 04 90 54 20 00
FAX 04 90 54 44 00
www.masdaigret.com
Part of the hotel is built into the cliff side, in keeping with the rocky-themed village above. Breakfast is served in the troglodyte dining room.
ℹ 17 🕐 Closed Nov.–March 🏊 🅿 🚫
🚫 All major cards

SOMETHING SPECIAL

🏨🍽 OUSTAU DE BAUMANIÈRE

This long-famous hotel beneath towering cliffs charms with three stone houses set on pretty grounds. The Michelin two-star restaurant is famous for its *gigot d'agneau en croûte* (lamb in pastry) and truffle ravioli.
$$$$$
MAUSSANE-LES-ALPILLES
TEL 04 90 54 33 07
FAX 04 90 54 4046
www.oustaudebaumaniere.com
ℹ 30 🕐 Closed Jan.–Feb.; restaurant also closed Nov.–Dec. & March, L Thurs.
🚫 🏊 🚫 🚫 All major cards

NÎMES

🏨🍽 HÔTEL D'ENTRAIGUES
$$ ✪✪✪
PLACE DE L'EVÊCHÉ, UZÈS
TEL 04 66 22 32 68
FAX 04 66 22 57 01
www.hoteldentraigues.com
Hardwood floors, simple furnishings, and warm ocher washes combine to create an intimate, relaxing atmosphere. Located in a collection of old town houses in central Uzès.
ℹ 36 🚫 🏊 🅿 🚫 All major cards

HOTELS
An indication of the cost of a double room without breakfast is given by $ signs.
$$$$$	over $300
$$$$	$250–$300
$$$	$150–$250
$$	$80–$150
$	under $80

RESTAURANTS
An indication of the cost of a three-course dinner without drinks is given by $ signs.
$$$$$	over $100
$$$$	$60–$80
$$$	$40–$60
$$	$25–$40
$	under $25

🏨🍽 HÔTEL LA BAUME
$$$ ✪✪✪
21 RUE NATIONALE
TEL 04 66 76 28 42
FAX 04 66 76 28 45
www.new-hotel.com
In old Nîmes, the New Hotels group has added a sensual, urban chic to this former *hôtel particulier*. A good location for visiting the city's monuments.
ℹ 34 🚫 🏊 🅿 🚫 All major cards

🍽 L'ENCLOS DE LA FONTAINE
$$$$
HÔTEL IMPERATOR
QUAI DE LA FONTAINE
TEL 04 66 21 90 30
Restaurant of the Hôtel Imperator favored by bullfighters at *féria* time. Try local specialties such as *brandade de morue* (creamy salt cod), *escabèche* (marinated fish), or sea bass with fennel compote.
🚫 All major cards

🍽 LE 9
$$
9 RUE DE L'ÉTOILE
TEL 04 66 21 80 77
Hidden away in the old town, this chic, theatrical restaurant serves Mediterranean-style cuisine till late.
🕐 Closed Nov.–April 🚫
🚫 CB, V

ST.-RÉMY-DE-PROVENCE

⊞ CHÂTEAU DES ALPILLES
$$$$ ✦✦✦✦
D31
TEL 04 90 92 03 33
FAX 04 90 92 45 17
www.chateau-des-alpilles.com
The castle, chapel, and farm-house all hold spacious, elegant rooms caringly restored and decorated with period furnishings by a mother-daughter duo.
🛏 22 🕑 Closed mid-Nov.–mid-Feb. 🏊 🅿 🌀
🌀 All major cards

⊞ LES ATELIERS DE L'IMAGE
$$$ ✦✦✦
36 BLVD. VICTOR HUGO
TEL 04 90 92 51 50
FAX 04 90 92 43 52
www.hotelphoto.com
This contemporary hotel uses photography as a central theme, and includes a private collection and gallery on the premises. The modern rooms are a wonder of sophisticated architectural style.
🛏 11 🕑 Closed Jan. 🏊 🅿
🌀 🌀 All major cards

⊞ SOUS LES FIGUIERS
$$$ ✦✦✦
3 AVE. TAILLANDIER
TEL 04 32 60 15 40
FAX 04 32 60 15 39
Old fig trees shade rustic and cool rooms perfect for siestas and lazy days in this quaint hotel in the heart of town. Most rooms have terrace or private garden. Art classes offered.
🛏 12 🕑 Closed Jan.–mid-March 🏊 🅿 🌀 🌀 MC, V

🍴 ALAIN ASSAUD
$$$
13 BLVD. MARCEAU
TEL 04 90 92 37 11
Thanks in part to its unassuming location, master chef Alain Assaud's kitchen is one of the better kept local secrets. The menu is set according to the freshest

produce available: asparagus in muslin sauce, filet of pork with carmelized onions, rhubarb tart.
🕑 Closed Wed., Thurs. L, & Sat. L 🌀 MC, V

🍴 LA MAISON JAUNE
$$$
15 RUE CARNOT
TEL 04 90 92 56 14
A St.-Rémy classic in an 18th-century town house, its menu features such delectables as roasted monkfish garnished with sundried tomatoes and cumin, with wines from Les Baux.
🕑 Closed Mon., Tues. L, & Jan.–Feb. 🌀 MC, V

🍴 LA GOUSSE D'AIL
$
6 BLVD. MARCEAU
TEL 04 90 92 16 87
The Garlic Clove gets rave reviews from just about everybody for its inexpensive gastronomical treats, family-run atmosphere, and occasional live music.
🕑 Closed Thurs.
🌀 All major cards

STES.-MARIES-DE-LA-MER

⊞ LE MAS DE LA FOUQUE
$$$$$ ✦✦✦✦
RTE. DU PETIT RHÔNE
TEL 04 90 97 81 02
FAX 04 90 97 96 84
www.masdelafouque.com
A traditional Camargue hotel, with large rooms, tiled floors, and wooden beams. Private terraces overlook the lagoon and park.
🛏 14 🅿 🕑 Closed Nov.–March; open during Christmas 🏊 🌀 All major cards

⊞ PONT DES BANNES
🍴 **$$$ ✦✦✦**
D570
TEL 04 90 97 81 09
FAX 04 90 97 89 28
www.pontdesbannes.com
Individual lodges constructed in the gardian tradition, with adobe walls and thatched roofs.

Inside, though, are handsome, modern interiors. Situated on the edge of the wetlands.
🛏 27 🏊 🅿 🌀 All major cards

🍴 LE BRÛLEUR DE LOUPS
$$$
9 AVE. LÉON GAMBETTA
TEL 04 90 97 83 31
One of the best spots in town to sample local seafood. Grilled sea bream with fennel butter and scorpion fish topped with a tomato-basil sauce are specialties.
🕑 Closed Tues. D, & Wed.
🌀 All major cards

■ AIX, MARSEILLE, & THE VAR

AIX-EN-PROVENCE

⊞ LE PIGONNET
$$$$$ ✦✦✦✦
5 AVE. DU PIGONNET
TEL 04 42 59 02 90
FAX 04 42 59 47 77
www.hotelpigonnet.com
A quintessential Provençal country château surrounded by exquisite gardens, just half a mile (800 m) from the old town. Local fabrics and furniture decorate the well-appointed rooms. Cézanne painted the Mont Ste.-Victoire from here.
🛏 52 🅿 🌀 🏊 🌀 All major cards

⊞ BASTIDE DU COURS
🍴 **$$$ ✦✦✦✦**
43-47 COURS MIRABEAU
TEL 04 42 91 57 56
FAX 04 42 91 57 51
www.bastideducours.com
Gorgeous bed-and-breakfast in a historic mansion along the Cours Mirabeau, with king-size beds fitted in fine linen. Its renowned eponymous restaurant serves deceivingly simple creations such as roast duck with pumpkin chutney.
🛏 5 🅿 🌀 🌀 All major cards

HOTELS & RESTAURANTS

🏨 **GRAND HÔTEL NÈGRE COSTE**
$$ ✪✪✪
33 COURS MIRABEAU
TEL 04 42 27 74 22
FAX 04 42 26 80 93
One of Aix's better values, this 18th-century town house has friendly service and quiet rooms.
🛏 37 🔄 🅿 All major cards

🍴 **LE CLOS DE LA VIOLETTE**
$$$$
10 AVE. DE LA VIOLETTE
TEL 04 42 23 30 71
Chef Jean-Marc Banzo runs Aix's top restaurant, blending artful presentation with his signature Provençal style; try the grilled sea bass stuffed with cured ham for starters.
🕐 Closed Sun.–Mon.
All major cards

🍴 **LE FORMAL**
$$$
32 RUE ESPARIAT
TEL 04 42 27 08 31
Hidden away on a quiet street beneath overhanging arches, this reconverted cellar promises romantic dining. Foie gras of duck accompanied with stewed apples and walnuts is the appetizer par excellence.
🕐 Closed Sun.–Mon.
MC, V

🍴 **LE PASSAGE**
$$
10 RUE VILLARS
TEL 04 42 37 09 00
www.le-passage.fr
Reine Sammut's hip restaurant-cum-culinary center (with cooking classes, wine cellar, and tea room) offers a rare combination: it's stylish, delicious, and affordable.
🕐 Closed Sat. L, & Sun.–Mon. AE, MC, V

🍴 **LES DEUX GARÇONS**
$
53 COURS MIRABEAU
TEL 04 42 26 00 51
Artists and intellectuals have frequented this classic terrace

café on the Cours Mirabeau since the 18th century.
All major cards

In Beaurecueil, along the Rte. de Cézanne:
🏨 **RELAIS DE STE.-**
🍴 **VICTOIRE**
$$ ✪✪✪
53 AVE. SYLVAIN GAUTIER
TEL 04 42 66 94 98
FAX 04 42 66 85 96
www.relais-sainte-victoire.com
Snuggled at the foot of Mont Ste.-Victoire, this comfortable, family-run manor features large rooms in Provençal style. The restaurant merits a detour in itself.
🛏 12 🔄 🅿 🏊
🕐 Closed Jan.; restaurant closed Sun. D, Mon., & Fri. L
AE, MC, V

LES ARCS

🍴 **LA VIGNE À TABLE**
$$$
N7
TEL 04 94 47 48 47
A local favorite for sampling Côtes de Provence vintages—the tasting room is just below the restaurant. Try the chicken breast with artichoke hearts or the sole in saffron sauce.
🕐 Closed Sun. D, & Wed.
MC, V

CASSIS

🏨 **LES ROCHES**
🍴 **BLANCHES**
$$$ ✪✪✪✪
RTE. DES CALANQUES
TEL 04 42 01 09 30
FAX 04 42 01 94 23
www.roches-blanches-cassis.com
White cliffs, an ivy-covered façade, gardens down to the sea's edge, and quiet ocean views make this a much sought-after locale. It's located several kilometers west of Cassis toward Les Calanques.
🛏 24 🔄 🅿 🏊 All major cards

🍴 **NINO**
$$
1 QUAI BARTHÉLEMY
TEL 04 42 01 74 32
One of Cassis' several alluring portside restaurants, offering seafood platters, grilled fish, and pasta, accompanied by crisp white wine from local vineyards.
🕐 Closed Mon.
All major cards

HYÈRES & ÎLES DES PORQUEROLLES

🏨 **LE MAS DU**
🍴 **LANGOUSTIER**
$$$$ ✪✪✪
CHEMIN DU LANGOUSTIER, ÎLE DES PORQUEROLLES
TEL 04 94 58 30 09
FAX 04 94 58 36 02
www.langoustier.com
This luxury island hotel, with its own vineyard, sits on a rocky spur overlooking the sea. Its Michelin one-star restaurant offers the light Provençal cuisine of chef Joël Guillet; meals served in the garden. Halfboard only. Tennis.
🛏 44 + 5 suites 🕐 Closed Oct.–May All major cards

🏨 **LE MANOIR D'HÉLÈNE**
🍴 $$$ ✪✪✪
ÎLE DE PORT-CROS
TEL 04 94 05 90 52
FAX 04 94 05 90 89
The island's only hotel, where D. H. Lawrence supposedly met the Englishwomen whose confessional conversations inspired Lady Chatterly's Lover. The restaurant offers a romantic terrace ideal for sunset-watching.
🛏 25 🕐 Closed Oct.–April
MC, V

🏨 **HOTEL DU SOLEIL**
$$ ✪✪
RUE DU REMPART, HYÈRES
TEL 04 94 65 16 26
FAX 04 94 35 46 00
www.hoteldusoleil.com
Simple rooms in an ivy-covered bastide set on 12th-century ramparts overlooking Hyères's vieille ville.
🛏 22 🅿 All major cards

🏨 Hotel 🍴 Restaurant 🛏 No. of guest rooms 🔄 No. of seats 🅿 Parking 🕐 Closed

🔟 LES JARDINS DE BACCHUS
$$$
32 AVE. GAMBETTA, HYÈRES
TEL 04 94 65 77 63
A good place to indulge, as the name implies. Swordfish, scampi, and other coastal specialties are prepared with flair and finesse. In the modern town.
🕒 Closed Sat. L, Sun. D, & all Mon. 🅰️ AE, MC, V

LA GARDE-FREINET

🏨 LA SARRAZINE
$$ ❂❂❂
D588
TEL 04 94 55 59 60
FAX 04 94 55 58 18
www.lasarrazine.com
A luxury hotel situated above the medieval village in the heart of the undeveloped Massif des Maures—a walker's paradise.
🔟9 🅱️ 🅿️ 🕒Closed Nov.–March 🅰️ MC, V

LORGUES

SOMETHING SPECIAL

🔟 CHEZ BRUNO
The restaurant where truffle king Bruno Clément created his black-diamond-based cuisine. Try the foie gras raviolis in truffle juice, roasted shoulder of lamb with truffles and potatoes, or the daube of wild boar.
$$$$
RTE. DES ARCS
TEL 04 94 85 93 93
🕒 Closed Sun. L, & Mon.
🅰️ All major cards

MARSEILLE

🏨 LE PETIT NICE
🔟 $$$$$ ❂❂❂❂
ANSE DE MALDORMÉ
CORNICHE J. F. KENNEDY
TEL 04 91 59 25 92
FAX 04 91 59 28 08
www.petitnice-passedat.com
Two luxurious Greek-style villas along the corniche are perfectly situated for contemplating the Mediterranean expanse—every room has sea views.

Gerald Passedat's eponymous restaurant offers contemporary cuisine with a regional twist: sea anemone beignets, for starters.
🔟 16 🅱️ 🅿️ 🔷 🅰️ All major cards

🏨 HÔTEL BOMPARD
$$$ ❂❂❂
2 RUE DES FLOTS BLEUS
TEL 04 91 99 22 22
FAX 04 91 31 02 14
www.new-hotel.com
A stately bourgeois house on hilly wooded grounds overlooking the sea, this lovely hotel is an oasis of calm. Rooms are decorated with Provençal flair.
🔟 46 🅱️ 🅿️ 🔷 🅰️ All major cards

🏨 HÔTEL DU RÉSIDENCE DU VIEUX PORT
$$$ ❂❂❂
www.hotelmarseille.com
10 QUAI DU PORT
TEL 04 91 91 91 22
FAX 04 91 56 60 88
Old-fashioned hotel with large bay windows and great views over the harbor. Rooms are spacious and equipped with modern amenities.
🔟 41 🅱️ 🅿️ 🔄 🅰️ All major cards

🏨 HÔTEL ALIZÉ
$$ ❂❂❂
35 QUAI DES BELGES
TEL 04 91 33 66 97
FAX 04 91 54 80 06
www.alize-hotel.com
Simple, comfortable rooms conveniently located off the harbor's main quay.
🔟 39 🅱️ 🅿️ 🔄 🅰️ AE, MC, V

🔟 UNE TABLE AU SUD
$$$
2 QUAI DU PORT
TEL 04 91 90 63 53
An up-and-coming gem tucked between the portside cafés, run by Alain Ducasse protégé Lionel Levy. There's no fish soup here, only the type of refined eating experience that you'd expect in Paris—with a southern

twist, of course. The puréed lobster and cèpes mousse served in a vodka glass hint tantalizingly at what's to come.
🕒 Closed Sun.–Mon.
🅰️ MC, V

SOMETHING SPECIAL

🔟 LE MIRAMAR
The Minguella family has been simmering pots of authentic bouillabaisse here for 40 years now. A classy, not-to-be-missed way of experiencing Marseille at its best.
$$$
12 QUAI DU PORT
TEL 04 91 91 10 40
🕒 Closed Sun.–Mon.
🅰️ All major cards

🔟 CAFFE MILANO
$$
43 RUE SAINTE
TEL 04 91 33 14 33
A chic little café whose inspired plats du jour are two steps ahead of the average French bistro.
🕒 Closed Sat. & Sun.
🅰️ All major cards

🔟 HONORÉ
$$
121 RUE SAINTE
TEL 04 91 33 08 34
For something different: classy French tapas served in a family-run home-deco workshop.
🕒 Closed Sun.–Mon., Wed. D, & Sat. L
🅰️ MC, V

ST.-TROPEZ

🏨 LE BYBLOS
🔟 $$$$$ ❂❂❂❂
AVE. PAUL-SIGNAC
TEL 04 94 56 68 00
FAX 04 94 56 68 01
www.byblos.com
The famous hotel where Mick Jagger married Bianca; designed like a village with sumptuous Moroccan decor, a chic nightclub, and two restaurants offering dinner only.
🔟 86 + 11 suites 🅿️

🅰️ Nonsmoking 🔄 Elevator 🅱️ Air-conditioning 🔷 Indoor/🔶 Outdoor swimming pool 🅶 Gym 🅰️ Credit cards   **KEY**

HOTELS & RESTAURANTS

🕀 Closed mid-Oct.–April
💳 🛇 💳 All major cards

🏨 LA PONCHE
$$$$$ ✪✪✪✪
PLACE RÉVELIN
TEL 04 94 97 02 53
FAX 04 94 97 78 61
Charming ensemble of former fishermen's cottages behind the port, with stylish, surprisingly large bedrooms.
🛈 13 & 5 suites 🕀 Closed Nov.– mid-Feb. 💳 🅿
💳 AE, MC, V

🏨 LE YACA
$$$$/$$$$$ ✪✪✪✪
1 BLVD. D'AUMALE
TEL 04 94 55 81 00
FAX 04 94 97 58 50
www.hotel-le-yaca.fr
Old Provençal house in the town center, built around a swimming pool and garden.
🛈 27 🕀 Closed mid-Oct.–Easter 💳 🅿 🛇
💳 All major cards

🍴 LE CAFÉ
$$
PLACE DES LICES
TEL 04 94 97 44 69
The former star-studded Café des Arts, whose adjoining restaurant in the back is reputedly still frequented by the occasional celebrity. The most regular patrons, however, are the boules players from the square out front.
💳 AE, MC, V

🍴 CAFÉ SÉNÉQUIER
$$
QUAI JEAN-JAURÈS
TEL 04 94 97 00 90
A favorite port café that's pricey but good for evening apéritifs and watching celebrities on yachts drinking theirs.
💳 No credit cards

🍴 LA TABLE DU MARCHÉ
$$
38 RUE CLEMENCEAU
TEL 04 94 97 85 20
Chef Christophe Leroy has added a gourmet note to many French standards: lobster and

macaroni au gratin, shepherd's pie with duck and foie gras.
💳 AE, MC, V

In Gassin:

🍴 BELLO VISTO
$$
PLACE DEI BARRYS
TEL 04 94 56 17 30
Perched in the hills overlooking the St.-Tropez peninsula, the Bello Visto has a view that defies believable. If you can peel your eyes away, enjoy a meal of grilled John Dory or rabbit sautéed with thyme.
🕀 Closed Tues. 💳 MC, V

In Ramatuelle:

🏨 VILLA MARIE
$$$$$ ✪✪✪✪
CHEMIN VAL RIAN
TEL 04 94 97 40 22
www.villamarie.fr
Luxurious new hotel in soft terra-cotta shades overlooking Pampelonne Bay. The pool has a waterfall. Spa.
🕀 Closed Oct.–March 💳
🛇 💳 All major cards

TOURTOUR

🏨 LE BASTIDE DE 🍴 TOURTOUR
$$$ ✪✪✪
MONTÉE ST.-DENIS
TEL 04 98 10 54 20
FAX 04 94 70 54 90
www.verdon.net
Sublime vistas from an exquisitely refurbished château outside one of the Var's loftiest villages. Surrounded by several acres of pine trees, olive groves, and lavender. Tennis.
🛈 25, 💳 🅿 🛇 🍽 📺
💳 All major cards

CÔTE D'AZUR: CANNES & AROUND

ANTIBES

🏨 AUBERGE 🍴 PROVENÇALE
$$$ ✪✪✪
61 PLACE NATIONALE
TEL 04 93 34 13 24
FAX 04 93 34 89 88

www.aubergeprovencale.com
This 17th-century abbey in old Antibes is now a quaint seaside hotel. The classy restaurant serves excellent seafood. Dine in the garden or inner courtyard.
🛈 7 💳 🅿 🕀 Closed mid-Nov.–mid-Dec.
💳 All major cards

🍴 LE CESAR
$$$
CHEMIN DE LA GAROUPE
TEL 04 93 61 33 74
Specialties include fish cooked in salt crust, pasta flambé, and artichoke ravioli. Just up a small staircase above Keller Beach.
🕀 Closed Oct.–March
💳 MC, V

🍴 OSCAR'S
$$
8 RUE DU DOCTEUR ROSTAN
TEL 04 93 34 90 14
Stone walls, copper cookware, and Roman-style sculptures set the tone for this cheery Italian seafood eatery in the old town. *Scampi tortellini*, scallop raviolis, and seaperch and lemongrass lasagna are some of the many seasonal delicacies.
🕀 Closed Sun.–Mon.
💳 V, MC

CHEZ MARGUERITE
$
31 RUE SADE
TEL 04 93 34 33 58
Mediterranean restaurant with paella and bouillabaisse in spring and summer, and various pasta dishes in the fall and winter.
🕐 Closed Mon.
🚫 AE, MC, V

At Cap d'Antibes:
DU CAP-EDEN ROC
$$$$$ ✪✪✪✪
BLVD. KENNEDY
TEL 04 93 61 39 01
FAX 04 93 67 13 83
www.edenroc-hotel.fr
Favored by Cannes film stars, this is the last word in luxury, especially the 1930s terrace and the pool hewn out of the rocks where Zelda Fitzgerald used to swim. Tennis.
🛈 121 + 9 suites 🅿
🕐 Closed Nov.–April 🚫
🏊 🏋

BIOT

LES TERRAILLERS
$$$$
11 RTE. DU CHEMIN-NEUF
TEL 04 93 65 01 59
Imaginative cuisine at this large farmhouse restaurant south of Biot has gained it one Michelin star. Try baby rabbit with *fines herbes*, foie gras ravioli with *fumet de morilles*, or monkfish with thyme butter.
🕐 Closed Wed.–Thurs., & Nov. 🚫 AE, MC, V

CAGNES: HAUT-DE-CAGNES

LE CAGNARD
$$$$ ✪✪✪✪
RUE SOUS BARI
TEL 04 93 20 73 21
FAX 04 93 22 06 39
Attached to the Grimaldi castle, the former haunt of artists and writers such as Modigliani, Renoir, and Antoine de St.-Exupéry. Rooms have a medieval touch.
🛈 26 🚫 🅿 Limited
🕐 Closed Nov.–mid-Dec.
🚫 All major cards

JOSY-JO
$$$
2 PLACE PLANASTEL
TEL 04 93 20 68 76
Bistro in the old town with rustic decor and a huge fireplace. Superb ingredients simply cooked such as peppers marinated in olive oil, and *petits farcis* (stuffed vegetables).
🕐 Closed Sat. L, Sun., & Dec.
🚫 🚫 AE, MC, V

CANNES

CARLTON INTER-CONTINENTAL
$$$$$ ✪✪✪✪
58 LA CROISETTE
TEL 04 93 06 40 06
FAX 04 93 06 40 25
www.intercontinental.com
The last word in luxury, the legendary Carlton is where film moguls do deals during the festival. The bathrooms are all marble, and many rooms have views overlooking the bay. Private beach.
🛈 295 + 18 suites 🅿 🚫
🚫 🚫 🚫 All major cards

MAJESTIC
$$$$$ ✪✪✪✪
10 LA CROISETTE
TEL 04 92 98 77 00
FAX 04 92 98 77 60
www.lucienbarriere.com
One of the mythic beachside resorts that packs in the film industry during festival time, with all the luxurious trappings one would expect..
🛈 305 🚫 🅿 🏊 🚫 🏋
🚫 All major cards

SPLENDID
$$$ ✪✪✪
4 RUE FELIX FAURE
TEL 04 97 06 22 22
FAX 04 93 99 55 02
www.splendid-hotel-cannes.fr
Cannes's oldest hotel is pleasantly unpretentious and an excellent alternative to some of La Croisette's larger resorts. Rooms are stylishly decorated. Ask for an ocean view.
🛈 34 🚫 🅿 🚫 AE, MC, V

HÔTEL DE PROVENCE
$$ ✪✪✪
9 RUE MOLIÈRE
TEL 04 93 38 44 35
FAX 04 93 39 63 14
www.hotel-de-provence.com
A secret oasis in the middle of Cannes, this charming hotel has clean, refreshing rooms in Provençal style. Only a hundred yards from La Croissette, it has access to a private beach.
🛈 30 🚫 🅿 🕐 Closed mid-Nov.–mid-Dec. 🚫 All major cards

LA PALME D'OR
$$$$
HÔTEL MARTINEZ
73 LA CROISETTE
TEL 04 92 98 74 14
Contemporary art deco decor and Riviera allure combine with an exceptional menu (rabbit with rosemary and chickpeas) to make this the top dining spot in Cannes.
🕐 Closed Sun.–Mon.
🚫 All major cards

LA BROUETTE DE GRAND-MÈRE
$$$
9 BIS RUE D'ORAN
TEL 04 93 39 12 10
Traditional French cooking, as good as grand-mère used to make. A convivial atmosphere, helped along by plenty of wine and roast quail.
🕐 Open D only; closed Sun.
🚫 MC, V

L'ECHIQUIER
$$$
14 RUE ST.-ANTOINE
TEL 04 93 39 77 79
An intimate, candlelit restaurant in Suquet that caters to stars and locals alike. The traditional standards include foie gras, bouillabaisse, sea bass, and magret de canard.
🕐 Open D only
🚫 All major cards

HOTELS & RESTAURANTS

🍴 LA SCALA
$$$
HÔTEL NOGA HILTON
50 LA CROISETTE
TEL 04 92 99 70 93
A fashionable restaurant with a terrace overlooking the Mediterranean, serving a gourmet Italian menu. Specialties include risotto with artichokes and foie gras, and pigeon with cèpes ravioli.
🍽 All major cards

🍴 LA MÈRE BESSON
$$
13 RUE DES FRÈRES
PRADIGNAC
TEL 04 93 39 59 24
A Cannes institution, this popular little bistro serves a different fish dish every day.
🕑 Closed Sun. 🅾
🍽 All major cards

GRASSE

SOMETHING SPECIAL

🏨 LA BASTIDE SAINT
🍴 ANTOINE
Jacques Chibois's two-Michelin-star restaurant is what first gave this 18th-century country house a name, but the regional-styled rooms are just as pleasantly luscious as the food. The menu includes artfully prepared lobster in black olive fondue, and lemon sea bream with truffle purée and hibiscus juice.
$$$$$ ✪✪✪✪
48 AVE. HENRI DUNANT
TEL 04 93 70 94 94
FAX 04 93 70 94 95
www.jacques-chibois.com
🛏 11 🚗 🅿 🍽 All major cards

🏨 CLOS DES CYPRÈS
$$$ ✪✪✪
87 CHEMIN DES CANEBIERS
TEL 04 93 40 44 23
FAX 04 93 40 83 09
www.closdescypres.com
Superb bed-and-breakfast in an 1880 house just outside Grasse with a perfumed garden and friendly welcome. Horseback riding, walking trails, tennis, and golf are all at the doorstep.
🛏 5 🚗 🅿 🍽 No credit cards

JUAN LES PINS

🏨 HÔTEL JUANA
🍴 $$$$$ ✪✪✪✪
LA PINÈDE, AVE. GALLICE
TEL 04 93 61 08 70
FAX 04 93 61 76 60
www.hotel-juana.com
Enchanting art deco monument dating back to 1931, with contemporary furnishings to match the state-protected facade. La Terrasse Christian Morisset boasts the Cap's best dining experience—try the baked turbot with truffles or clam and supion canelloni in squid ink.
🛏 40 🍴 🅿 🚗 📺 🕑
Hotel closed mid-Dec.–mid-Jan.; restaurant closed L & Nov. 🍽 All major cards

🏨 DES MIMOSAS
$$ ✪✪✪
RUE PAULINE
TEL 04 93 61 04 16
FAX 04 92 93 06 46
Quiet, 19th-century house with large modern rooms, many with balconies, and a shady garden.
🛏 34 🕑 Closed Oct.–late April 🚗 🍽 AE, MC, V

MOUGINS

🏨 LE MAS CANDILLE
🍴 $$$$$ ✪✪✪✪
BLVD. CLÉMENT REBUFFEL
TEL 04 92 28 43 43
FAX 04 92 28 43 40
www.lemascandille.com
18th-century farmhouse transformed to theraputic getaway complete with a spa—gorgeous accommodation in a tranquil country setting. Two restaurants on the premises.
🛏 39 🍴 🅿 🚗 🕑 Closed Jan. 🍽 All major cards

🏨 LE MOULIN DE
🍴 MOUGINS
$$$$$
AVE. NOTRE-DAME-DE-VIE
TEL 04 93 75 78 24
This one-Michelin-star restaurant, with its sculpture-filled garden founded by Roger Vergé—the chef celebrated for his cuisine du soleil—is now run with equal panache by Alain Llorca, former chef of the Negresco in Nice.
🕑 Closed Mon.
🍽 All major cards

🍴 L'AMANDIER DE
MOUGINS
$$$
PLACE DU COMMANDANT
LAMY
TEL 04 93 90 00 91
Roger Vergé's less exclusive counterpart to the famous Moulin, though this doesn't mean the cooking—rack of lamb served with zucchini flower risotto, for example—is any less delightful. Cuisine du soleil cooking classes also take place here.
🍽 All major cards

ST.-PAUL-DE-VENCE

🏨 LE ST.-PAUL
$$$$$ ✪✪✪✪
86 RUE GRANDE
TEL 04 93 32 65 25
FAX 04 93 32 52 94
www.lesaintpaul.com
Secluded, exquisitely furnished 16th-century town house, within the village walls.
🛏 15 + 3 suites 🍴 🍽 All major cards

🏨 LE HAMEAU
$$$ ✪✪✪
528 RTE. DE LA COLLE
TEL 04 93 32 80 24
FAX 04 93 32 55 75
www.le-hameau.com
Excellent family hotel with large swimming pool and secluded location; some rooms have a private terrace.
🛏 19 🍴 🅿 🚗 🕑 Closed Nov.–Dec. 🍽 All major cards

KEY 🏨 Hotel 🍴 Restaurant 🛏 No. of guest rooms 🍴 No. of seats 🅿 Parking 🕑 Closed

SOMETHING SPECIAL

🍴 COLOMBE D'OR
🏨

Dine on the terrace at this celebrity-haunted hotel-restaurant amid a priceless collection of art donated as payment for meals and rooms by Picasso, Calder, Braque, and more. Try the serving of 15 hors d'oeuvres and the soufflés. Reserve rooms in advance.

$$$$ ✪✪✪
PLACE DES ORMEAUX–PLACE DE GAULLE
TEL 04 93 32 80 02
FAX 04 93 32 77 78
www.la-colombe-dor.com
🛏 16 + 10 suites 🕐 Closed Nov.–late Dec. 💳 All major cards

VALLAURIS

🍴 LE MANUSCRIT
$$$
224 CHEMIN LINTIER
TEL 04 93 64 56 56
An old perfume distillery with a romantic garden, nostalgic décor, and classic Provençal menu.
🕐 Closed Sun. D & Mon.–Tues. 💳 AE, MC, V

VENCE

🏨 CHÂTEAU DU
🍴 DOMAINE ST.-MARTIN
$$$$$/$$$$ ✪✪✪✪
AVE. DES TEMPLIERS
TEL 04 93 58 02 02
FAX 04 93 24 08 91
www.chateau-st-martin.com
Built on the site of a Knights of Templar fort, the large suites of this contemporary château have Louis XV-style furnishings, with balconies overlooking the Mediterranean. The one-Michelin-star restaurant serves up excellent roast prawns in balsamic vinaigrette and grilled turbot with cocoa bean and apricot purée.
🛏 38 🏊 🅿 ❄ 🕐 Closed mid-Oct.–mid-Feb. 💳 All major cards

🍴 LA TABLE D'AMIS
$$$
689 CHEMIN DE LA GAUDE
TEL 04 93 58 90 75
Celebrated chef Jacques Maximin runs this modest restaurant out of his home in Vence, proving you don't have to pay top dollar to sample some of France's most creative cooking. Desserts are particularly elaborate—such as candied eggplant with ginger ice cream.
🕐 Closed Mon.–Tues.
💳 AE, MC, V

◼ CÔTE D'AZUR: NICE TO MENTON

BEAULIEU-SUR-MER

🏨 LA RÉSERVE
🍴 DE BEAULIEU
$$$$$ ✪✪✪✪
5 BLVD. DU MARÉCHAL LECLERC
TEL 04 93 01 00 01
FAX 04 93 01 28 99
www.reservebeaulieu.com
Fabulous Riviera hotel on the seafront, founded by the famous James Gordon Bennett, proprietor of the *New York Herald Tribune*. It's called La Réserve for the seawater tank (*réserve*), where the chef used to keep live fish in. The restaurant, which has one Michelin star, still specializes in fish.
🛏 33 🅿 🕐 Closed mid-Nov.–mid-Dec. ❄ Some rooms 🏊 💳 All major cards

🍴 LES AGAVES
$$$
4 AVE. MARÉCHAL FOCH
TEL 04 93 01 13 12
Located in the former Palais des Anglais, this small restaurant serves memorable meals, thanks to that little something extra. Favorite dishes are curried scallops and lobster and mango salad.
🕐 Open D only
💳 AE, MC, V

COARAZE

🏨 AUBERGE DU SOLEIL
🍴 $ ✪
5 CHEMIN CAMIN DE LA BEGUDA
TEL 04 93 79 08 11
FAX 04 93 79 37 79
Located nearly 2,100 feet (640 m) above sea level, this simple hotel situated in one of Nice's *villages perchés* is a good choice for a quiet getaway. A walker's paradise.
🛏 8 🏊 🅿 🕐 Closed Nov.–March 💳 AE, MC V

ÈZE

🏨 CHÂTEAU DE LA
🍴 CHÈVRE D'OR
$$$$/$$$$$ ✪✪✪✪
RUE DU BARRI
TEL 04 92 10 66 66
FAX 04 93 41 06 72
www.chevredor.com
High atop the eagle's nest village of Èze, this collection of restored, stone village houses clusters around the original manor house. Rooms are luxurious, including pink-marble bathrooms. The gourmet restaurant's menu changes with the seasons; plate glass windows look out on stunning sea views all aound.
🛏 33 🏊 🅿 ❄ 🏋
🕐 Closed Nov.–March
💳 All major cards

MENTON

🏨 HÔTEL DES AMBASSADEURS
$$$$ ✪✪✪✪
3 RUE PARTOUNEAUX
TEL 04 93 28 75 75
FAX 04 93 35 62 32
www.ambassadeurs-menton.com
This stately, pink-colored belle époque palace dates from 1865. Its interior is decorated in warm Provençal colors, with many rooms having small balconies. Private beach.
🛏 49 🅿 ❄ 💳 All major cards

HOTELS & RESTAURANTS

🏨 HÔTEL AIGLON
🍴 $$$ ❍❍❍
7 AVE. DE LA MADONE
TEL 04 93 57 55 55
FAX 04 93 35 92 39
www.hotelaiglon.net
A belle époque villa has been converted into this lovely hotel, showcasing a rococo-gilt lobby and luxurious gardens. Rooms are well appointed; ask for a garden view in summer.
🛏 29 ⛱ 🅿 ❄ 🕐 Closed mid-Nov.–mid-Dec. ⚫ All major cards

🍴 LE BOUQUET GARNI
$$
I RUE PALMARO
TEL 04 93 35 85 91
This sun-drenched terrace is two steps from the local market—there's no doubts about the freshness of the produce here. Some favorites: stuffed zucchini flowers, gnocchi, and "veggies from Dad's garden."
🕐 Closed Sun.–Mon. ⚫ No credit cards

🍴 L'ULIVO
$
21 PLACE DU CAP
TEL 04 93 35 45 65
Convivial Italian trattoria serving a variety of pasta dishes. Steamed mussels are a specialty.
🕐 Closed Mon. & Thurs. ⚫ MC, V

MONACO: MONTE-CARLO

🏨 HERMITAGE
$$$$$ ❍❍❍❍
PLACE BEAUMARCHAIS
TEL 377 98 06 40 00
FAX 377 92 16 38 52
A luxurious belle époque palace with a huge, glass-domed winter garden, opulent restaurant, and terrace of cool marble.
🛏 209 + 18 suites 🅿 ❄ ⚫ All major cards

🏨 HÔTEL METROPOLE
$$$$$ ❍❍❍❍
4 AVE. DE LA MADONE
TEL 377 93 15 15 15

FAX 377 93 25 24 44
www.metropole.mc
Historic palace renovated in 2004 to include a spa and even more sumptuous rooms. Gardens are an oasis of calm in the heart of Monte-Carlo.
🛏 146 ⛱ ❄ 🅿 ⬆ 🍽 ⚫ All major cards

🏨 HÔTEL COLUMBUS
$$$$ ❍❍❍
23 AVE. DES PAPALINS
TEL 377 92 05 90 00
FAX 377 92 05 91 67
www.columbushotels.com
The bourgeois answer to Monaco's old-fashioned, aristocratic tradition. Modern, chic, and seductively comfortable.
🛏 192 ⛱ ❄ 🅿 ⬆ 🍽 ⚫ All major cards

🍴 BAR ET BOEUF
$$$$$
AVE. PRINCESSE GRACE
TEL 377 98 06 71 71
To the French, sea bass-and-beef is the Anglo equivalent of surf and turf. This Ducasse-branded restaurant whips out fusion variations including stir-fried beef with artichokes and bass baked with eggplant and zucchini.
🕐 Closed L & mid-Sept.–mid-May ⚫ All major cards

🍴 LOUIS XV
$$$$$
HÔTEL DE PARIS
PLACE DU CASINO
TEL 377 98 06 88 64
Monaco's most famous restaurant, a three-Michelin-star establishment presided over by the celebrated Alain Ducasse. If you need to look at the prices, don't go. Typical dishes might be Provençal vegetables with black truffles, or pigeon with *foie gras de canard*.
🕐 Closed Tues., Wed. (except D mid-June–late Aug.), 2 weeks in Feb., & Dec. ⚫ All major cards

HOTELS
An indication of the cost of a double room without breakfast is given by **$** signs.

$$$$$	over $300
$$$$	$250–$300
$$$	$150–$250
$$	$80–$150
$	under $80

RESTAURANTS
An indication of the cost of a three-course dinner without drinks is given by **$** signs.

$$$$$	over $100
$$$$	$60–$80
$$$	$40–$60
$$	$25–$40
$	under $25

🍴 CAFÉ DE PARIS
$$$
PLACE DU CASINO
TEL 377 98 06 76 23
Monte-Carlo's front-and-center brasserie with an enormous terrace and extravagant fin-de-siècle interior.
⚫ All major cards

NICE

🏨 BEAU RIVAGE
$$$$$ ❍❍❍❍
24 RUE ST.-FRANÇOIS-DE-PAULE, 06300
TEL 04 92 47 82 82
FAX 04 92 47 82 83
www.nicebeaurivage.com
Ideally located on the edge of the old town, with views over the sea, this large hotel has its own private beach club. It was here that Matisse stayed on his first few visits to Nice. Ask for a room overlooking the sea.
🛏 118 ❄ ❄ ⚫ All major cards

SOMETHING SPECIAL

🏨 NÉGRESCO
The most famous and expensive hotel in Nice. This magnificent belle époque building on the Promenade des Anglais has sumptuous furnishings and impeccable

service. As grand as it gets—look for the vast Baccarat chandelier.

$$$$$ ✪✪✪✪
37 PROMENADE DES ANGLAIS
TEL 04 93 16 64 00
FAX 04 93 88 35 68
www.hotel-negresco-nice.com
🛈 134 & 18 suites 🚭 🛉
🚭 All major cards

🏨 HI
$$$$
3 AVE. DES FLEURS
TEL 04 97 07 26 26
www.hi-hotel.net
This new boutique hotel with postmodern design and informal service offers themed bedrooms for music lovers, computer freaks, or movie fans. No restaurant but DIY bar on each floor.
🛈 38 🚭 All major cards

🏨 LA PÉROUSE
$$$$ ✪✪✪✪
11 QUAI RAUBA-CAPÉU
TEL 04 93 62 34 63
FAX 04 93 62 59 41
For a sea view that won't break the bank. Flowery terrace and garden restaurant.
🛈 64 🛉 🏊 🚭 All major cards

🏨 HÔTEL WINDSOR
$$$ ✪✪✪
11 RUE DALPOSSO
TEL 04 93 88 59 35
FAX 04 93 88 94 57
www.hotelwindsornice.com
Individually designed rooms in sleek postmodern hotel three blocks from the beach. With hammam, massages, and tropical garden.
🛈 57 🏊 🅿 🛉 🛗
🚭 AE, MC, V

🍽 JOUNI
$$$
60 BLVD. FRANCK PILATTE
TEL 04 97 08 14 80
www.jouni.fr
Jouni has trimmed down the Côte's decadence in favor of more refined tastes like pumpkin risotto, grilled fish of the day, and orange soufflé. Reserve.
🚭 MC, V

🍽 LE COMPTOIR
$$
20 RUE ST.-FRANÇOIS-DE-PAULE
TEL 04 93 92 08 80
A 1930s-style bar/restaurant, particularly good for late night dining or for a light meal after the opera.
🛗 Closed Sat. L & Sun.
🚭 MC, V

🍽 LA MÉRENDA
$$
4 RUE TERRACE
This tiny bistro is famous for its traditional Niçois dishes: stockfish, beignets, stuffed sardines, beef daube. No phone and no booking. Get there early to reserve a table.
🛗 Closed Sat. & Sun. Aug., & late Nov.–mid-Dec. 🛉
🚭 No credit cards

🍽 LE SAFARI
$$
1 COURS SALEYA
TEL 04 93 80 18 44
Big café with Mediterranean blue shutters, close to the market on Cours Saleya. Great for alfresco dining. Try the deep rich calamari daube, or *bagna cauda*, a hot anchovy dip with raw vegetables.
🚭 All major cards

🍽 TERRES DE TRUFFES
$$
11 RUE ST.-FRANÇOIS-DE-PAULE
TEL 04 93 62 07 68
Chef Bruno Clément's boutique selling truffle-related products. The truffle-tasting bar inside has appetizers in addition to full course meals—look for tortellini soup with truffles and the ever popular truffle ice cream.
🛗 Closed Sun. 🚭 All major cards

PEILLON

🏨 AUBERGE DE LA
🍽 MADONE
$$$ ✪✪✪
2 PLACE AUGUSTE ARNULF
TEL 04 93 79 91 17

FAX 04 93 79 99 36
Top pick of the tiny hotels dotting Nice's backcountry. With views looking out onto the village, and a restaurant serving local specialities.
🛈 20 🛗 Closed mid-Oct.–Dec.; restaurant closed Wed. 🚭 MC, V

ST.-JEAN-CAP-FERRAT

🏨 GRAND HÔTEL DU
🍽 CAP FERRAT
$$$$$ ✪✪✪✪
BLVD. DU GÉNÉRAL DE GAULLE
TEL 04 93 76 50 50
FAX 04 93 76 04 52
www.grand-hotel-cap-ferrat.com
One of the Riviera's legendary grand hotels, secluded in its own tropical gardens overlooking the sea, with a private funicular down to a terrace and the seawater pool. Magnificent interior furnishings and a Michelin one-star restaurant. Tennis.
🛈 44 + 9 suites 🅿
🛗 Closed Oct.–April 🛉
🚭 All major cards

🏨 ROYAL RIVIERA
🍽 $$$$$ ✪✪✪✪
3 AVE. JEAN MONNET
TEL 04 93 76 31 00
FAX 04 93 01 23 07
www.royal-riviera.com
A 1904 belle époque residence, with contemporary furnishings that animate the gorgeous neo-Hellenic interior. Private beach and gardens.
🛈 77 🏊 🛎 🛉 🛗 Closed mid-Nov.–mid-Jan. 🚭 All major cards

🏨 HÔTEL LE PANORAMIC
$$$ ✪✪✪
3 AVE. ALBERT 1ER
TEL 04 93 76 00 37
FAX 04 93 76 15 78
www.hotel-lepanoramic.com
All rooms in this friendly, quiet hotel have balconies facing the Mediterranean sunrise.
🛈 20 🛗 Closed Nov.–Dec.
🚭 All major cards

ALPES PROVENÇALES

BARCELONNETTE

 AZTECA
$$ ●●●
3 RUE FRANÇOIS ARNAUD
TEL 04 92 81 46 36
www.azteca-hotel.fr
Centrally located 19th-century villa with Mexican-style rooms. Free shuttle to the ski slopes in season.
🛏 27 **P** 🕒 Closed Nov.
◈ MC, V

BREIL-SUR-ROYA

🏨 **CASTEL DU ROY**
🍴 **$$ ●●**
RTE. DE L'AIGARA
TEL 04 93 04 43 66
FAX 04 93 04 91 83
www.castelduroy.com
The most comfortable choice for those visiting the Vallée des Merveilles. Simple rooms, but the peaceful setting in the forested slopes just outside of town make for a lovely stay.
🛏 19 ◪ **P** 🕒 Closed Nov.–April ◈ MC, V

DIGNE-LES-BAINS

🏨 **LE GRAND PARIS**
🍴 **$$ ●●●●**
19 BLVD. THIERS
TEL 04 92 31 11 15
FAX 04 92 32 32 82
www.hotel-grand-paris.com
A 17th-century monastary has been transformed into a luxurious retreat with a superb restaurant. Tennis and golf available.
🛏 20 **P** ◪ ⬛ ▦ 🕒 Closed Dec.–March ◈ All major cards

LANTOSQUE

🏨 **HOSTELLERIE DE**
🍴 **L'ANCIENNE GENDARMERIE**
$$ ●●●
D2565, TOWARD PARC NATIONAL DU MERCANTOUR
TEL 04 93 03 00 65
FAX 04 93 03 06 31

www.hotel-lantosque.com
One of the Maritime-Alpes' most upscale hotels began as a police station—though you get no sense of its past in its cozy rooms. Rooms blend antique furnishings with modern tastes.
🛏 8 ◪ 🕒 Closed Nov.–Feb. ◈ MC, V

LA-PALUD-SUR-VERDON

🏨 **HÔTEL DES GORGES DU VERDON**
$$$ ●●●
LA PALUD
TEL 04 92 77 38 26
FAX 04 92 77 35 00
www.hotel-des-gorges-du-verdon.fr
Ideally situated near the edge of the Gorges du Verdon, this excellent mid-range choice has modern, colorful rooms with sweeping views.
🛏 27 **P** ◪ 🕒 Closed Nov.–March ◈ MC, V

MOUSTIERS-STE.-MARIE

SOMETHING SPECIAL

🏨 **LA BASTIDE DE**
🍴 **MOUSTIERS**

Alain Ducasse transformed this 17th-century farmhouse into one of Provence's most beautiful country inns. Guests are allowed to wander freely throughout the premises, including the kitchen and vegetable garden. The one-Michelin-star restaurant is worth a trip in itself.
$$$/$$$$ ●●●●
CHEMIN DE QUINSON
TEL 04 92 70 47 47
FAX 04 93 70 47 48
www.bastide-moustiers.com
🕒 Closed Dec.–Feb. ◈ All major cards

🍴 **LES SANTONS**
$$$
PLACE DE L'ÉGLISE
TEL 04 92 74 66 48
A tiny Michelin one-star restaurant with gorgeous views of the village church and

stream. Run by the celebrated Alain Ducasse, its most famous dish is the lavender-honey roast chicken. Reservations are essential.
🕒 Closed Mon. D & Tues. mid-Nov.–mid-Feb. ◈ All major cards

ST.-DALMAS-DE-TENDE

🏨 **LE PRIEURÉ**
🍴 **$ ●●**
RUE JEAN MÉDECIN
TEL 04 93 04 75 70
FAX 04 93 04 71 58
www.leprieure.org
Serving fresh trout and magret de canard, this is one of the better restaurants near the Vallée des Merveilles. Pleasant rooms available.
🛏 24 **P** 🕒 Closed Nov.–March ◈ AE, MC, V

TRIGANCE

🏨 **CHÂTEAU DE**
🍴 **TRIGANCE**
$$$ ●●●
CHEMIN DE QUINSON
TEL 04 94 76 91 18
FAX 04 94 85 68 99
www.chateau-de-trigance.fr
Perched dramatically over the village, this medieval castle was restored in the 1960s with period decor. Breakfast on the rooftop terrace, with dinner available in the ancient armory. Near the Gorges du Verdon.
🛏 10 **P** 🕒 Closed Nov.–March ◈ All major cards

VALENSOLE

🏨 **HOSTELLERIE DE LA**
🍴 **FUSTE**
$$$ ●●●●
LIEU-DIT DE LA FUSTE
TEL 04 92 72 05 95
FAX 04 92 72 92 93
www.lafuste.com
This 17th-century farmhouse was converted into an oasis of luxury amid fields of lavender, almond trees, and sun-drenched hills. Excellent service.
🛏 12 **P** ◪ 🕒 Closed mid-Nov.–mid-Dec. 🕒 Some rooms ◈ All major cards

SHOPPING IN PROVENCE

Provence has been marketed to the outside world for centuries, so it's not surprising that many of its traditional products are already well known even to first-time visitors. Lavender, *herbes de Provence*, and olive oil all bespeak the intense sunlight and distinctive aromas of the area. Handicrafts are prolific as well: terra-cotta *santons*, woven baskets, and Provençal linens to name a few examples. In addition to these regional products are numerous department stores and chic boutiques, catering to the well-heeled international clientele that has made Provence and the Côte d'Azur a home away from home for the past several decades. Nice, Cannes, St.-Tropez, and Aix-en-Provence are the top cities in which to window shop and see the latest in French fashion trends.

Markets

Markets are still the best way to shop in Provence. Most towns and villages have at least a weekly market, and in bigger cities they may even be daily. They usually start early in the morning and close at noon—if you want to see them at their bustling best, go early. Much of the fruit and vegetables are likely to be locally grown; look for signs saying *du pays*. The livestock section is not for the tender-hearted, as cages full of live ducks, geese, and chickens wait to be carried home for dinner. Look for local delicacies such as cheese, honey, olives, charcuterie, regional pastries (*fougassettes* in Grasse, *navettes* in Marseille, *calissons* in Aix) and of course, spices and herbs.

Weekly flea markets

Provence has several flea markets (*marchés aux puces* or *brocantes*) selling secondhand goods, antiques, and local curios. Again, you need to arrive early to find the bargains.
Aix-en-Provence
Place du Verdun
Tues., Thurs., Sat.
Cannes
Rue Forville
Mon.
Marseille
Ave. du Cap Pinède
Sun.
Nice
Cours Saleya
Mon.
Nîmes
Blvd. Jean-Jaurès
Mon.

Dégustations

Dégustation means "tasting." All over France you will see signs inviting you to sample the local produce, particularly the wine. You are not obliged to buy, but it would be thought uncivil not to purchase at least one bottle.

Opening hours

Food stores, especially bakers (*boulangeries*), open early, around 7 a.m. Small stores and department stores (*grands magasins*) usually open at 9 a.m. Most stores close for lunch between noon and 2 or 3 p.m., staying open until 7 or 7:30 in the evening. Hypermarkets will usually stay open all day until quite late.

Many stores close on Mondays; food shops, and especially bakers, open on Sunday mornings, when it is fun to watch everyone buying their tarts and cakes for Sunday lunch.

Payment

Supermarkets accept credit cards, but smaller stores often do not. Check the signs on the door before you go in. Some traders are reluctant to accept payment by American Express cards or traveler's checks.

Exports

Most purchases include TVA (VAT or value-added tax) at a base rate running currently at 19.6 percent, rising to as high as 33 percent on luxury items. Visitors from outside the European Union may claim back TVA if they spend more than 300 euros in one place. Ask the store for a completed *bordereau* (export sales invoice), which must be shown, together with the goods, to customs officers when you leave the country. You then mail the form back to the retailer, who will refund the TVA—though this may take some time.

WHAT TO BUY

ANTIQUES & FLEA MARKETS

The best place for serious antique hunting is l'Isle-sur-la-Sorgue, where more than 300 dealers have set up shop (open Sat.–Mon.), in addition to the huge weekly antique flea market on Sundays along the quays of the Sorgue River. The items on sale range from furniture and paintings to curios and clothes.
Le Village des Antiquaires
2 bis ave. de l'Égalité
L'Isle-sur-la-Sorgue
Tel 04 90 38 04 57
Close to 100 antique dealers are stuffed into this market space, specializing in everything from china to bathroom furnishings.

ENGLISH-LANGUAGE BOOKS
Antibes Books
24 rue Aubernon
Antibes 06600
Tel 04 93 34 74 11
Book in Bar
1 bis rue Cabassol
Aix-en-Provence 13100
Tel 04 42 26 60 07
Cannes English Bookshop
11 rue Bivouac Napoléon
Cannes 06400
Tel 04 93 99 40 08
The Cat's Whiskers
30 rue Lamartine
Nice 06000
Tel 04 93 80 02 66
Scruples
9 rue Princesse Caroline
Monaco 98000
Tel (377) 93 50 43 52
Shakespeare
155 rue Carreterie
Avignon 84000
Tel 04 90 27 38 50

HANDICRAFTS

Ceramics
Pottery has been a regional export since Roman times. The art began to die out around the turn of the 20th century, but underwent a major renaissance following the end of World War II. Picasso was largely responsible for its popular rebirth in Vallauris along the Côte d'Azur; Moustiers-Ste.-Marie specializes in the altogether different tradition of faïence, meticulously painted tableware. There are many pottery shops here along route de Riez.

Fayences de Moustiers
18 rue du Marché
Nice 06300
Tel 04 93 13 06 03
For Riviera vacationers unable to make the trip to Moustiers, this Nice boutique has a quality selection of faïence.

Galerie Madoura
Rue Georges et Suzanne Ramié
Vallauris 06220
Tel 04 93 64 66 39
www.madoura.com
Limited-edition ceramic plates and vases, based on original Picasso designs from 1947–1971.

Galerie Sassi-Milici
65 ave. Georges Clemenceau
Vallauris 06220
Tel 04 93 64 65 71
www.sassi-milici.com
Ceramics individually decorated by international artists.

Syndicat des Potiers
Rue Jean Gerbino
Vallauris 06220
Tel 04 93 64 88 30

Fabric
The brightly printed *indiennes* fabrics have been used as tablecloths, curtains, and sheets throughout Provence since the 18th century. Decorated with local motifs (sunflowers, poppies, etc.), they were traditionally made in Orange. Today, you can find fabric shops in most major towns.

Les Indiennes de Nîmes
2 blvd. des Arènes
Nîmes 30000

Tel 04 66 21 69 57
Sells home accessories and clothing; fabric by the meter also available.

La Maison des Lices
2 & 18 blvd. Louis Blanc
St.-Tropez 83990
Tel 04 94 97 64 64
Fine linens and other household products.

Les Olivades
15 rue M. Reinaud
Aix-en Provence 13100
Tel 04 38 33 66
www.les-olivades.com
The largest traditional fabrics manufacturer with stores in all the major towns of Provence. See website for other locations.

Souleïado
18 blvd. de Lices
Arles 13200
Tel 04 90 96 37 55
Traditional linens with outlets also in Les Baux and St.-Rémy.

Terre et Provence
26 rue de la République
Avignon 84000
Tel 04 90 85 56 45
Dinnerware, pottery, and fabrics.

Glass
Blown glass didn't become Biot's specialty until 1956, when Eloi Monod opened La Verrerie de Biot. It's particularly known for its *verre à bulles,* glass incorporating tiny bubbles of air into its design.

Cristallerie d'Èze
8 rue Principale
Èze 06360
Tel 04 93 41 20 34
Crystal and glassware.

La Verrerie de Biot
Chemin des Combes
Biot 06410
Tel 04 93 65 03 00
www.verreriebiot.com
Glassblowing factory with products for sale in the showroom; guided tours also available.

Paper
Vallis Clausa, Moulin à Papier
Chemin de la Fontaine
Fontaine-de-Vaucluse 84800
Tel 04 90 20 34 14
An old-fashioned paper mill here

is used to produce handmade paper and related products.

PERFUME
The three main perfume houses of Grasse all sell individual perfumes and gift sets created by their parfumeurs-in-residence. If you'd like to sample the scents on a more level playing field, Poilpot Thierry in Nice offers a large collection of locally made perfumes.

Florame
34 blvd. Mirabeau
St.-Rémy 13210
Tel 04 32 60 05 18
Essential oils, aromatherapy, and soaps in the Musée des Arômes.

Fragonard
20 blvd. Fragonard
Grasse 06130
Tel 04 93 36 44 65

Galimard
73 rte. de Cannes
Grasse 06130
Tel 04 93 09 20 00

Molinard
60 blvd. Victor Hugo
Grasse 06130
Tel 04 93 36 01 62

Poilpot Thierry
10 rue St. Gaétan
Nice 06300
Tel 04 93 85 60 77

SANDALS
Les Sandales Tropéziennes
16 rue Georges Clemenceau
St.-Tropez 83990
Tel 04 94 97 19 55
Handmade leather sandals since 1927.

SANTONS
The terra-cotta Provençal figurines known as santons were originally made for Nativity scenes, although the repertoire of *santonniers* (santon makers) has expanded to include all the traditional village *métiers,* from the baker to the scissors grinder. Each December in Marseille is the region's largest santon fair, the best place to see the work of different craftspeople. Otherwise, visit one of the following family-run workshops, all of whom make each santon by hand.

Arterra
3 rue du Petit Puits
Marseille 13002
Tel 04 91 91 03 31
Creative and tastefully made
santons. In the Panier quarter.
L'Atelier d'Art
2 blvd. Emile Combes
Aubagnes 13400
Tel 04 42 70 12 92
Though not on the usual tourist
route, Aubagnes is home to
several respected santon
workshops.
Pinocchio
Rue de la Pise
Èze 06360
Tel 04 93 41 21 30
An interesting collection of
accessories for dolls and
marionettes.
Santons Devouassoux
Le Grand Vallet
Meyrargues 13650
Tel 04 42 57 51 10
Santons Fouque
65 cours Gambetta
Aix-en-Provence 13100
Tel 04 42 26 33 38
www.santons-fouque.com
One of the most acclaimed
santon workshops of Provence.

SOAP
The highly successful L'Occitane
chain found its niche exporting
the aroma of Provence with
soaps, creams, and other
beauty products. When the
French think of Provençal
soap, however, the first image
that springs to mind is the
olive-green block of *savon de
Marseille*, first produced in the
17th century. One hundred
percent biodegradable and
recommended for sensitive
skin, savon de Marseille today
is available in various scents
and sizes. It's sold in most
pharmacies and beauty
supply stores.
Compagnie de Provence
1 rue Caisserie
Marseille 13002
Tel 04 91 56 20 94
Carrying the time-honored
cubes of Marseille soap.
L'Occitane
21 rue Grande
Manosque 04100

Tel 04 92 72 41 02
www.loccitane.com
The home store of the renowned
producer of Provence-related
beauty supplies.
**Savonnerie Marius Fabre
Jeune**
148 ave. Paul Bourret
Salon-de-Provence 13300
Tel 04 90 53 24 77
Like Marseille, Salon-de-Provence
was also a major producer of
soap in the 19th century.

FOOD & WINE

**Chocolate, jams,
& pastries**
Delectable chocolates,
homemade jams, candied
fruits, honey, and a mind-
boggling variety of pastries
are just some of the many
sweets that southern France
has perfected over the
years.
La Bonbonnière
54 rue Sous Préfecture
Apt 84400
Tel 04 90 74 12 92
Candied fruits, jams, and
chocolate.
Calissons du Roy René
330 rue Guillaume du Vair
Aix-en-Provence 13545
Tel 04 42 39 29 89
Aix's own almond-flavored
calissons and other pastries.
Carroussel des Confitures
2 rue du Vieux Collège
Menton 06500
Tel 04 93 57 21 00
Locally produced jams & honey.
Chocolatier Schies
125 rue d'Antibes
Cannes 06400
Tel 04 93 39 01 03
La Chocolatière du Panier
35 rue Vacon
Marseille 13001
Tel 04 91 55 70 41
Confiserie Bono
280 allée Jean-Jaurès
Carpentras 84200
Tel 04 90 63 04 99
Candied fruits and jams.
Confiserie Florian
14 quai Papacino
Nice 06300
Tel 04 93 55 43 50
The most well-known producer

of candied fruits on the Riviera.
Four des Navettes
136 rue Sainte
Marseille 13007
Tel 04 91 33 32 12
One of Marseille's oldest
bakeries, specializing in boat-
shaped navettes.
Pâtisserie Bergèse
18 rue Lafayette
St.-Rémy-de-Provence 13210
Tel 04 90 92 01 97
Sinful delights including cakes,
chocolate, and nougat.
Puyricard
Ave. Georges de Fabry
Aix-en-Provence 13100
Tel 04 42 28 18 18
Chocolate and other sweets.
Venturini Fougassettes
1 rue Marcel Journet
Grasse 06130
Tel 04 93 36 20 47
Sweet flat breads flavored with
orange blossom.

**Herbs & other
specialties**
Most herbs can be found
at local markets, though in
the lavender country around
Sault and Valensole, you can
also buy lavender-related
products (including honey)
direct from the farmers
themselves at roadside stalls.
Little sachets of herbes de
Provence are ubiquitous in
tourist shops.
Alziari
14 rue St.-François-de-Paule
Nice 06100
Tel 04 93 85 76 92
Actually an olive oil producer,
Alziari also sells about
everything one could ever want
from inland Provence: herbs,
soaps, honey, and tapenade.
**Boutique de l'Abbaye de
Lérins**
Île St.-Honorat 06400
Tel 04 92 99 54 00
The place to buy the famous 45-
herb liqueur made by the monks,
and other regional products.
Cannolive
16 rue Vénizélos
Cannes 06400
Tel 04 93 39 08 19
Inland Provençal specialties.
Les Délices du Luberon

1 ave. du Partage des Eaux
L'Isle-sur-la-Sorgue 84800
Tel 04 90 20 77 37
Tapenades, sun-dried tomatoes,
and pesto.
L'Herbier en Provence
Montée La Castre
St. Paul 06570
Tel 04 93 32 91 51
Musée de la Lavande
Rte. de Gordes
Coustellet 84220
Tel 04 90 76 91 23
Extensive boutique full of
lavender-related items.
Au Père Blaize
4 rue Méolan
Marseille 13001
Tel 04 91 54 04 01
Pharmacy and traditional
herbalist.

Olive oil
The best place to buy olive
oil is from *moulins à huile,*
oil presses, which are often
signposted off backroads
throughout Provence. The two
major areas of olive cultivation
center around St.-Rémy and
Nyons (in the Vaucluse), though
mills exist even along stretches
of the Riviera.
Château d'Estoublon
Rte. de Maussane
Fontvieille 13990
Tel 04 90 54 64 00
Fad'Oli
46 rue des Arènes
Arles 13200
Tel 04 90 49 70 73
Moulin de la Brague
2 rte. de Châteauneuf
Opio 06650
Tel 04 93 77 23 03
Moulin à Huile Conti
138 rte. de Draguignan
Grasse 06130
Tel 04 93 70 21 42
Moulin à Huile Lottier
102 ave. des Acacias
Menton 06500
Tel 04 93 35 79 15
Moulin Jean-Marie Cornille
Maussane-les-Alpilles 13520
Tel 04 90 54 32 37

Pastis
Provence's anise-flavored
apéritif of choice (and direct
descendant of absinthe) does

not go down well with
everyone. If lazy afternoons
spent sitting outside cafés
have you converted, however,
the two major brand names in
the industry are Ricard and
Pernod. Bottles are available in
all supermarkets.

Wine
Some of the finest French
wines originate in Provence,
and the opportunity to stop in
and visit individual *domaines*
and walk off with a crate of a
wine you'd never find anywhere
else is one of the great delights
of the area. The *maisons des
vins* listed below are good
starting points to sample the
regional appellations.
Caveau du Gigondas
Place du Portail
Gigondas 84190
Tel 04 90 65 82 29
Comprehensive selection of
local wines.
Château Vignelaure (Côteaux
d'Aix)
Rte. Jouques
Rians 83560
Tel 04 94 37 21 10
**Domaine de la Ferme
Blanche** (Vignoble de Cassis)
D559
Cassis 13260
Tel 04 42 01 00 74
Domaine de la Genestière
Chemin de Cravailleux
Tavel 30126
Tel 04 66 50 07 03
**Domaine des Terres
Blanches** (Côteaux des Baux)
Off D99
St.-Rémy 13210
Tel 04 90 95 91 66
Domaine de Trévallon
(Côteaux d'Aix)
Chemin Romain Arles
St.-Rémy 13210
Tel 04 90 49 06 00
Maison des Vins (Côtes de
Provence)
N7
Les Arcs 83460
Tel 04 94 99 50 20
Maison des Vins (Côtes du
Rhône)
6 rue Trois Faucons
Avignon 84000
Tel 04 90 27 24 00

**Vignerons de Beaumes de
Venise**
Quartier Ravel
Beaumes-de-Venise 84190
Tel 04 90 12 41 00
Vinadéa
8 rue Marechal Foch
Châteauneuf-du-Pape 84230
Tel 04 90 83 70 69
www.vinadea.com
Comprehensive selection of local
wines.
La Vinothèque
18 rue Jean Reboul
Nîmes 30900
Tel 04 66 67 20 44

Reading wine labels

AOC Appellation d'origine
contrôlée. Guarantees that
a wine is produced according to strict standards, coming from a defined area and
made from certain grape
varieties. AOC wines will
be the most high quality.

Cru Classé High-quality
classification used by only a
few appellations (including
Côtes de Provence).

Grand Cru Great noble
vintage.

VDQS Vins Délimité de
Qualité Supérieure. The
second highest classification—superior quality wine.
The label has a VDQ icon
in the lower left corner and
also specifies its type of
grape.

Vin de pays A higher-class
table wine guaranteed to
have at least originated in a
certain region.

Vin de table Basic French
table wine, made without
indication of origin or grape
variety.

ENTERTAINMENT & ACTIVITIES

ENTERTAINMENT

Entertainment possibilities vary from sophisticated opera billings to traditional bullfights, with several towns transforming ancient Roman monuments into impressive outdoor venues. Nonstop festival lineups ensure something for everyone, with jazz concerts, gypsy pilgrimages, photography exhibits, and theater performances year-round. Casinos and movie theaters round off the list of after-dark entertainment choices, and, for the real night owls, there are always the clubs of Marseille, St.-Tropez, Cannes, and Nice.

Bullfights

Known as *tauromachie* in French, the bullfights staged in the Roman arenas of Arles and Nîmes are an excellent way of experiencing a real slice of traditional Provençal life. Decidedly less gruesome than the bullfights of Spain, it's for the most part the *raseteurs*, not the animals, who get hurt. The best times to see a bullfight are the Féria Pascale (Easter weekend), Fête des Gardians (March 1), and the Cocarde d'Or, in July. Tickets are available at the ticket office of the arena in question; otherwise you can also ask the tourist office for more information.

Casinos

Casinos are all part of the allure of the French Riviera, the most famous and over-the-top of them all being Le Casino, in Monte-Carlo.
Casino de Bandol
2 place Lucien Artaud
Bandol 83150
Tel 04 94 29 31 31
Casino du Golfe
Promenade Port
Cavalaire-sur-Mer 83240
Tel 04 94 01 92 40
Casino de Grasse
Blvd. Jeu de Ballon

Grasse 06130
Tel 04 93 36 91 00
Casino Ruhl
1 Promenade des Anglais
Nice 06000
Tel 04 97 03 12 22
Le Casino
Place du Casino
Monte-Carlo, Monaco
Tel (377) 98 06 21 21

Cinema

The interest that the French display in cinema is on par with the attention that other cultures devote to professional sports, and Provence is no exception. The following theaters screen movies in V.O., meaning they're shown in their original language with French subtitles. Not only will you find Hollywood's latest blockbusters, but also independent and classic films that rarely make it to the big screen elsewhere. Cannes's world-famous Festival International du Film takes place each May, but without some sort of relevant credentials, getting a seat borders on impossible.
Cinéma Mazarin
6 rue Laroque
Aix-en-Provence 13100
Tel 08 92 68 72 70
Cinéma Mercury
16 place Garibaldi
Nice 06300
Tel 08 36 68 81 06
Cinéma Olympia
16 rue Pompe
Cannes 06400
Tel 04 93 39 13 93
Cinéma Renoir
24 cours Mirabeau
Aix-en-Provence 13100
Tel 08 92 68 72 70
Cinéma Rialto
4 rue de Rivoli
Nice 06000
Tel 08 92 68 00 41
Cinéma Utopia
4 rue Escaliers Ste.-Anne
Avignon 84000
Tel 04 90 82 65 36

Cinéma Les Variétés
37 rue Vincent Scotto
Marseille 13001
Tel 04 91 90 36 67
Entrevue
23 quai Marx Dormoy
Arles 13200
Tel 04 90 93 37 28
Bookstore, hammam, and movie theater.

Opera, ballet, & classical music

In addition to the main opera houses and classical music venues listed below, be on the lookout for signs posted outside town churches and cathedrals, which make for intimate and enchanting concert spaces. During the summer months a seemingly infinite number of music festivals take place throughout the south, many staged in spectacular outdoor locations such as the Roman theater in Orange.
Ballet National de Marseille
20 blvd. Gabès
Marseille 13008
Tel 04 91 32 73 27
Opéra de Marseille
2 rue Molière
Marseille 13001
Tel 04 91 55 11 10
In a 20th-century art deco building downtown.
Opéra de Monte-Carlo
Place du Casino
Monaco 98000
Tel (377) 98 06 28 00
Opéra de Nice
4 rue St.-François-de-Paule
Nice 06300
Tel 04 92 17 40 40
Opera and music concerts in Vieux Nice.
Opéra-Théâtre
1 rue de Racine
Avignon 84007
Tel 04 90 82 81 40
Built in 1847, boasting a year-round bill of opera, music, and theater performances.
Palais de l'Europe
8 ave. Boyer
Menton 06500
04 92 41 76 50
Menton's cultural center, hosting a variety of operas, ballets, and music concerts.

ENTERTAINMENT & ACTIVITIES

Théâtre Antique Centre Culturel
14 place Silvain
Orange 84100
Tel 04 90 51 17 60
Ticket office for events staged in Orange's majestic Roman theater, including the Chorégies music festival in July and Aug.
Théâtre du Jeu de Paume
17 rue de l'Opéra
Aix-en-Provence 13100
Tel 04 42 99 12 00
Beautiful 18th-century theater with a varied program.

ACTIVITIES

A wide variety of activities can be pursued in Provence and along the Mediterranean, ranging from the inert (lying on the beach) to the extreme (bungee jumping). Virtually everywhere in the region you can walk, ride, and play golf, and the coasts offer a huge variety of marine and bathing activities. Most towns have excellent public swimming pools and sports facilities.

A good place to pick up general information is the local tourist office. However, for a more comprehensive guide to sporting activities—be it cycling, sailing, hiking, or scuba diving—check in with the departmental tourist offices (Comité Départemental de Tourisme) listed below.
Alpes de Haute Provence
19 rue du Dr.-Honnorat
Digne-les-Bains 04005
Tel 04 92 31 57 29
www.alpes-haute-provence.com
Alpes Maritimes
55 Promenade des Anglais
Nice 06000
Tel 04 93 37 78 78
www.guideriviera.com
Bouches-du-Rhône
Les Docks Atrium
10 place Joliette
Marseille 13002
Tel 04 91 56 47 00
www.crt-paca.fr
Hautes Alpes
8 bis rue Capit de Bresson
Gap 05000
Tel 04 92 53 62 00
www.hautes-alpes.net

Var
1 blvd. Maréchal Foch
Draguignan 83003
Tel 04 94 50 55 50
www.tourismevar.com
Vaucluse
12 rue Collège de la Croix
Avignon 84000
Tel 04 90 80 47 00
www.provenceguide.com

Ballooning

Hot-air ballooning is a unique and thrilling way to discover the Provençal landscape. Rides usually last from 1 to 2 hours.
Montgolfière Provence Ballooning
Le Mas Fourniguière, Joucas
Gordes 84220
Tel 04 90 05 76 77
Provence en Ballon
Chemin Colombier
Barbentane 13570
Tel 04 90 95 54 50

Bird-watching

The main magnet for serious birders is the Camargue wetlands, home to hundreds of migrating bird species for part of each year. Within the protected area are two facilities offering an introduction to the flora and fauna of the region, as well as walking trails.
Maison du Parc Naturel Régional de Camargue
Mas du Pont de Rousty
D570, Pont de Gau
Tel 04 90 97 86 32
Parc Ornithologique de Pont de Gau
D570, Pont de Gau
Tel 04 90 97 82 62

Boat trips

Isles de Stel
12 rue Amiral Coubert
Aigues-Mortes 30220
Tel 04 66 53 60 70
Boat trips through the Camargue.
Trans Côte d'Azur
Quai Amiral Infernet
Nice 06300
Tel 04 92 00 42 30
Glass-bottomed boat trips along the coast.

Bungee jumping

One of the highest bungee-jumping spots in Europe is the Pont de l'Artuby, 600 feet (180 m) above the water, in the Gorges du Verdon.

Canyoning

Canyoning (also known as canyoneering) is an increasingly popular adventure sport that involves the descent of relatively inaccessible mountain streams through the use of climbing equipment and techniques.
AET Nature
Foussa
Breil-sur-Roya 06540
Tel 04 93 04 47 64
Canyoning, rafting, and climbing in the Roya Valley.
Aqua Viva Est
12 blvd. République
Castellane 04120
Tel 04 92 83 75 74
Aventures et Nature
La-Palud-sur-Verdon 04120
Tel 04 92 77 30 43
Base Sport et Nature
Brec
Entrevaux 04320
Tel 04 93 05 41 18

Cycling

Cycling is a French passion that ranks up there with (and stands in direct contrast to) the regional *boules* obsession. People are surprisingly helpful when it comes to accommodating bicycles, and most medium-size towns have at least one bike shop, with both rental and repair services. A growing interest in mountain biking (known in French as VTT) has brought about a new spin on the traditional sport.
Holiday Bikes
www.holiday-bikes.com
French bike rental chain, with numerous locations throughout Provence. They rent both road bikes and mountain bikes.
Vélo Loisir en Luberon
13 blvd. des Martyrs
Forcalquier 04300
Tel 04 92 79 05 82
Cycling information and rentals for the Luberon area.

Golf
There are surprisingly more golf courses in the region than one would expect, especially given the arid climate. Nonetheless, it is a sport that has a long history here, beginning with European vacationers in the late 1800s.
Golf Club Aix-Marseille
Domaine de Riquetti, Les Milles
Aix-en-Provence 13290
Tel 04 42 24 20 41
One of the oldest courses in Provence, built in 1935.
Golf des Baux
Domaine Manville
Les-Baux-de-Provence 13520
Tel 04 90 54 40 20
Golf du Grand Avignon
Les Chênes Verts
Vedène 84270
Tel 04 90 31 49 94
Golf du Roquebrune
D7, Les Issambres
Roquebrune-sur-Argens 83520
Tel 04 94 19 60 35
Golf du Ste.-Maxime
Rte. du Débarquement
Ste.-Maxime 83120
Tel 04 94 55 02 02
Golf de Servanes
Rte. de Servanes
Mouriès 13890
Tel 04 90 47 59 95
Provence Country Club
Rte. de Fontaine-de-Vaucluse
Saumane-de-Vaucluse 84800
Tel 04 90 20 20 65

Horseback riding
For information on serious horseback riding in the Camargue and other areas, contact the centers below.
Centre Équestre de la Ville de Marseille
33 Traverse Carthage
Marseille 13008
Tel 04 91 73 72 94
Centre de Tourisme Équestre Brenda
Mas St. George (Astouin)
Les-Stes.-Maries-de-la-Mer 13460
Tel 04 90 97 52 08
Nouveau Club Hippique des Antiques
3 rue Étienne Astier
St.-Rémy 13210
Tel 04 90 92 30 55
Horseback riding through the Alpilles and Dentelles.

Nudism
Topless sunbathing is more or less the norm on all of the Côte d'Azur's beaches, although naturalists will have to make for the enclave on Île de Levant, an island off Hyères.
Héliopolis Île du Levant
Hyères 83411

Rafting & canoeing
Most of Provence's rivers are reined in by at least one dam, if not more. Nevertheless, white-water rafting and kayaking is possible on some stretches in Haute-Provence and is an excellent way to see the Europe's deepest canyon, les Gorges du Verdon.
Aboard Rafting
8 place de l'Église
Castellane 04120
Tel 04 92 83 76 11
Action Aventure Rafting
12 rue Nationale
Castellane 04120
Tel 04 92 83 79 39
Eau Vive Evasion Rafting
Place Revelly
Annot 04240
Tel 04 92 83 38 09
Kayak Vert
La Beaume
Fontaine-de-Vaucluse 84800
Tel 04 90 20 35 44
For relaxed day trips downstream to L'Isle-sur-la-Sorgue. Fishing supplies are also available.
Kayak Vert Camargue
Petites Armelles, ave. Arles
Les-Stes.-Maries-de-la-Mer 13460
Tel 04 90 97 80 32
Renting canoes and kayaks for paddling trips through the Camargue.
Maison du Canoë, Kayak, et du Rafting
Le Four à Chaux, Pont Martinet
Méolans 04340
Tel 04 92 85 58 29
Paddling activities in the Ubaye Valley.

Rock climbing
Jagged limestone outcrops and cliff faces make up the majority of the region's impressive climbing sites. The Calanques,

the Gorges du Verdon, the Dentelles de Montmirail, Buoux in the Luberon, and the Vallée des Merveilles all have classified routes, some with bolted climbs. A Provençal variant of the sport is the Via Ferrata—a kind of high-altitude ropes course, popular throughout the Alps. Check the following locations for more information, rental gear, and guides.
Association Lei Lagramusas
La-Palud-sur-Verdon 04120
Tel 04 92 77 38 02
Aventures et Nature
La-Palud-sur-Verdon 04120
Tel 04 92 77 30 43
Base Sport et Nature
10 rue Fontaine
Castellaine 04120
Tel 04 92 83 11 42
Comité Départemental de la Montagne et de l'Escalade
Place Capitaine Arnaud
Mezel 04270
Tel 06 20 96 79 88
Club d'Escalade de Quinson
Quinson 04500
Tel 04 92 74 40 04

Sailing, windsurfing, & other water sports
There's no shortage of choice along the coast when it comes to renting water skis, Jet Skis, or sailing equipment. The local tourist offices will have a list of the various companies that provide these services.
Nautique 2000
Port Gallice
Juan-les-Pins 06160
Tel 04 93 61 20 01
Riviera Fun Sail
1987 ave. Pélissier
Antibes 06600
Tel 06 03 71 46 78
Team Water Sport
Coco Plage
Quartier Pampelonne
Ramatuelle 83350
Tel 04 94 79 82 41
Waterskiing, windsurfing, and other related water sports in the St.-Tropez area.

Scuba diving
There are a large number of fascinating dives off the coast, from the shipwrecks

surrounding offshore islands to the quiet and mysterious coves of Les Calanques. Several schools offer either certification courses and first time *plongée baptîme* dives. To rent equipment on your own, you will need to prove you are certified.

Centre Cassidain de Plongée
3 rue Michel Arnaud
Cassis 13260
Tel 04 42 01 89 16
Henri Cosquer's school organizes dives in the turquoise inlets of Les Calanques.

Féderation Française d'Études et des Sports Sous Marins
24 quai Rive-Neuve
Marseille 13007
Tel 04 91 33 99 31
Departmental center for scuba diving.

Porquerolles Plongée
ZA Porquerolles
Île de Porquerolles 83400
Tel 04 98 04 62 22
A variety of dives for all levels and ages off the Îles d'Hyères. They also offer snorkeling and certification courses.

Skiing
Skiing in Provence's Alps doesn't quite compare with the larger Alps farther northeast, although the lift tickets here are generally much less expensive.

Isola 2000
Office de Tourisme
Tel 04 93 23 15 15
Seventy-four miles (120 km) of trails.

St.-Étienne du Tinée
Office de Tourisme
1 rue Commune de France
Tel 04 93 02 41 96
Eighty miles (130 km) of trails.

Spas
Roman influence and natural hot springs have no doubt influenced the tradition of steamy relaxation in southern France, although these days you're just as likely to find shiatsu, aromatherapy, and meditation alternatives on the *carte* in addition to the time-tested saunas and hot baths.

La Bastide de Gordes & Spa
Rte. de Combe
Gordes 84220
Tel 04 90 72 12 12

Thermes de Dignes les Bains
29 ave. Thermes
Digne-les-Bains 04005
Tel 04 92 32 32 92

Thermes de Gréoux
Rue Eaux Chaudes
Gréoux-les-Bains 04800
Tel 04 92 70 40 01

Les Thermes Marins
2 ave. Monte-Carlo
Monaco 98000
Tel (377) 98 06 68 00

Thermes Sextius
55 cours Sextius
Aix-en-Provence 13101
Tel 04 42 23 81 82

Walking & hiking
Provence is a great place to get out and walk through the countryside and wilderness. Despite massive development along the coast, the rugged terrain and growing environmental concern throughout the region has ensured that pockets of wilderness remain intact.

The most spectacular hikes are along the Calanques near Marseille, around the Dentelles in the Rhône Valley, perched-village hopping in Nice's backcountry, the rolling chestnut and pine forests of the Massif des Maures behind St.-Tropez, and the Gorges du Verdon and the Vallée des Merveilles in the Provence Alps.

Hiking trails are known as Grande Randonée, GR for short. Tourist offices will have information on the local GRs, otherwise contact the organizations below for more detailed information, maps, and lists of alpine lodges. Bear in mind that backcountry hiking is generally forbidden at the height of summer due to the threat of forest fires.

Club Alpin Français
14 ave. Mirabeau
Nice 06000
Tel 04 93 62 59 99

Comité Départemental de la Randonnée Pédestre
4 ave. de Verdun
Cagnes-sur-Mer 06800
Tel 04 93 20 74 73

Destination Merveilles
10 rue des Mesures
Villeneuve Loubet 06270
Tel 04 93 73 09 07
Guided tours to the Vallée des Merveilles.

FURTHER READING
Countless books have been written about Provence. Here is just a sampling:

Collected Short Stories (1990), by Somerset Maugham. Includes "The Fact of Life" and "Three Fat Women from Antibes," which take place in Provence by the Cap-Ferrat resident.

The Count of Monte Cristo (1845) and *The Man in the Iron Mask,* by Alexandre Dumas. Two classics set partly in 19th-century Marseille.

A Little Tour in France (1885), by Henry James. A lively and personal account of James's solo trip through France, including nine chapters about Provence.

Loser Takes All (1955), by Grahame Greene.

Perfume (2001) by Patrick Suskind. The fascinating, horrifying tale of a gifted young boy in 18th-century Grasse who sets out to create his own perfume.

Provence (1935) by Ford Maddox Ford. A florid, rambling account of Provence between the wars.

Tender is the Night (1934), by F. Scott Fitzgerald. The decadent '20s Jazz Age on Cap d'Antibes.

Two Towns in Provence (1983), by M.F.K. Fisher. Fisher's classic and unforgettable portraits of Aix-en-Provence and Marseille.

Wine & War (2002), by Don and Petie Kladstrup. How French winemakers saved the nation's vineyards from WWII invaders.

ILLUSTRATIONS CREDITS

All photographs by Gerard Sioen/ Anzenberger except for the following:

Cover (r), Jean-Pierre Pieuchot/Getty Images. 9, Gianni Dagli Orti/CORBIS. 26, Stapleton Collection/CORBIS. 27, Bettmann/CORBIS. 28-29, Gail Mooney/CORBIS. 31, Swim Ink/ CORBIS. 33, Bettmann/CORBIS. 39, Bettmann/CORBIS. 41 CORBIS KIPA. 43, Underwood & Underwood/CORBIS. 44, Robert Leslie/drr.net. 140, Christina Anzenberger-Fink/Anzenberger. 62, Bertrand Rieger/Getty Images. 113, DR-IAP/ age fotostock. 147 (low le), Gail Mooney/ CORBIS. 147 (low rt), Robb Kendrick. 158-159, Gianni Dagli Orti/CORBIS. 164, Christina Anzenberger-Fink/Anzenberger. 171, Christina Anzenberger-Fink/ Anzenberger. 178-179, Christina Anzenberger-Fink/Anzenberger. 182, Christina Anzenberger-Fink/Anzenberger.

Published by the National Geographic Society
John M. Fahey, Jr., *President and Chief Executive Officer*
Gilbert M. Grosvenor, *Chairman of the Board*
Nina D. Hoffman, *Executive Vice President; President, Book Publishing Group*
Kevin Mulroy, *Senior Vice President and Publisher*
Marianne Koszorus, *Design Director*
Elizabeth L. Newhouse, *Director of Travel Publishing*
Cinda Rose, *Art Director*
Carl Mehler, *Director of Maps*

Staff for this book:
Barbara A. Noe, *Series Editor and Project Manager*
Kay Kobor Hankins, *Designer*
Chris Anderson, *Illustrations Editor*
Christopher Pitts, *Researcher*
Lise Sajewski, *Editorial Consultant*
Matt Chwastyk, Thomas L. Gray, Nicholas P. Rosenbach, and XNR Productions, *Map Edit, Research, and Production*
R. Gary Colbert, *Production Director*
Mike Horenstein, *Production Manager*
Meredith Wilcox, *Illustrations Assistant*
Connie D. Binder, *Indexer*
Dana Chivvis, Lawrence Porges, Jack Brostrom, *Contributors*

Staff for 2008 edition
Christopher Pitts, *Researcher*
Lynsey Jacob, *Editorial Assistant*
Carol Stroud, Ruth Thompson, Meredith Wilcox, *Contributors*

Artwork by Maltings Partnership, Derby, England (pp. 50–51 & 72–73).

National Geographic Traveler: Provence & the Côte d'Azur, 2nd edition (2008)
ISBN: 978-1-4262-0235-3

NATIONAL GEOGRAPHIC
TRAVELER
A Century of Travel Expertise in Every Guide

AVAILABLE WHEREVER BOOKS ARE SOLD